SOCIAL WORK IN A CHANGING WORLD

For practice teachers (field educators) and social work students throughout the world

Social Work in a Changing World

An International Perspective
on Practice Learning

Edited by

Mark Doel
Steven Shardlow

Published by
Arena
Ashgate Publishing Limited
Gower House
Croft Road
Aldershot
Hants GU11 3HR
England

Ashgate Publishing Company
Old Post Road
Brookfield
Vermont 05036
USA

British Library Cataloguing in Publication Data

Social work in a changing world:
   an international perspective on practice
   learning
   1. Social service   2. Social service –
   Evaluation
   I. Doel, Mark   II. Shardlow, Steven, 1952–
   361.3

Library of Congress Catalog Card Number: 96-84402

ISBN 1 85742 343 7

Typeset in Palatino by Raven Typesetters, Chester
and printed in Great Britain by Biddles Ltd, Guildford

Contents

Part Two – Teaching and Learning

Part Three – Case Studies

List of figures and tables

Acknowledgements

All edited books rely upon the contribution of a large number of people, many of them unknown by name to the editors. So it is with this book. For that reason, we would like to thank not just our contributors, but also all those persons who have helped them, perhaps with the development of their ideas, the technical aspects of getting print onto a page or in other supportive ways. We wish to thank the Cultural Initiative/Open Society in Moscow for commissioning this book, as part of the series Social Work in a Changing World, edited by Shulamit Ramon (the full series was originally published in Russian). In particular, we wish to thank Teodor Shanin and Victor Galizin, without whom the book would never have come into being, and everybody else from the Transformation Project of the Humanities and the Social Sciences who helped to make the publication of this book possible. Very special thanks to Shulamit Ramon, who has provided a constant source of enthusiasm for the project, and we thank her for her encouragement and editorial advice. We wish to acknowledge the help of many people, but we wish to mention by name: Antonina Dashkina and Tony Widmer from the Russian-European Social Innovation Trust for their help in many ways; John Warwick for supplying materials to us, and Vitaly Slastonen, Mikhail Rybakov and Boris Shapiro for inspiring us about Russia. Finally, we would like to thank Marg Walker for her secretarial help in completing this book.

Foreword

Shulamit Ramon

Since the end of the 1980s we have witnessed considerable political, economic, social and cultural change in East, West and Central Europe. The scope and depth of change has been particularly dramatic in the post-Communist countries, of which Russia is the biggest and the most influential. In response to these changes it is not accidental that the Transformation Project of the Humanities and the Social Sciences of the Soros Cultural Initiatives Foundation in Moscow included the introduction and development of social work as one of its core activities. A cornerstone of the Transformation Project's work to promote the development of social work has been to initiate the development of a range of materials such as books and videos that can be used by social work educators and practitioners in Russia. This book by Mark Doel and Steven Shardlow was commissioned as part of a series of books (originally published in Russian and for which I was overall series editor) dedicated to the coverage of social work values, knowledge and skills, in the context of different needs, wishes, client groups, and social contexts.

The uniqueness of social work lies in the attempt to offer a personalized service which holds together the psycho-social levels of our existence through the efforts of professionally qualified workers who also act as intermediaries between the service user and the state. Usually, social workers are not policy-makers, though they may and, in my view, should attempt to influence policy decisions. Social workers are accountable to their employers, but their first and foremost loyalty is to defending vulnerable people in our society. They do so in a variety of ways, which are based on knowledge of how people develop, interact, change, learn, become motivated or despair; of how societies influence the lives of individuals, and of how to tread that fragile boundary between influence, coercion and enabling people to determine their choices and to put these into practice.

They are successful at times, and unsuccessful at others. Therefore, knowledge of the evaluative evidence on social work is crucial to improving its effectiveness, as well as to ensure that newcomers to social work will learn from mistakes made in Western social work, and will not need to repeat the same mistakes, only to make their own, new mistakes.

An important component of social work is the belief that usually we do not know what is the best choice for another person, that the individual knows better than anyone else what is good for them, even when they need to know a lot more about alternative possibilities, the relative advantages and disadvantages of alternative courses of action, and even when they need to learn how to make decisions.

Social work does not exist in isolation from specific political and cultural contexts. Therefore, the form which social work should take in any one country must be tailored to the context of that country; imitation of models of social work used elsewhere is unlikely to work well without such adaptation – so, too, with social work education and practice learning. This book is a bold contribution to the promotion of diverse and valid forms of practice learning in different societies, expecting that we can all learn from each other and then develop a unique response particular to our culture and history.

Preface

Mark Doel and Steven Shardlow

The origins of this book are to be found in the overthrow of the Communist regime in Russia in 1991. It may seem a little strange, even pretentious, for a book about practice learning in social work to make such a claim. However, the fact remains: after 1991, social work and social work education were introduced to Russia. Creating a new profession and the infrastructure to support it is by no means easy in a society making the transition to both a market economy and democracy. 'Yes,' we can hear our readers say, 'but where does this book fit in?'

The original idea for this book and the series of which it forms a part (this book is one of several originally commissioned by the Transformation Project of the Humanities and the Social Sciences for publication in Russian to promote the development of social work and social work education) was a response to the difficulty of setting up social work education in countries with no previous experience of social work. The purpose of this book is to collect together different examples and experiences from around the world of various aspects of practice learning about social work, in order to help inform the development of practice learning in Russia. However, the material has relevance beyond the Russian context – in fact, wherever social work is taught and wherever students learn about social work practice in social work agencies.

Establishing meaningful communication across national, linguistic and cultural boundaries is not easy. As you would expect, the authors in this book use a wide range of different concepts to describe and analyse social work practice learning. Many of these concepts are particular to their country; even the *central* concepts of this book are described differently. We decided that we would not seek to impose any single conceptual framework on the text of the book. Thus we did not require that all authors use a specific terminology. Instead, each author uses those concepts to discuss practice learning that are consistent with their own experience. (Moreover, all authors are writing in a personal capacity; there is no sense in which their views should be taken to represent either the views of their institution or of their country generally.)

Do these differences really matter? Of course, some differences are more significant than others. An important one concerns the title and function of the person in a social work agency who has responsibility for a student's learning – who is called variously, in North America, a *field instructor*, *field supervisor* or *field educator*. A person holding the same responsibility in the United Kingdom or New Zealand, for example, would be called a *student supervisor*, or more recently, a *practice teacher*. The significant question is, although these terms signify the same role, do they conceal differences in the way that individuals who occupy the role conceive of their relationships with students and responsibilities for learning? The answer to this question seems to be 'yes': the terminology is a key to a proper interpretation of this role.

This example illustrates one of the major difficulties in bringing together a collection of materials from different countries and cultures. If even the simplest of terms are different, can we be sure that when those are translated into familiar concepts in our own culture, we really understand the meaning? We have to work hard to remind ourselves that we are engaged in a highly complex process of transferring ideas from one context to another. To help understand the various concepts employed in this book, we have included a detailed glossary which links together clusters of terms used in the book, in language that we hope is simple and straightforward. Our intention is to avoid imposing uniformity where none exists, and to steer clear of 'conceptual imperialism'.

Thinking about the variety of concepts employed within the book soon leads to another vexed question – the difficulty of referring to both men and women in an inclusive way when using the singular pronoun. Using *he/she* or *(s)he* is clumsy, so we have tended wherever possible to use the plural form *they*.

Our enthusiasm for this book, great at the outset, has grown as we have read the work of our fellow authors and worked with them to produce the finished version. As editors, we consider it an honour to be involved with a project that has been designed to draw together examples of practice learning from around the world. We hope the book is interesting to all who have a commitment to practice learning, and that it will encourage those who are actively involved in teaching students in practice settings to contribute to any future volume.

1 Introduction to the context of practice learning: An overview of key themes

Mark Doel and Steven Shardlow

Importance of practice learning

Wherever in the world social work is practised, there is a need to provide education for those who wish to become social workers. The nature and form of social work education across the world may be as diverse as the varieties of social work practice. However, placements (periods of learning spent in social work agencies) seem to be an essential part of social work courses. All participants in social work education, whether students, practice teachers (field instructors) or tutors (academic social work teachers), seem unanimously to favour placements:

> ... you need placements. I do not think it would be worth having a course without placements ... (Student)

> I feel that practice placements are essential, I don't see how you can theoretically learn to work with people. (Practice Teacher)

> Without the practice the whole course is meaningless. (Tutor)

At least this was the conclusion Syson and Baginsky (1981: 172) drew from a research study. Placements are popular for many reasons, and they serve a variety of purposes in the process of social work education. It is difficult to conceive of effective social work education that adequately prepares students for work with clients without some form of practice-based learning. It seems logical, even common sense, that learning a discipline such as social work requires the development of practical skills, and that it is necessary to spend some time with others to observe and to practise. Only then can students have the opportunity to refine and develop their abilities under controlled conditions in direct work with clients.

Social work takes many different forms around the world – with individuals, families, groups and communities, focusing on individual casework, advocacy, benefits advice and social development work – but it remains essentially a practical activity. In addition to an opportunity to acquire practice skills, placements provide an opportunity for students to develop a sense of their own professional identity, to use and acquire relevant knowledge for practice and to help them to develop a sense of professional values.

The central concern of this book is to examine how best to help students learn about social work practice while they are on placement in social work agencies. To maximize the potential of this type of learning, some key conditions are necessary.

First, students need to be given pieces of work such that they are responsible, under guidance, for ensuring that the following processes are completed: planning, intervention, evaluation and review. If students *only* observe others carrying out social work and do not have the opportunity to practise social work themselves, their learning will be impeded. There is an important place in social work education for observational placements and to see others modelling social work practice; however, neither this type of placement nor observing others practise social work are sufficient to enable students to learn about how to practise social work themselves. They need the opportunity to practise. This is evident in many other areas of our lives: for example, if we wish to learn how to use a computer, we can learn something about computers by watching others and listening to explanations; however, only when we run our fingers over the keyboard and try to make the computer respond to our wishes do we really learn how to use the machine. The same principles apply to learning about social work.

Second, each student needs to have one person in the agency who is responsible for their learning – a practice teacher (this is the term used in the United Kingdom, in North America the term 'field educator' is preferred – please see the glossary for a more detailed discussion of the range of different terms used to describe this role). The practice teacher will frequently have only one student at any one time, although there are different models where practice teachers have several students at once. Whether the practice teacher has only one or several students, the learning relationship is highly personalized, and considerable attention can be given to the learning needs of the individual student. This is in direct contrast to much of higher education, where students may have little direct, personal access to teachers. There are differing opinions about how the practice teachers should practise their craft of teaching and helping students learn about social work practice – the provision of high-quality practice teaching is the subject matter of this book.

There are some elements that are essential to good practice teaching:

- Practice teachers can best help the student when they regard themselves as *teachers*. Perhaps this requires some explanation. It is only relatively recently in the United Kingdom that this has been the case. For many years, most practice teachers did not emphasize the active teaching function of their role but saw themselves as passive supervisors of the students' work. Often, they were helping students to practise what they had learned at university, rather than actively teaching students about social work practice. Now an increasingly important aspect of being a practice teacher is to do just what the term suggests – *teach*.
- Practice teachers are also co-ordinators of learning opportunities: they are organizers or commissioners, but not necessarily the sole providers of teaching. Hence, many practice teachers draw upon the abilities of their colleagues within the social work agency to teach some aspects of social work to students, in addition to teaching students themselves.
- The relationship between students and practice teachers is built upon foundations of openness and negotiation. This will never be an easy or simple task, as practice teachers must carry the responsibility for examining a student's practice competence. Hence, it is inevitable that many students will experience some anxiety about the nature of this relationship. Thus it is essential that models of practice learning be used creatively to empower the learner. This can only be achieved where there is a climate of openness and mutual trust.

We believe this form of learning through high-quality practice teaching to be a fundamental and essential part of good social work education. Without high-quality practice learning, social work students cannot be adequately equipped for the real world of social work.

A complete programme of social work education will include both class-based theoretical learning, most usually taught in a university or similar institution of higher education, and practice learning taught in a social work agency. These two different types of learning opportunity are provided by very different organizations, and there may well be tension between the university and the agency in any social work programme. If this tension helps students to develop a critical focus to their practice, it is valuable and useful. Consider the following:

Example

> *Tariq, a Muslim student, has a placement in a social work agency that provides care for children who cannot live with their parents: the care is provided sometimes by substitute families and sometimes in homes for children. The practice in the agency challenges the research findings that he has been pre-*

sented with about how to provide high-quality care, so practice provides a critical edge for theory. Likewise, his understanding of the needs that the children have is shaped by his knowledge of child development gained at university before the placement, and he can use this knowledge to inform his thinking. Also, both the practices of the agency and the material presented at university are different to his own personal and religious views. Hence, theoretical knowledge helps to inform and structure his practice and vice versa, and these tensions promote learning.

Ideally, the knowledge and learning gained in one learning environment interact with knowledge gained in the other environment. Through this process, theory and practice interact with each other and help to create a social work practitioner who is engaged with the many dimensions of social work. To achieve this type of balance, there is a need for mutual planning and co-ordination between the university and the agency. This can be achieved in a variety of ways through many different structural arrangements. Where this joint approach to the provision of learning for students is absent, it is more likely that students' experiences will be *ad hoc*, inconsistent and lacking a clear focus.

Key concerns about practice learning

If we accept that placements are essential for social work courses, a number of questions come immediately to mind:

- how to develop effective and efficient systems for practice learning – how to create placement opportunities for students?
- what to teach during a placement?
- how to structure the student's learning?
- how to examine a student's competence to be a social worker?
- how the university and the social work agency should interact, and who has the power to determine important issues about the structure of practice learning?
- what kind of education and training to provide for practice teachers (field educators)?

A further consideration is how to do these things in ways that are fair and open. The authors in this book develop a number of different themes in response to some of these and other questions. We would like to highlight some of the most significant debates arising from these questions which find expression in this book.

Indigenous and external influences on practice learning

The extent to which social work and social work education should draw upon the local and indigenous traditions of any society rather than being influenced by international ideas and trends is a major theme evident in many of the contributions in the book.

In Chapter 3, Terry Sacco describes a tension in South Africa between views that derive from traditional beliefs arising from a collectivist philosophy of life, in which the individual is part of a network in harmony with nature, and an individualistic society regulated by the belief that people are consumers who can dominate nature. Similar ideas are explored by Harry Walker (Chapter 5), with respect to Maori cultures in New Zealand. Both argue for social work students to be freed from a possible tyranny of dominant modes of thinking that reflect global economic power. Yet it is not just social work students who need to think about such issues: these influences are also felt by teachers and clients.

Such issues are not confined to those societies in which white colonialists have oppressed black or native populations. In Chapter 10, Ivo Reznicek describes different traditions of learning: those deriving from the Austro-Hungarian Empire and those of American social work education. His chapter describes the search for compromises between the different traditions. In a similar vein, Iris Shuk-fong Ng-Wan (Chapter 12) analyses differences in approaches to learning, grounded in cultural history and recent experiences. She explores the modifications made to teach a course, first developed in Hong Kong, for potential practice teachers in the People's Republic of China.

Wherever social work education has been introduced, be it India, the People's Republic of China, the Czech Republic, the Russian Federation, New Zealand or South Africa, these tensions are evident. The discussion takes a different form in different chapters, but the underlying themes are evident. In countries where social work and social work education are recent innovations, social work educators need to think carefully about such issues if they are to avoid developing a social work practice and forms of social work education that do not fit with the historical and cultural traditions of their society.

Societies where social work has been established for some time also need to consider these debates. They can perpetuate oppression by attempting to export inappropriate paradigms of social work education, and they need to develop and adapt to the changing cultural context at home. Of course, these concerns do not imply that we should each isolate ourselves and our traditions of social work education; there is much to be learned from the experiences of others, as long as they are considered carefully and examined so that we can all decide for ourselves about their relevance to our own approaches to social work education.

Social work education and society

The form of social work that develops in any society is shaped by the prevailing social, economic and cultural forces. The same is true of social work education. However, social work education may or may not be useful in preparing students for practice in any society. There can be a misfit between the requirements of practice and the knowledge, skills and values that students acquire during the educational process, leaving students poorly equipped to face the rigours of social work practice. How to make social work education relevant for students remains a challenge that confronts all social work educators. All of the authors address this concern, directly or indirectly.

In Chapter 4, Bart Grossman and Robin Perry describe the current mismatch between social work, social work education and clients' realities in the United States, where much social work activity is devoted to the affluent rather than the poor, and where a large number of students actively choose not to work with poorer people. Yet the extent of poverty is such that massive social work intervention is required. They argue for the need to shift the nature and form of social work education. In contrast, R.R. Singh (Chapter 11) describes the evolution of social work education through a close involvement with social problems and how the interaction between providing a social work service and social work practice has resulted in a creative synthesis. In Postscript, by Andrey Panov and Evdokia Kholostova, we understand how the evolving structures for social work education are shaped by the broader systems of education. Taking yet another perspective on this issue, Lesley Hughes and Karen Heycox (Chapter 7) argue the importance of proper procedures and structures to measure students' professional competence, in order to ensure that society is protected from incompetent practitioners.

Organizational relationships

The nature and quality of organizational arrangements are key determinants in the success of practice learning. In shorthand, this is the 'social work agency/educational establishment relationship'. The use of placements as a form of learning requires that there should be some liaison between the teaching institution and the practice agency. This relationship may take a variety of different forms, and these are highlighted by Gayla Rogers in her comparative analysis in Chapter 2. She looks at the United Kingdom model, where social work agencies and universities jointly provide social work education through formal partnership arrangements. In contrast, Ivo Reznicek (Chapter 10) describes how personal and informal relationships have been essential in locating and providing placements in the Czech Republic. The question is raised as to who has the power to define the type of placement arrangements and the way that these will operate. The advantages of self-selection arrangements are advocated strongly by Harry Walker (Chapter 5). Throughout the book, there are many different examples of how these relationships are constructed and maintained, with indications of the possible consequences of different arrangements.

Theory and practice

Closely related to organizational relationships is a debate and discussion about the function of the placement in relation to the student's social work education. Is the placement the opportunity to put into practice what has already been learned in an academic context? Is it an opportunity to observe practice, do practice or combine both? These are not the only possibilities; in Chapter 6, Mark Doel and Steven Shardlow suggest that practice should form and shape a student's learning through the medium of a practice curriculum, and that the learning on a placement is of a very particular nature.

Learning in class situations and learning in practice environments each have their own unique and distinct features as well as similarities. The dialogue between the two settings can become a creative interchange for learning. In part, the function that the placement has in the construction of learning will be defined through the nature of the relationship between the educational institution and the social work agency, and their respective beliefs about the function of the placement in mediating theory and practice.

How to help students and practice teachers to learn

Learning is at the core of this book: not just with regard to how students in agencies can be helped to learn about social work practice, but how practice teachers can be prepared to teach them. The book explores a number of approaches to learning; for example, Harry Walker (Chapter 5) and Iris Shuk-fong Ng-Wan (Chapter 12) draw upon Freire's theories of conscientization to inform their approach to practice learning, while Marion Bogo (Chapter 8) looks at a range of learning theories to consider how adults can best be helped to learn. Mark Doel and Steven Shardlow (Chapter 6) approach the question by looking at methods of learning and structures to support it.

Most importantly, Svein Bøe (Chapter 9) reminds us of the need to listen to the views of both practice teachers and students about their experiences of learning and teaching. Only by taking these views seriously and using them to help build on existing practice can we hope to develop new and better forms of practice learning.

Overview of the organization of the book

The book is divided into three parts. The first part, *Frameworks*, introduces a range of different concepts and ideas as a base for considering subsequent sections of the book. The second part of the book, *Teaching and Learning*, focuses on the experiences of those involved in the processes of social work education and also offers ideas about how social work educators can promote learning. In the final part of the book, *Case Studies*, case examples focus on the experiences of four countries in developing an aspect of practice learning.

We hope that this will be the first of a number of volumes focusing on practice learning in an international context; in particular, we would like to see a future book with contributions from field instructors and practice teachers.

Part One

Frameworks

2 Comparative approaches to practice learning

Gayla Rogers

Introduction

From an overall historical standpoint, there has been an enduring conviction that carefully supervised practice learning is a fundamental, vital and indispensable component of social work education, and has been since its formalization as an academic discipline. It is often cited as the most important and significant aspect of professional development (Butler and Elliott, 1985; Kadushin, 1992; Thompson, Osada and Anderson, 1990; Towle, 1954; Young, 1967). Yet a number of authors report that the practice teaching component is a neglected area of educational concern (Brennen, 1982; Shatz, 1989). It is well recognized that 'knowing about', however sophisticated the knowledge, falls short of the responsibilities of a profession, which must include 'knowing how'. According to Kadushin (1992: 11), 'Skills imagined and enacted vicariously in the mind in the class can only be practised in the flesh in the living interchange with a client.' Only in the translation of knowledge into practice, acquired through experiential and practice learning, can social work education achieve professional justification. 'Theoretical knowledge and practical ability thus constitute the twin pillars around which the whole educational edifice is constructed' (Evans, 1987: 83). Through practice learning on their course, students begin to adopt the values and world-view that characterize the profession, and begin to internalize that professional role as part of their identity (Rogers and McDonald, 1989a).

Practice teachers' importance and position within the curriculum has rarely been questioned and has often been the focus of study in both the United Kingdom and North America (Kadushin, 1992; Gardiner, 1989). In spite of the fact that social work may be defined and practised differently throughout the world, there appears to be consensus about the issues and challenges social work courses face regarding the practice learning component of their programmes and the role of the practice teacher. Social workers

11

who are practice teachers have much in common with their counterparts in other countries in terms of practice learning, perhaps more so than on any other social work-related topic. There is something universal in the struggle to help students integrate theory and practice. Regardless of how the context of politics, culture and geography influences the nature and choice of the theory and the definition and scope of the practice students are attempting to integrate, such integration appears to be a universal expectation.

This chapter illuminates the salient issues and challenges facing social work educationalists with regard to practice learning. It begins with the theory/practice and integration/linkage debates. Other recurring themes identify these challenges: practice teachers' roles and responsibilities; the development and maintenance of high-quality placements, and the contributions from adult and higher education.

Practice teachers provide one-third to one-half of a student's professional education and are seen as integral to social work courses. It is apparent that practice teaching has become and continues to evolve into a legitimate and distinct area of study and research (Gardiner, 1989). An international study (Raskin, Skolnick and Wayne, 1991) to examine social work field instruction received responses from 51 countries and found that the quality of field instruction emerged as a major concern everywhere. Much of how practice learning and teaching is researched, analysed and examined is related to political, economic and social factors, and to a lesser extent to pedagogical and philosophical factors. These are the factors that create different meanings and place different emphases and importance on what are, in fact, similar issues and challenges.

Common ground: Issues and challenges

All programmes of social work education want students to have a valid and valuable practice learning opportunity within their course where they can learn 'about' practice as well as 'how to' practise under the guidance and supervision of a competent practice teacher. The issues this creates and the challenges it poses to social work course administrators, faculty, practice teachers, agency administrators and students alike have some elements in common. For example, the transfer of knowledge from the classroom to the placement, the acquisition and application of skills and the development of a professional identity are considered to be the essential learning processes in practice learning, regardless of country of origin (Gardiner, 1984a; Pettes, 1967; Rodway and Rogers, 1993; Sawdon, 1986; Skolnik, 1989; Tolson and Kopp, 1988).

Similarly, the relationship between the student and the practice teacher, the methods used to teach, supervise and assess, and the availability and relevance of practice opportunities all have an impact on the teaching–learning process. It is through these processes that students acquire a professional identity and the perceptual lens of a social worker. Social work courses struggle universally with the turnover and training of practice teachers, the shortage of good-quality placements, the challenge of working collaboratively with the practice community, dealing fairly and effectively with weak or failing students, and providing adequate resources for the practice teaching component of the social work course.

The integration and transfer debate

Practice learning is the component of a course that is undertaken in an agency under the supervision of a practice teacher. For many students struggling to make sense of the theoretical perspectives of the course, the placement enables them to extend their own learning, and it will often set the pattern for future working methods and professional practice (Thompson, Osada and Anderson, 1990). This discussion appears to be of vital importance, because the integration of theory and practice and the transfer of learning have not only been driving forces in curriculum development but have also been salient to the continued efforts of accrediting bodies to improve social work courses and the qualifications of their graduates.

The split: Theory versus practice

There have, over the years, been difficulties in establishing a workable partnership between 'town and gown', between education and training, in the face of differing expectations, values and practices. Agencies accuse courses of failing to provide the sort of workers they require, countered by charges from course organizers that the people they have trained 'are not being employed in the correct way' (Blyth, 1980: 28). This epitomizes the historic split between theoretical classes and practice teaching on social work courses. The split between theory and practice, according to Evans (1987), is largely a product of the institutional structure of social work. In attempting to bridge that gap, there are discussions on the integration of theory and practice (Paley, 1984, 1987); the relevance of theory for practice (Harris, 1983; Sibeon, 1989–90); the transfer of learning (Gardiner, 1984a, 1987), and the role of practice teaching in social work education (Casson, 1982; Syson and Baginsky, 1981).

Integration of theory and practice is considered difficult due to the fact that students move back and forth between the academic setting and the placement. This split results in a 'tandem model' of curriculum design (Davies, 1981) and has been the subject of much debate and concern for social work educators (Hutchison, 1977; Parsloe, 1977; Timms, 1970). Hearn (1982) argues that there is a problem in defining what 'theory' and 'practice' actually mean. These terms have come to be understood as 'theory' meaning what is learned on courses and 'practice' as what is done in agencies.

The relationship between theory and practice

Sibeon (1982) suggests that the relationship between theory and practice mirrors the division of labour between colleges and agencies. Payne (1990: 4) argues that the 'debate about theory and practice links is one of the manifestations of a continuing struggle for influence over the definition of the nature of social work'. He suggests that there are three ideological traditions in the development of social work which represent differing positions about theory and practice and the struggle for occupational control:

- the pragmatic tradition, associated with work in official agencies;
- the socialist tradition, concentrating on the reform aspects;
- the therapeutic tradition, dealing with individualized needs.

In the UK, the Central Council for Education and Training in Social Work (CCETSW) requires training programmes to develop their courses in partnership with employers. This is a model which provides managers with a direct opportunity to influence the content of practice, but Howe (1990–91) believes that this will result in managers exerting too much control over the definition of social work and the content of training. He fears that social workers will be 'trained rather than educated [and] become skilled functionaries rather than expert professionals' (1990–91: 49). What is important is to examine how, in actuality, theory seems to influence practice, as this underlies the distinction between technician and professional.

Some writers claim that researched knowledge and practice can inform each other (Paley, 1984). However, Carew (1979) found that few social workers used theory explicitly in their work, and that although most thought it was important, its use provided a framework rather than a guide to action. In an important series of studies, Curnock and Hardiker (1979; Hardiker, 1981) show that workers use theoretical knowledge inexplicably and advocate the notion of 'practice theories ... which refer to the process of using and integrating professional experience and knowledge in a skilful and ethical manner' (Curnock and Hardiker, 1979: 38). The problem with this notion, as Paley (1984: 21) points out, is 'how do we discriminate between this process and the process of integrating professional experience and knowledge in an unskilful or unethical manner?' Cocozzelli and Constable (1985), in an American study, confirm the British finding that general approaches to clients, rather than explicit use of theory, constitute the most common relationship between theory and practice.

Barriers to integration

There is a temptation to think that the argument is solely between practitioners and academics. Sheldon's (1978) distinction, referred to by several authors, between the 'theoretical sub-culture' and the 'practice sub-culture' certainly supports that view, as he sees the practice sub-culture becoming increasingly anti-intellectual. Thus the rift between scientific theory and practice wisdom is replayed in the tension between education and training, classroom learning and practice learning. Interestingly, a study by Coulshed (1986: 126) concludes with the recommendation that 'further studies need to be undertaken to investigate ways in which all students can become competent practitioners by devoting more of their time and energies to the academic part of professional training'.

A factor which adds to difficulties in integrating theory and practice is the large number of disciplines from which social work theory has traditionally been drawn (Barbour, 1984) and the fact that there is no theoretical consensus in social work (Whittington and Holland, 1985). With the expansion of theoretical perspectives available to social work in recent years, the problem of how to incorporate material into the academic and practice curricula without reducing content to merely token levels has intensified. With generic content superseding specialist training, the difficulties experienced by students appear to be compounded when faced with applying generic concepts in very specific practice contexts.

Solutions to integration difficulties

CCETSW's solution to integrating general theories within specific practice settings lies in the requirement of the Diploma in Social Work (DipSW – the British social work qualification) that students apply their core social work knowledge and skills in a placement of a 'particular' practice during the second year of their course. Another solution to the split between academe and practice and the sheer vastness of the knowledge base is the belief in the potential power of the transfer of learning (Whittington, 1986), which is more than simply a concept and – judging from the number of articles – is of profound importance. Harris (1983) notes that while transfer of learning is not a recent conception, it acquired special significance for social work educators when it appeared in CCETSW regulations for the award of the CQSW (CCETSW, 1981) and has continued to appear as a requirement for the DipSW (CCETSW, 1991a: 19).

Transfer of learning involves a capacity to comprehend specific experience at a level of abstraction that allows its general characteristics to be applied to other experiences that share only some of the features of the original (Harris, 1983). This ability is seen to be fundamental to a competent social worker, suggesting that course teachers and practice teachers consciously teach for transfer. Gardiner's work (1984a, 1984b, 1989), which appears to be a key reference for other authors, seeks to advance the understanding of the concept of transfer and suggests how courses can be designed to equip students for practice in a wider range of situations than they have encountered during training. Echoing Harris and Gardiner, Gray (1986) believes that the practice teacher has a crucial role in helping students to make patterns from experiences, to transfer learning to new situations and, especially, to understand how they transfer that learning. 'Transfer holds the prospect of preserving genericism in a complex world of specialised needs and suggests a way of designing programmes that are not only defensible educationally and professionally, but are also of manageable content and realistic length' (Whittington, 1986: 574–5).

Rothman (1977) believes that for the profession to mature fully, the approach to practice learning has to shift from a situation in which education is controlled by practitioners emphasizing skills and apprenticeship to one in which education is under university control, wherein intellectual concepts and principles are given greatest emphasis. This notion was taken to the extreme in the 1960s, when several American schools developed teaching centres using college-based practice teachers instead of the long-standing approach of using agency practitioners, launching a long debate about whether practice teachers should be based in agencies or colleges (Cassidy, 1969).

One Canadian school operated a college-based model until very recently. A study of this programme provided evidence that the priorities of university-based practice teachers are more likely related to the goal of the development of an autonomous professional, whereas agency-based practice teachers' priorities are related to the service goals of getting the job done (Rachlis, 1988). Today, the vast majority of practice learning is done in social agencies, and the majority of practice teachers are agency-based. The vestiges of the struggle to maintain an educational focus within a practice setting using practitioners as educators can be seen in the increased efforts to develop educational resources and articulate clearly-defined roles for academic faculty and practice teachers.

The role of the tutor in integration

The approach a course takes to the tutor/liaison role also affects the transfer of knowledge from the classroom to the placement and the integration of theory and practice. The tutor/liaison is the individual assigned the role of linking the student and practice teacher with the university or social work course. Several authors have indicated that the tutor/liaison function is central and critical to facilitating the linkage between the placement and classroom (Faria, Brownstein and Smith, 1988; Rogers and McDonald, 1989a; Rosenblum and Raphael, 1983; Rosenfeld, 1988). 'The linkage function serves to enhance the practicum, so that it is not merely an apprenticeship but also develops into an educational experience' (Smith, Faria and Brownstein, 1986: 68). The tutor/liaison carries the 'major responsibility for making any practice learning situation work' (Gordon, 1982: 118). The tutor/liaison role has been called the 'single most important link between class and field' (Fellin, 1982: 112). Rogers and McDonald (1989a) found that the single most important coefficient predicting practice teachers' perception of students being prepared for professional practice was help with the learning process from the tutor/liaison. It is apparent that the model and approach taken by a social work course, and in particular the involvement of the tutor/liaison, has an impact on integration, transfer of learning and the quality and effectiveness of practice learning. The approach or model of practice learning that a social work course adopts influences the role of the practice teacher.

Practice teachers: Roles and responsibilities

'The role of the practice teacher as the bridge between academic and practice sub-cultures is ripe for creative development' (Sawdon, 1991: 79). Sawdon and Sawdon (1987: 4) raise two important questions regarding the factors that make for a good practice learning experience:

- To what extent are the agencies in collaboration with educational institutions able to offer a suitable learning environment for the development of student potential and practice competence?
- To what extent do the individual parties involved have the knowledge, skills and commitment to make use of and develop that environment?

Gardiner's (1989) study appears to support the view that students learn best with practice teachers who are clear enough and confident enough about their own practice and knowledge base to adapt their teaching in response to the students' learning needs and learning style. In examining helpful and unhelpful practice teaching styles from students' perspectives, Secker (1992: 13) found the most helpful style was 'when teachers were warm and reassuring, and challenged the students to develop and justify their own ideas about cases, rather than telling them what to think'. This style requires time, patience and a 'hands-on' approach to allow the process of learning and reflecting to unfold.

There is general agreement in the literature on the four key functions of the practice teacher role: *manager, teacher, enabler* and *assessor* (Collins and Ottley, 1986; Fisher, 1990; Pettes, 1979). All four functions entail a range of associated tasks which change with the phases of the placement process. In order to promote students' learning and to engage effectively in the monitoring and assessment tasks, Fisher (1990) offers a framework within which to locate and develop helpful supervisory skills based on the key elements of respect, feedback, challenge and modelling. The skills that are most likely to influence students' learning are: encouraging self-criticism; encouraging open discussion; understanding student feelings; particularizing student concerns; sensing student feelings, and clarifying purpose (Knight and Glazer-Semmel, 1990). These skills suggest that the primary function of the practice teacher is one of enabling the student to develop into an autonomous professional and combines elements of the mentor, therapist and teacher role.

Rosenblatt and Mayer (1975), surveying students' responses to their field instructors, found four objectionable supervisory styles affecting their relationships with field instructors. One is constrictive, where the field instructor is too controlling; the second is amorphous, where there is a lack of clarifying feedback; the third style is unsupportive, and the fourth is therapeutic, where evaluating the student's work is bypassed in favour of focusing supervision on the student's personality.

The practice teacher–student relationship

Not only is the role important, but also the relationship between the student and the practice teacher plays a critical role in the teaching/learning process. Fortune maintains: 'The instructor–student relationship often is the most intense, growth producing (or growth retarding), and memorable experience of a student's education' (Fortune et al., 1985: 93). It has been argued that the core qualities for effective practice teaching lie in the practice teacher's own competence as a social work practitioner (Fisher, 1990). But training programmes can only do so much and cannot compensate for qualities which are not there at the outset. 'The success of the placement hinges not only upon formal working agreements, good supervision and the completion of assessed work, but also on the relationship between practice teacher, student and tutor and the unspoken rules of engagement which underlie these activities' (McBeath and Webb, cited in Bell and Webb, 1992: 30).

From a student's point of view, there is a need to balance being supportive with focusing on the tasks. This opens up for discussion the question of how much personal growth and work on one's own developmental issues needs to be completed as a part of practice learning, and furthermore, raises the question of how much of the personal growth is to be facilitated, directed and subsequently assessed by the practice teacher. Practice teaching could, in advancing the personal/emotional growth agenda, look more like therapy than learning. Although, in justifying this inclusion, some would argue that 'clinical learning', by definition, incorporates personal self-examination, resulting in personal/emotional growth in order for the student to learn how to use one's self effectively in development as a professional (Rubenstein, 1992; Saari, 1989). The approach taken by a practice teacher can be placed on a continuum ranging from viewing the student as a learner to viewing the student as a new, inexperienced worker to viewing the student as a client. How students are viewed is closely related to how practice teachers understand their role and responsibilities.

Supervision versus teaching

In the United Kingdom, there has been a shift away from the notion of 'supervision' to more active 'teaching' on the part of the practice teacher, resulting in a more structured, time-consuming and demanding involvement. Consider, for example, the implications of having to produce evidence that their students have achieved their competencies (CCETSW, 1991b). Problems of a different sort emerge in North America. The notion of field supervisors as 'teachers' has not been strongly advocated, as rarely in North America are they referred to as 'practice teachers'. Often, the terms 'field supervisor' and 'field instructor' are used interchangeably. More recently, the term 'field educator' has begun to appear. Perhaps this is indicative of a shift more in line with British thought regarding the recognition of the educational versus supervisory role inherent in practice teaching.

Enhancing practice teaching

In recent years in the United Kingdom, there has been a growing emphasis on improving the supply, quality and effectiveness of practice placements. In response to this concern, a national framework has been created to plan the teaching, assessing and accrediting of practice teachers. The National Organisation for Practice Teaching has worked alongside CCETSW to encourage the development and recognition of practice teaching (Mitchell, 1992). This development has been supported by the introduction of training for practice teachers with the aim that all practice teachers will gain the Practice Teaching Award.

Despite the massive effort to develop, approve and offer practice teaching training courses, a fundamental problem remains in the UK. There continues to be a chronic shortage of good practice teachers and practice placements

(Borrill, O'Sullivan and Sleeman, 1991). Researching into this issue, Bell and Webb (1992) attempt to redress what they perceive to be a neglected area in the social work literature: the perceptions, both positive and negative, of practice teachers about taking students on placement. They found that the rewards and costs of taking on a student were similar to what others have established (Gray, 1987; Slater, 1992). The rewards include: satisfaction from working with the student; contribution to the development of social work practice; the prospect of promotion, and status conferred by the validation of their own practice. The negative features include: lack of resources and support; inadequate preparation and understanding of programme providers' expectations; superficial divisions of labour between colleges and agencies; a non-user-friendly environment; the sense of isolation, and lack of recognition.

Even though there are many able and experienced social workers who would make ideal practice teachers, they have neither the time nor the incentive to take on the extra responsibility (Mitchell, 1992). Weinstein (quoted in Mitchell, 1992: 21) believes that some of the main stumbling-blocks are workload relief and the cost of training. Training, she states, 'is labour intensive because ... each practice teacher trainee has to have someone supervising their practice and observing them supervising a student'.

New practice teachers may react negatively to having their work with students scrutinized and assessed, especially if there is no organizational recognition of their efforts in terms of status and salary (Davies and Kinoch, 1991). It is possible that the accreditation system will reduce the numbers of practice teachers, since some may be selected out, others may be deterred by the process, others may not be allowed study leave, and others may consider it pointless to undertake the work involved only to have to fit in taking a student on top of their regular workload (Fisher, 1990). Furthermore, concern is being expressed over the cost and amount of time given to practice teacher training programmes at a time when agency commitments and resources are under pressure (Sawdon, 1991). These concerns appear to echo the past with reference to Brandon's (1976) comments about the widening gulf between educators and practitioners in his criticism of the poor quality of supervision available for students and the number of social work educators who have become disillusioned with the directions of the profession.

Practice teachers are the key

The role of the practice teacher is, in many ways, unique for its opportunity for practitioners to both demonstrate and discuss social work practice. The practice curriculum is presented in the form of objectives, competencies and/or outcomes. However, it usually is left to the practice teacher to implement the practice curriculum within the context of the agency setting, according to policies of the educational institution and adapted to the individual needs of the student. Faced with the competing demands of practice and education – and little time for either – the practice teacher must find the most expeditious methods.

In North America, practice teachers (field supervisors) without the benefit – or even in spite of the benefit – of a course on practice teaching select teaching methods based on: how they were taught; what they think will be most effective; what fits with their practice orientation and world-view; what suits the organization's culture and policies, and what will get the job done.

Regardless of how the role is defined, practice teachers are seen as essential to a social work course but are often viewed as peripheral to the faculty (academic teaching staff). There are loud criticisms regarding the under-resourcing of the practice learning component of social work courses on both sides of the Atlantic, which has a profound effect upon the availability of practice placements and the quality of practice learning.

Developing and maintaining high-quality placements

The availability or lack of high-quality practice learning opportunities has been the subject of much debate and research for many years. Related to this are a number of studies that reveal inconsistencies in the provision, training and support of practice teachers (Johnson, 1989; Perry, 1990; Raynor, 1992). Problems such as inadequacy of supply owing to pressure on agencies, the absence of quality monitoring in practice teaching and the turnover of practice teachers are recurrent themes in the UK, Canada and the USA. For example, Perry (1990) found that insufficient places are made available and that provision is too dependent on the goodwill of practice teachers.

Approaches to placement provision

Two approaches to placement provision have been identified as (1) the 'agency obligation' approach, where senior management commits to providing placements as a core activity and placements are seen as a mainstream responsibility of the organization, and (2) the 'grace and favour' approach, where placements are seen as a favour done for colleges, and practice teaching is seen as a marginal activity (Raynor, 1992: 25). In this approach, placements depend on personal contacts and whims of individuals (Grimwood and Fletcher, 1987). When practice teaching is seen as an activity that social workers are expected to carry out in addition to their normal workload, as an optional extra, practitioners rarely agree to take on this commitment more than once or twice. The result is a high rate of turnover among qualified social workers. Syson and Baginsky (1981: 32), summarizing the situation in the early 1980s in their major study of practice placements, noted 'CCETSW's concern that an overall shortage of placements combined with a high turnover of practice teachers might be limiting the number of opportunities available to courses'.

A comprehensive survey of practice teaching in Wales found deficiencies in the supply of certain kinds of placements, wide variations in agency provision and an uneven pattern of placement support (Raynor, 1992). Statutory agencies may regard the educative function as a further burden to their already stretched resources or as an add-on to their main function of providing direct social services. Tensions increase further if the finite resources available for direct service delivery are redirected for training, as the benefits of training are not always readily apparent.

Resource issues: The British response

Agency constraints coupled with a national shortage of placements have created a culture where there is an inevitable compromise between willingness to take a student versus the quality and competence of the practice teacher. From the point of view of practice teachers, the 'most widespread and deeply rooted concern amongst [them] was the lack of time and space to do the job properly' (Williamson et al., 1989: 32). This echoes earlier studies where few practice teachers had any workload relief in return for taking students (Syson and Baginsky, 1981). The high turnover rate of practice teachers has been attributed to limited recognition, abuse of goodwill, and new awareness of the critical demands of the task (Clapton, 1989).

A major problem in addressing the resource issue, however, is the lack of empirical evidence relating to the demands which providing student placements makes on practice teachers. One study found that 'student placements can make a positive contribution to practice teachers and teams in terms of providing a stimulus, a source of challenge and reappraisal of various aspects of professional and organisational practices, which can be quite highly valued' (James, Morrissey and Wilson, 1990: 108). These points have previously been debated by others, who have concluded that the costs to the agency and the team of having a student are outweighed by the benefits (Shardlow, 1988; Slater, 1992).

Agencies sometimes justify placements on the grounds that the student will provide an extra pair of hands. This argument is highly spurious, since students' contributions to the agency are offset by the time and energy agency staff spend in providing adequate supervision and assessment (Blyth, 1980). The assumption that the traditional model of practice teaching, the one-to-one arrangement, is superior and the most preferable arrangement needs to be challenged in light of the costs, the turnover of practice teachers and the demand for placements. The lack of qualified staff in some placements and the number of placements required by courses led to the creation of 'long-arm' supervision arrangements (Foulds, Sanders and Williams, 1991). Initially, they developed as a way of circumventing CCETSW regulations, but it is likely that variations of this model might provide a basis for cost-effective practice teaching where the accredited practice teacher manages and co-ordinates a range of learning experiences for a number of students, involving a variety of staff who may or may not be accredited. Practice teaching may also be seen as a step to other supervisory or managerial positions, so social workers may undertake student supervision for career development reasons, rather than out of interest. Practice teaching is unlikely to develop any level of expertise until it is seen as a worthwhile activity in itself and not simply a launching-pad for careers in management.

Resource issues: The North American perspective

In North America, practice teachers most often volunteer for the job and are not rewarded financially by the social work course provider or the agency. Only in some cases does the agency provide some release time from regular duties, which only partially compensates for the amount of time the practice teacher devotes to this task. In essence, both the agency and the practice teacher donate their time to the training of social work students. Maintaining a pool of competent practice teachers and motivating them to continue to take students is a common problem.

There is evidence of concern about the high turnover rate among practice teachers in North America. Watt and Thomlison (1981) found that 47 per cent of their national sample of Canadian field instructors were in their first or second year of instructing students. Rogers and McDonald's (1989b) study found that 35 per cent of the field instructors were in their first year and 53 per cent had supervised for less than two years. Bogo and Power's (1992) study found that 46 per cent of first-year field instructors did not volunteer to take another student in the following year. Lacerte, Ray and Irwin (1989) found that 45 per cent of their sample in one American school were instructors for one to two years.

Practice teacher turnover has important implications for universities, agencies and students (Bogo and Power, 1992: 178–9):

> A high turnover rate is costly because it requires considerable time for recruitment of new field instructors. Schools that offer training for new field instructors require continuous resources to provide training and agency release time from client service for staff to attend training.

Retention of practice teachers is an issue which needs to be addressed through long-term strategies. Three factors have been found significant in influencing intent to continue as a field instructor: agency support, faculty support and intrinsic aspects such as enjoyment of teaching, learning new ideas and contributing to the profession (Rosenfeld, 1988). Given the realities of social work practice today, Shapiro (1989: 238) suggests that practice teachers are especially vulnerable to burn-out through trying to meet 'agency and university expectations, juggling needs of students and clients, and striving to integrate roles as educators and social workers ... field instructors may feel torn between bolstering clients above the survival level and providing a solid educational experience for social work students'.

Generally, schools of social work in Canada and the USA rely on a voluntary, collaborative partnership between the university and the placement agency. The university has relied on the agency's goodwill, and the agency has relied on its professional staff's commitment to students. However, 'expecting individual social workers to absorb the extra workload demands for institutional commitments to professional education appears to be an unfair practice' (Bogo and Power, 1992: 188). Interestingly, Bogo and Power found that agency support for decreased workload had no significant effect on intent to continue or not.

Contributions from adult and higher education

In the early 1970s, Malcolm Knowles (1970) popularized the concept of andragogy, which identified learning principles relevant to adults. This was seen as a major breakthrough in learning theories applicable to social work education, and several authors applied these principles to field education, encouraging their adoption into field instruction practices (Clancy, 1985; Gelfand et al., 1975; Hersh, 1984; Knowles, 1972; Siporin, 1982). Since the literature in social work supported the acceptance of the student as an adult learner, a search began for suitable instructional strategies. The premise was that teaching methods needed somehow to match the learning style of the student in the practicum setting in order to maximize learning, professional development and preparation for practice (Kruzich, Friesen and Van Soest, 1986). Learning typologies evolved, illuminating various types of learners and learning styles through the use of inventories or scales which would suggest the most appropriate learning/teaching strategy (Berengarten, 1957; Gregorc, 1982; Kolb, 1976; Myers, 1976).

Subsequent research on learning styles in social work education has underscored their importance in identifying students' preferences (Kadushin, 1976); in teaching direct social work practice (Papell, 1978); for individualizing training (Austin, in Munson, 1979), and their relevance to clinical supervision (Fox and Guild, 1987). Various procedures for making accurate educational diagnoses or assessments of students were promoted, often citing Towle (1954) as the pioneer in the assessment of the student as a learner (Goldmeier, 1983; Lemberger and Marshack, 1991; Webb, 1988). This literature suggests that the social work profession has, to a certain extent, verified that students learn in different ways, and that learning is more effective when teaching is consonant with the student's style. Ramsden's (1985) research has shown that there is no single learning approach, style or orientation which is, of itself, the best; what is desirable is that the learner selects appropriate strategies for matching personal goals and talents with the nature and demands of the learning task.

Competency-based approaches

The move toward competency-based educational principles and practices has been fostered by more rigorous accreditation standards and increasing accountability requirements in practice. This has prompted programmes of social work education to state clear educational objectives and performance criteria that are measurable and observable. Practice teachers, in operationalizing this curriculum and applying these standards in practice learning, use educational supervision that is goal-directed (St John, 1975); structure- and criteria-guided (Dwyer and Urbanowski, 1981); competency-based and task-centred (Larsen and Hepworth, 1982), and problem-focused (Basso, 1987). In doing so, practice teachers use direct teaching methods that enable them to evaluate students' skills and effectiveness accurately while ensuring quality of service. The emphasis is on structured and clearly stated learning plans, practice assignments that are carefully sequenced, and supervision focused on outcomes. The value of this approach is that students become much clearer about what they are supposed to learn. The educational objectives become the evaluation criteria (Arkava and Brennen, 1976). However, social work practice is complex and multi-faceted, which begs the question: can it all be encompassed in specific behavioural objectives? Increasing behavioural specificity tends to increase the number of objectives which need to be examined and assessed. As the number of objectives increases, so does the ability to manage the task, which in turn could reduce both the practicality and perhaps the relevance of the objectives.

Recent contributions from higher education

Recent developments in higher education have highlighted concepts and practices with great potential for social work education. Some of this work, such as the work of Donald Schön (1983, 1987), has already been examined and applied in a social work education context. Papell and Skolnik (1992) use

Schön's concepts to present a paradigm relevant to social work education. Kondrat (1992a, 1992b) uses Schön's work on reflective practice for the professions to supplement her conceptual schema for examining epistemological differences among formal, substantive and critical forms of rationality involved in professional knowledge, professional learning and field education.

Schön (1987: 38) suggests that educating professionals for practice in situations of uncertainty, uniqueness and value conflict is accomplished by the 'reflective practicum'. Through a combination of the student's learning by doing, learning through interactions in the form of a 'reciprocally reflective dialogue' (p. 40) with a coach, and learning by exposure and immersion, students are able to 'use the process of reflection-in-action (the thinking of what they are doing while they are doing it) to combine the competence and artistry embedded in effective practice' (p. 13). Relating this directly to social work education are the notions of educating autonomous practitioners, as opposed to training technicians. For example, Hamilton and Else (1983) note that field instructors need to help students learn to think for themselves, bring knowledge to bear in unpredictable situations and be creative in responding to unique problems.

Brookfield (1986: vii) rejects the school of thought in which 'the facilitation of adult learning is seen as a non-directive, warmly satisfying provision of a resource to a learner, who is fully cognizant of her learning needs and in command of her learning activities'. Instead, he argues for 'a new concept of facilitation that incorporates elements of challenge, confrontation and critical analysis of self and society' (p. 125). The contrasting personalities, philosophies and conflicting priorities of field instructor and student interact continuously. This educational transaction occurs in the context of the agency's culture and structure, clients' problems and issues, and the prevailing political/social/economic climate. The field instructor, using these principles, is less concerned with student satisfaction and more concerned with creating a collaborative learning environment where 'the student is challenged to critically reflect upon her actions and re-examine underlying beliefs, values and theoretical constructs' (Brookfield, 1986: 143).

Mezirow et al. (1990) suggest that contemporary learning theories have given surprisingly little attention to the frames of reference and assumptions that influence the way adults perceive, interpret and act on their experiences. They present a transformation theory of adult learning that challenges prevailing theory and mainstream approaches to adult education. This critical reflection can facilitate transformative and emancipatory learning and promote lifelong learning. There is a growing body of literature on adult women's development and feminist pedagogy (Belenky et al., 1986). This research suggests that educational norms and approaches may not serve men and women equally. Educational practices that focus specifically on meeting the needs of women, both as learners and as developing adults, can inform and support models and methods of social work education (Taylor and Marienau, 1995). Thus there is much research and writing in the higher and adult education arena that is ripe for testing in social work contexts.

Summary discussion

Several substantive themes emerge from comparing approaches to practice learning. Discussions of integration of theory and practice and the transfer of learning permeate the literature in both the United Kingdom and North America. In the UK, this exchange is part of a deeper debate regarding professional educational versus technical training. In North America, integration reflects the approach to practice learning taken by a particular school of social work and the educational methods and teaching strategies employed by the practice teacher. The topic appears to be of considerable importance to practice learning, but the nature and focus of the discussion is quite different.

Practice teaching methods

There is concern and debate in both countries regarding the selection and use of practice teaching methods that are distinct from job supervision techniques and also distinct from therapeutic interventions. The challenge is to treat students as learners, not as employees or clients. This applies to the assessment practices which are argued to require procedures different from job performance appraisals or techniques that measure emotional/personal growth.

In the UK, this thrust has evolved through the shift from 'supervisor' to 'practice teacher' and shifts in the validation and accreditation strategies for professional and higher education. Changes in course requirements that specify areas of students' knowledge and abilities which have to be demonstrated are complemented by the explicit expectations that educational institutions and agencies will work closely together in course planning and in the selection and assessment of students and practice teachers. The national training courses for practice teachers provide content on teaching and learning for professional competence. Whether these educational methodologies for adult learners are being applied, and whether they do produce a 'new' and 'improved' practice teacher and consequently a more competent social work practitioner, remains to be seen.

In North America, training practice teachers is conducted on a college-by-college basis, in widely varying amounts. There is literature available to assist schools to help their practice teachers select and use appropriate instructional methods to maintain an educational focus, but there is no national perspective on how this is done or even how important it is in relation to the education of social workers.

Practice teacher turnover and partnerships

Both in the United Kingdom and North America, concern is expressed about the turnover of practice teachers, the shortage of practice teachers and their need for training. This problem is seen to be endemic to the management and organization of field placements in the UK. Solutions are found in senior management taking more responsibility for ensuring that practice teaching is a valued activity and in CCETSW's accrediting of practice teachers through the Award. In North America, the problem is located in the school of social work's inability to motivate, recognize and support field instructors. Solutions are expressed in the provision of perks by schools to field instructors and making field instructors feel more connected and committed to the school. Rarely are solutions seen in terms of relationships with senior management, although there is discussion of partnerships and working collaboratively with the community.

The concept of 'partnership' in North America is not the same as the notion implied by CCETSW's commitment to partnerships as expressed by 'programme providers'. Whether the British consortia bring 'town and gown' together so that social workers are more 'competent in practice' or whether instead this leads to employer-defined training and an anti-intellectual, de-professionalized ethos remains to be seen. In North America, social work courses are only beginning to develop ways to allow the practice community to comment and have some input into the curriculum (see Chapter 4). When courses involve members from the social work community on advisory or other committees, engage in joint research projects and invite practitioners into the classroom, they are seen to be working collaboratively with the community. North Americans operate partnerships with specific organizations such as those delivering child welfare services, in order to enhance staff by increasing the number of them with social work degrees. These partnerships are very limited and not typical of the way degree-granting programmes in social work normally operate.

The value in comparing approaches

In certain respects, there is much that North Americans can learn from the study of British practice teaching. In particular, the advancements in anti-discriminatory and anti-oppressive practice extend the Canadian and American work in multi-cultural and multi-racial educational policies. The accreditation of practice teachers elevates their role and place in the social work course as well as ensuring a minimum expectation in their work with students. The Practice Teaching Award is also seen as a solution to the turnover and shortage of practice teachers. It is possible to envision the development of a recognized qualification for practice teachers in both Canada and the United States as a goal for schools of social work and individual practitioners.

On the other hand, there are some things the British can glean from the study of practice learning in North America. In North America, social work degrees, the BSW, MSW and DSW (PhD Social Work), are recognized as both professional and academic qualifications, whereas in the United Kingdom, the DipSW (or its predecessor, the CQSW or CSS) is the professional qualification in social work, and it is separate from any other academic degree. In North America, there is a clear continuum and progression from a community college social service diploma to a university degree at the Bachelor, Master and then Doctoral level, and there is also less debate or confusion surrounding the education versus training of social workers. The word 'training' does not appear in the discussion of social work education in North America, nor is its future tied in any way to the employers' satisfaction with the end product of the course. Practice learning is seen as one of several integral components of the social work degree. Those who believe that the practice learning component is more important than any of the other components may wish it was given the status and priority it is granted in the United Kingdom. However, it may be that its importance is in relation to the other components of policy, research, human behaviour and practice methods, and that they all contribute equally to the professional education of social workers. This point may be worth consideration in the United Kingdom and may help advance the position of social workers in British society as a professional body with specific academic credentials. The separation of the DipSW social work qualification from a hierarchy of academic degrees is worthy of re-examination and may be the key to deciding that social work is a profession, not a vocation.

In summary, practice learning is a core component of social work education. It is complex, multi-faceted and multi-dimensional, as it involves so many stakeholders. This component requires resources and considerations that are different from any other component of the social work curriculum. Its success and outcomes depend on inter-personal, intra-system and inter-system relationships, which in turn require collaboration, co-operation and mutual understanding. Practice teachers need support, development opportunities and rewards. Practice placements need to feel a sense of ownership and accept some responsibility for practice learning. Educational institutions need to listen and be responsive to the changing environments in the agencies, they need to understand the meaning of partnerships and share the responsibility for practice learning with practice placements. Students need a chance to develop a professional identity, to learn the practice behaviours, knowledge and values of competent practitioners, and to learn what it means to be a social worker.

The challenges we face are not insurmountable, but they appear to be universal. There is much we can learn from each other. In comparing approaches, we may find ourselves jointly creating responses and solutions that are locally applicable and globally relevant.

3 Towards an inclusive paradigm for social work

Terry Sacco

Introduction

This chapter explores some ideas regarding the development of an inclusive approach to practice and teaching. It is a discussion which raises some questions concerning the basic assumptions which underlie social work practice and teaching. All social workers practise within a set of assumptions which underpin their perceptions of the world and their engagement with the world. It is vital that these basic assumptions are questioned so that social workers do not take their perspective for granted and fall into the error of believing that the ways of others are deficient or lacking.

Social work practice rests on conceptions of people: what they are; what they need in order to grow and find fulfilment, and how they cope with the challenges that life presents. The assumptions to be explored concern the universe, the nature of humanity and human knowing, and human needs.

The Western paradigm

According to Saleeby (1994), human beings can only make sense of the world by creating meaning through the development of symbols. In many ways, it is our culture which shapes who we think we are, what we think we are doing and where we think we are going. Culture provides us with an interpretive system where meaning is given to experience: 'Culture is the means by which we receive, organise, rationalize and understand our particular experiences in the world' (Saleeby, 1994: 352).

Western culture has dominated the development of social work knowledge. What are the assumptions about the universe and the source of knowledge that have been woven into the fabric of Western culture? What are the assumptions

31

regarding what it is to be human, and how have human needs been defined?

Assumptions about the world and the source of knowledge

The Western understanding of the world derives its insights from science, particularly the natural sciences. Western development of knowledge has been shaped fundamentally, in its aims, values and methods, by science and the environment and culture that science and technology have created (Poertner, 1994; Shutte, 1993). The dominant 'truth' of the Western world regards knowledge as coming from objective reality (Saleeby, 1994). Truth and fact are perceived to be identical. The scientific paradigm regards knowledge as originating from outside the self, discovered through detaching the self from the environment to observe and analyse 'reality' objectively (Gowdy, 1994). This paradigm regards reality as that which can only be understood by science, which includes 'a set of procedures combining experiment, quantification, atomism, and the mechanical philosophy. The world is seen as a collection of matter and motion, obeying mathematical laws' (Berman, cited in Gowdy, 1994: 363).

Scientific inquiry has been considered the only pathway to true knowledge. Thus, understanding human nature and the problems of living fall under the domain of scientists, rendering people dependent on experts to explain and oversee their life experiences (Gowdy, 1994). Scientific knowledge is so imaginatively stimulating and potentially useful that it is easy to understand the way in which it has come to be the paradigm of all valued knowledge (Shutte, 1993). The aggregate of all the sciences can seem to constitute the only real knowledge worth having in a scientific culture. If any knowledge falls outside science, then, in principle, it is not something 'knowable'. According to Shutte (1993: 35), this attitude has given rise to its own myth, a total picture of the universe and all that can be hoped for and all that can be undertaken:

> The myth includes a view of reality in both macroscopic and microscopic terms: the ultimate framework of reality in space and time, and the ultimate elements that constitute each real thing and determine how it acts. As such it also provides a vision of all that we can reasonably hope or do. The gap between the microscopic limit of physics and the macroscopic framework of cosmology is filled in by all the detail of the other sciences, to increase the imaginative power of the picture and make it more immediately relevant to our own lives.

Assumptions about our humanity

For Shutte (1993), the conceptions of human beings which arise from Western thinking are twofold.

The first view is highly individualistic and associated with liberal democracy and free-market economics. Each individual is rather like an atom: separate, autonomous and constrained only by forces imposed on it from without. Morality is perceived as an essentially private matter. Social regulation is in place to prevent interference by others. In this view, there is virtually no such thing as a common human nature. Everyone is different, and the only thing held in common is the capacity to originate action, the negative freedom to choose. The individual can be the subject of rights. However, these rights are not derived from a human nature held in common, rather they are the product of consent by all interested parties.

A second conception of human beings is collectivist in character. According to this view, humanity subsists primarily in the social whole rather than in a diversity of individuals. In so far as people participate in the whole, they can acquire humanity. This humanity is specified by whatever place a person occupies within the system of social institutions that make up society; there is no humanity that transcends the whole realm of institutions as such. The social whole itself is conceived as a kind of organism. There is no question of a freedom or independence for its members. In this instance, freedom is the lack of constraint produced by co-operation in common life, the overcoming of all kinds of conflict. In this conception, morality becomes the will of the powerful, the class or the party or the state. Shutte (1993: 44) perceives that 'both [conceptions] fail to recognise a dimension of persons that transcends the scope of scientific knowability . . . for this reason they are led to deny the existence of human nature common to all persons'.

Human needs

Arising from the dominant Western cultural point of view, human needs are based on the assumption that each individual needs a 'decent' standard of living, education, housing, medical care and social services, and that the provision of universal services would lead to the elimination of poverty, the advancement of underprivileged groups and the narrowing of gaps in income, education and employment (Eisenstadt and Ahimeir, cited in Barretta-Herman, 1994).

The resulting general view and set of values within the dominant Western culture are materialist, liberal-capitalist, utilitarian and atheist (Shutte, 1993). It is a world-view that separates body, mind and soul (Gowdy, 1994). The essence of identity is captured in Descartes' dictum 'I think, therefore I am', and freedom is found in independence. It is a culture which is product- and outcome-oriented. The quest for knowledge involves logical deductions, is consciously delimited in scope and field, and researched through a stated or implied literary-based discourse.

Impact on social work

Social work has been profoundly influenced by Western thought, values and views of persons and the universe.

From the dominant Western perspective, key assumptions are that professional acts are rational acts (Constable, 1983); that professional activity is instrumental problem-solving through the application of rigorous and scientifically tested and derived methods, where the professionals are the experts (Gowdy, 1994), and that effective practice or 'good' practice must be rooted in an established theoretical foundation, without which the quality of practice suffers (Goldstein, 1986). A resulting view is the separation of 'scientific' knowledge from all other forms and sources of knowledge, and a hierarchy of educators over students, researchers over practitioners and of practitioners over clients. Faver (1986) argues that the use of a scientific method to create a technology of practice has led to a separation from discussions of social work values and goals which are fundamental to social workers' practice: 'In accepting positivism, we have allowed the discourse in social work to be controlled by the language and assumptions of science' (Faver, 1986: 22).

Kelman (cited in Gowdy, 1994: 366) notes that the emphasis on control and manipulation in social scientific methods 'may in itself contribute to people's sense of alienation and helplessness'. Saleeby (1994) identifies a helper myth which is rooted in the scientific paradigm, where social work education and research provides the armament, the theory and techniques to discover what the problems of others are, and where the helper maintains inter-personal distance and dispassionate concern. What often happens is that the social workers impose on clients their version of the situation, and the clients surrender their own knowledge. Saleeby (1994) concludes that the 'global truth' claims of the proponents of 'objective reality' have subjugated and displaced other forms of knowledge.

Paradoxically, from the Western paradigm, social workers have learnt ways in which to become distanced from real engagement with the world of suffering. Social workers have learnt to mistrust their intuitive knowledge and trust only that which has been researched and documented. Gowdy (1994) says that when the process of personal knowing and learning is thwarted, knowledge becomes disembodied, appearing to be conferred on authorities from even higher authorities. Saleeby (cited in Gowdy, 1994: 366) believes that this happens when personal sources of knowledge are denied: 'we lose ownership of and sensitivity to, our organismic capacities and sensations, we lose our roots in nature and are forced to dwell in an empty past or dread anticipation of the future'. This loss of a personal source of knowledge is the key precondition for political and social oppression.

By its very nature, social work is about deepening a personal sense of humanity and valuing the humanity of others. However, much of the profession has been built on a knowledge base and has developed methodologies and techniques which have failed in this endeavour. Looking at the dominant Western paradigm, there has been a failure to value and account for multiple ways of knowing, for transcendence, for understanding people as the real source of knowledge and for an understanding of humanity which provides the means of answering the most pressing questions of meaning and value.

Towards an inclusive paradigm

From this author's point of view, the question that should be asked is: *How can social workers, educators, students and clients be freed from the constraints of the dominant mode of thinking and practising?*

As a beginning, it is necessary to embrace a cosmology which allows for the mystery, the fascination, the awe and the unknowability of life. Social workers need to become open to the never-ending search for truth from *a variety of sources*. It is also important to embrace a view of life which takes for granted the frayed edges, the messiness, the complexity and the unfathomability of the human experience. A view of humanity which connects humans at the deepest ground of being alive with all that lives needs to be developed. In addition, a faith in social work which gives space for the expression of the fullest humanity must be cultivated.

Views of the universe and of humanity

> This we know, the earth does not belong to man, man belongs to the earth. This we know, all things are connected, like the blood which unites one family. All things are connected. Whatever befalls the earth, befalls the sons of the earth. Man did not weave the web of life. He is merely a strand in it. Whatever he does to the web, he does to himself (Chief Seattle).[1]

In his letter to Governor Isaac Stevens, Chief Seattle describes a picture of the universe which has as its foundation the profound knowledge that all of life, all that life has inherited and all that life comes to be, is connected and springs from the same source. It is an all-embracing view of the universe which can contribute to the development of a living cosmology.

Drawing from Fox (1988), 'cosmology' can be defined as meaning three things: it is the story about the origins of the universe; it is mysticism – a psychic response to being in the universe; and it is art – the images which awaken body, soul and society. Cosmology needs these elements to come alive: a joyous response to the awesome fact of being in the universe, and the expression of that response by the art of living.

Within the African context, traditional African thinking offers under-standing of human nature and human flourishing which resonates with Chief Seattle's vision of the web of life, which has been lost in the midst of Western 'advancement' and which has to be reclaimed if humans are to live with hope and find human fulfilment.

The African philosopher Sengor (1966: 4) describes African notions of the universe where reality is perceived to be a:

> network of life forces which emanate from God and end in God, who is the source of all life forces. It is God who vitalizes and devitalizes all other beings, all other forces . . . the African conceives the world beyond the diversity of its forms, as a fundamentally mobile yet unique reality that seeks synthesis.

Traditional Native American teachings also testify to this search for syn-thesis:

> Our values teach us that mental, physical, and spiritual disease is caused by disharmony within the individual, or by disconnection to the family, community, nature, or the greater universe. When we live in harmony we interrelate with others and nature in a holistic manner. We see ourselves as part of the *Whole*.[2]

Likewise, in traditional African thought there is a conviction that human beings transcend the realm of the merely material. This can be understood through African conceptions of the fundamental energy of the universe and of what it is to be human. Each living person as well as all living things are filled with divine energy which is a vital force (Setiloane, 1986). This vital force, this divine energy, of all that lives is in communion and is in dynamic participation. Sengor (cited in Ba, 1973: 74) suggests that Africans have a cer-tain emotive sensitivity, 'an effective rapport with the forces and forms of the universe, a direct and immediate contact with *the Other*'.

In addition, personhood is only attainable in community: 'The most cherished principle is to include rather than separate' (Setiloane, 1986: 10). This is the single most important concept within African traditional life. Belonging in community is the root of being human. In Africa, *I belong, there-fore I am*. 'To be human is to belong to the whole community' (Mbiti, 1971: 2). In the African view, 'it is the community which defines the person as person, not some isolated static quality of rationality, will or memory' (Menkiti, cited in Shutte, 1993: 46). The implication of this view is that in order to develop as persons, people need to be empowered by others.

One of the African myths provides a metaphor which gives expression to this belonging in community. A myth explaining genesis in Africa is known as 'the hole in the ground myth'. This myth accounts for the arrival of men, women, children and animals – all together as a community – on earth from a hole in the ground, having been escorted by Loowe, to fulfil the will of Divinity.

Belonging in community and being a vital force in participation is made possible by *seriti*. *Seriti* is perceived in essence as 'dignity', although translation of the term cannot capture the full meaning. If all of life is connected through *seriti*, then the dignity of all life must be upheld if people are to uphold their own. For, if the dignity of all of life is not upheld, then the dignity of all humanity is lost. Human beings can only be free through dependence and interaction with life. According to Shutte (1993), this paradox of freedom-in-dependence does indeed express an important truth about human nature. Human capacity for free self-realization requires a certain kind of influence of other persons if it is to develop towards fulfilment. Shutte (1993) presents this development in three stages: from the basic capacity for self-consciousness and self-determination that makes people human, through increasing self-knowledge and self-affirmation to a progressively greater ability for self-transcendence and self-donation in relationship with others. The process of finding fulfilment is made possible by virtue of complex inter-personal transactions with others.

Individual freedom and community with others need not be seen as opposed. The unity of individual and community will only be realized if the way in which people transcend the realm of the merely material is understood.

Working out an understanding of human beings and personal development that incorporates traditional African conceptions of humanity is a way of dealing with the oppositions in Western thinking between both materialism and dualism, and individualism and collectivism. The inter-personal transaction that brings about individual growth reveals a kind of personal energy or power that is certainly not physical in any way, but which is embodied and expressed in physical reality. The fact that individual freedom is shown to depend on personal relationships with others for its exercise, growth and fulfilment provides an alternative to both the individualistic and the collectivist approach to society and politics (Shutte, 1993).

Implications for social work

Social workers have critiqued the dominant Western mode of thinking, researching and practising and have contributed to the search for alternative approaches to social work (Gowdy, 1994; Saleeby, 1994; Goldstein, 1986; Faver, 1986).

Drawing from traditional African and Native American views of the universe, where synthesis and harmony are valued, an inclusive paradigm in social work teaching and practice can be sought: an inclusive paradigm which embraces an understanding that the knowledge social workers seek resides in the process of knowing self and others. The path towards an inclusive paradigm described by social workers (Gowdy, 1994; Saleeby, 1994; Goldstein, 1986; Faver, 1986) sits well with the traditional African and Native American views of the universe.

Berman (cited in Gowdy, 1994) proposes that social workers develop a participating consciousness in which there is a recognition that the universe and all that is in it is alive and inter-related. People come to know the world through full participation, through letting go of control and through identifying with the world. This process involves personal knowing, which can only be developed with 'passionate participation of the knower in the act of knowing' (Polanyi, cited in Gowdy, 1994: 365) and with care of the soul and soul language which is essential to human knowing. *Soul* is not a thing, but a quality or a dimension of experiencing life and self. It has to do with depth, value, relatedness, heart and personal substance. Care of the soul is a continuous process that concerns itself with attending to the small details of everyday life, as well as to major decisions and changes (Moore, 1992).

The development of personal knowing is what Gowdy (1994) calls the path with a heart. She refers to Schön, who perceives this process to be 'knowing-in-action'. This means that intelligence resides within the act of using body, mind and soul to meet the challenges of life. For Gowdy (1994), coming to know any aspect of the world as unique is a process in which the heart, as much as actions and mind, participates. This means that sources of knowledge which are sensory and intuitive need to be embraced. As social workers begin to trust their gut responses and the sources of personal knowledge, social workers can begin trusting those of others.

Letting others and the context speak

As social workers expose themselves to the wonder, the mystery and the open-endedness of life and do not feel compelled to take control and find solutions for the challenges that face others, they will be able to let others speak. In letting others speak, Goldstein (1986) offers a common-sense, humanistic and reflective approach which is fundamentally respectful of the constructions people give to their own lives and experiences. According to Goldstein (1986), theory and practice can only be guided by a worker's openness to the client's own story. Human beings build themselves into the world by creating meaning, and these meanings are given expression through stories and narratives. This echoes Saleeby's (1994) constructivist approach, which requires that social workers ground professional understanding and actions in the stories and the meaning systems of those whom social workers serve. Developing a constructivist approach becomes imperative when work with people who are oppressed within a culture or context is considered.

People who are oppressed surrender their own narratives and stories, or suppress them and accept the social worker's interpretations, narratives and theory.

Saleeby (1994) points out that some local knowledges have been subjugated and displaced by the dominant truth. Local knowledges exist but are denied any credibility and any possibility of expression within the wider context. Very often, local knowledges are not articulated because they have been part of an oral tradition which has presented history, mythology and religious concepts metaphorically. Social workers must help with the 'insurrection' of these local, subjugated knowledges in the lives of others and let these knowledges inform both practice and teaching:

> If one truly listens to what a client is saying – not for the purpose of pigeonholing him into a diagnostic category or pinning a sociological label on him – one begins to know some of the basic recurring questions arising out of the human dilemma. (Saleeby, 1994: 353)

It can be difficult to hear and respect the accounts of others, particularly if they are in socially subordinate positions. However, there are some international examples which provide conviction and hope for those whose knowledges have been subjugated in the face of cultural imperialism.

Barretta-Herman (1994) traces the social welfare department's restructuring process in New Zealand in 1986. Here, social work practice has been undergoing radical change, and every familiar social work activity is being re-examined in the light of joint decision-making and resource-sharing with communities. In the New Zealand context, these communities particularly include the Maori *whanau* (extended family), *hapu* (sub-tribe) and *iwi* (tribe). This process has signalled the move towards community as provider within a welfare society of social service delivery. The department's principal social worker noted that changes which have occurred in social work practice include the development of culturally sensitive practice models, the establishment of Maori and Pacific Island teams, the involvement of local *iwi* in recruitment and selection of staff, the development of strong links with the Maori community, and the promotion and funding of preventive, community-based services as determined by locally-based communities (Barretta-Herman, 1994). Arising from the position of letting the context speak, the passage of the Children, Young Persons and their Families Act in 1989 provides for *whanau* conferences that have clearly reduced the power of the state and professional social workers to make decisions for children and which place that responsibility in the hands of the *whanau*.

Another example of letting the context speak comes from Sherraden and Martin's (1994) discussion on social work with immigrants in the United States of America. They argue that immigrants utilize informal caregiving, which provides effective support and is seen as an important source of community identity and strength. Social workers can make their services more accessible by working with informal caregiving resources. A specific example which Sherraden and Martin (1994) cite comes from a Puerto Rican community in New York City, which reclaimed barren land to build an estimated fifty *casitas* fashioned in the style of Caribbean peasant housing. These *casitas* are gathering points, social clubs, community centres and garden spots. Sciorra (cited in Sherraden and Martin, 1994: 371) says that 'the *casita* is not merely a nostalgic lament for an idealized past but a form of community organization whereby control of one's immediate environment is achieved through the use of traditional expressive culture'. Each *casita* is a natural locale for social work practice, and in this instance, one *casita* serves as an 'office' for a professional social worker.

As a final example, the author would like to draw from her own experience in Gauteng, South Africa, to show how differently people cope with the challenges of life. Workshops were conducted with school teachers from different communities where the most pressing problem has been living and coping with violence and the pervasive violent nature of South African society. What was striking was the ways in which people cope with living with violence. These coping strategies have been fundamentally shaped by the cultures and communities from which they gain meaning. The teachers from a Western cultural background generally coped with living with violence by retreating from activities which brought them into contact with people, and gained strength from solitude, quiet and restful activities. However, teachers from African communities and backgrounds gained courage and strength from activities which brought them into contact with others. Their strength and will to go on, in the face of fear, were rejuvenated by praying, singing and being in community.

The author's contention is that letting others and the context speak is a powerful process which contributes to a deeper understanding of human nature, a deeper experience of what it means to be human, and ultimately, to a more appropriate social work practice.

Conclusion

In working towards an inclusive paradigm, social workers open themselves to becoming engaged with the struggle of knowing and to the process of learning from self and others. Social workers can then begin living with vision, courage, wisdom and love. The teaching and practising stance is likely to be humanized, engaged, but also hesitant and critical. Hesitation is necessary, as it expresses a consciousness of the mystery of being, the dignity of every person and all that lives. It provides a moment for consulting the soul.

In conclusion, the language of the soul is described by Toor (1994: xii):

> We need to awaken the language of the soul, and speak to it every day. We need to be with other people who are alive, who are asking real questions, who are not playing at life (yet who know how to play, how to laugh, how to weep, how to dare, and do not hold back loving). When we start to learn the language of the soul, we'll begin to take more risks, be brutally honest with ourselves, be real with others; we'll take off our *persona* and throw it into the sea. We'll sing over our food, hum at the office, make waves when life gets cramped, and refuse to give in to the old voices that plunder the power in the heart. Soul language is generic and all-inclusive. No one can teach us that language; it has to come from within. It has to come from self-knowing, hard work, sacrifice, from *Kenosis* (humbling oneself, emptying out the past).

Notes

1   An excerpt from Chief Seattle's letter to Governor Isaac Stevens on surrendering the land of his people, the Dwamish, in 1854. The letter is reproduced in Vincent Busch (1989) *Hope for the Seeds*, Quezon City, Philippines: Claretian Publications.
2   Marilyn Youngbird (1994) in the preface to Djohariah Toor's *Songs from the Mountains*, New York: St Martin's Press.

4 Re-engaging social work education with the public social services: The California experience and its relevance to Russia

Bart Grossman and Robin Perry

Introduction

In 1991, social work emerged as a certified profession with higher education requirements in the Russian Republic. Social work in Russia is currently rooted in 'a perception that social problems are a matter of demographics and social structure' (Imbrogno, 1994: 94). However, increased attention is being paid to the need for direct practice interventions as well as policy development. In the United States, emphasis on direct intervention has combined with other factors to create a profession of social work increasingly alienated from a mission of service to the poor. This article describes the evolution of the disconnection of American social work from the poor, and efforts to re-commit social work and social work education to practice focused on the neediest clients. Such disengagement need not be repeated as the profession emerges in Eastern Europe and Russia. Some of the techniques employed to re-engage social work and social work education with the public social services in the USA suggest alternative paths of development that may better fit emerging democracies.

The disengaged profession

From the late 1970s until recent years, the profession of social work in the USA has become disconnected from its traditional focus on the needs of the poor and the institutions that address these needs – typically the publicly-supported social services. Training for social work has increasingly meant preparation for careers serving middle-class clients in private practice. As social work participation in private practice has increased, the profession's involvement in public and non-profit agencies has declined, to the extent that

43

many key public institutions have become de-professionalized. De-professionalization is associated with increased bureaucratization, decreased individualization of services and increased focus on maintenance and protection rather than prevention and rehabilitation. Moreover, lack of professional assessment increases the frequency of bad choices that may result in harm to children and other vulnerable client populations.

This chapter will focus on the following key questions:

- How did this disengagement between social work and the publicly-supported agencies come about in the United States?
- What has been the role of social work education in fostering disengagement?
- What has been done, or could be done, to re-focus social work education in the United States?
- How could the development of social work education in Russia avoid the pitfalls of the US experience?

The erosion of the relationship between social work and the poor has many causes, including: the decline of governmental and public commitment to social change; the deterioration of working conditions in the public agencies; the popularity of psychotherapeutic and personal growth techniques in the profession and in the culture, and the lack of fit between content in social work education and current practice realities in publicly-supported agencies. However, it is important to understand that the relationship between social work education and the public services in the USA has never been positive.

The profession arose in the voluntary agencies at the end of the nineteenth century, a time when government played a small role in the social services. The development of social work education was linked to the search for a knowledge base upon which to develop the early ideas of 'scientific charity'. At first, the search focused on the social sciences, chiefly economics and sociology. By the 1930s, teachings were integrated from psychiatry and Freudian psychoanalysis, which tended to focus on intra-psychic problems and individualistic solutions. By the 1950s, the clinical perspective dominated, and the focus of intervention became not the community or even the person in the environment, but rather the internal conflicts and psychological history of the 'patient' (Grossman, Laughlin and Specht, 1992).

Graduate social work education and the public social services

Throughout the Depression and the two world wars, the social work profession maintained its primary commitment to the sponsorship of social services under non-governmental auspices and to an individualistic practice. It was only with the 1962 amendments to the Social Security Act that the federal government began to provide financial support to the states for social casework services. These provisions were broadened year by year. In 1974, the addition of Title XX to the Social Security Act established the framework for the states to offer comprehensive, universal social services. The states made considerable strides in that direction until the passage of the 1981 Omnibus Budget Reconciliation Act.

With the growth in public agency involvement in social services, one would have expected a simultaneous increase in social work education involvement with these settings. For a time, this was the case. Title XX supported collaborative projects between schools and public agencies. Agency-based field units in which instructors, often agency staff hired by schools, provided on-site supervision and coursework became common. However, these developing partnerships were undermined by a powerful combination of blows.

The first, from the left, attacked the public agencies as tools of oppression designed to 'regulate' the poor, not to alleviate poverty. This attack was often directed from the schools and transmitted in the most extreme form by students who went to the agencies with a mission not to help, but to overthrow the oppressors of the poor. This anti-poverty critique, while based in palpable realities, was exploited by the right. A string of conservative presidents and governors undertook the dismantling of the American welfare state, and a conspicuous casualty was funding for professional education. Although enrolment in Master of Social Work (MSW) programmes increased by 67 per cent from 1969 to 1990, federal student support decreased by 69 per cent, and state and county support decreased by 51 per cent. This left/right combination all but ended the relationship between social work education and public social services.

The disengagement between social work and the publicly-supported agencies can be seen through many indicators. About 25 to 30 per cent of social workers are involved in private practice nationally, primarily with middle-class clients. Public child welfare, mental health and other publicly-supported agencies charged with serving the poor and disadvantaged report enormous difficulty attracting and retaining MSWs. Nationally, less than 20 per cent of child welfare workers currently hold the MSW. New recruits to the profession do not necessarily plan careers serving the poor. In Rubin and Johnson's (1984) study of MSW students entering practice, more than 50 per cent indicated that they were preparing for careers in private practice with middle-class clients. In a recent study (Santangelo, 1992) of the entering class in the graduate schools of social work in California, students were asked to choose between two statements of mission:

1   'Social work should devote most of its attention and resources to the problems of the poor' or
2   'Social work should devote equal attention and equal resources to all social class groupings.'

In 1991, 70 per cent of the respondents chose the latter.

Re-engagement

In the late 1980s, a change began to occur in the United States. After a decade or so of keeping a guarded distance, public agencies and schools of social work began tentatively to explore new connections. The reasons for this exploration were manifold, including:

- Increasing numbers of social workers were achieving top leadership positions in public agencies.
- The job market was growing in response to the growth of recognized social problems like child abuse, AIDS, drug abuse, teenage pregnancy and homelessness.
- Many public agencies no longer had internal training divisions, and many turned to the universities for assistance in developing in-service education.
- In some states, the availability of MSWs for public employment was not keeping pace with the demand. (In California, for example, MSWs employed in public child welfare declined from 32 per cent in 1986 to 23 per cent in 1991, while the number of child welfare positions increased substantially.)
- Highly-publicized deaths in placement and other failures were creating pressure in the courts, congress and state legislatures for efforts to re-professionalize child welfare services.
- Key pieces of legislation like the Family Support Act changed the focus of intervention, creating a need for new professional training.
- Funders were increasingly interested in supporting school–agency coalitions rather than funding either sector independently, as a mechanism to enhance the quality of services.
- In some states, changing demographics created a situation of marked ethnic disparity between clients and workers. In California, for example, children in foster care are 37.9 per cent African-American, 20.6 per cent Hispanic, 2.4 per cent American Indian and less than 1 per cent Asian (Harris, Kirk and Besharov, 1993). In contrast, the distribution of direct service workers in California is 19 per cent African-

American, 16.4 per cent Hispanic, 0.01 per cent American Indian and 6.1 per cent Asian (CalSWEC, 1991).

Perhaps most significantly, schools and agencies faced a common enemy in the 1980s strong enough to unite them – a political attack on the very idea of governmental support for the social services. However, as schools and agencies began to explore partnerships and coalitions, they encountered significant differences in approach and culture that created barriers to co-operation.

Barriers to collaboration

As Alicea (1978) points out, 'Coalitions are characterized not only by unity but also by diversity of interests . . . the concept of coalition entails simultaneously both . . . centripetal and centrifugal forces.' In the case of school–agency partnerships, barriers arise from differences in organizational culture and past experiences with collaboration.

Reward systems

University reward systems put considerable emphasis on the professional and scholarly achievements of individuals. This value-system contrasts with the organizational, problem-solving orientation of the agency. It is extremely difficult for individuals to move between these frames of reference. Practitioners who take jobs in schools, for example, are often perplexed by the lack of clarity about collective goals and performance standards and the lack of hierarchical supervision.

Knowledge and theory

The most stereotyped version of these differences holds that university faculty rely on empirical and theoretical knowledge, whereas practitioners draw knowledge from precedent, experience and intuition. Thus, faculty members may fail to appreciate that formal research alone cannot answer all questions. Practitioners may overvalue their own experience, assuming it will be highly generalizable.

Constraints and sanctions

Each organizational culture has constraints and sanctions that are unfamiliar to the other. In addition, schools of social work in the USA operate under the constraint of the Council on Social Work Education (CSWE) and the

Academic Senate of each institution, both of which make changes slowly through complex deliberative processes. Agencies, on the other hand, are pushed and pulled by political and economic forces at many levels. Turnover of upper-level personnel is quite high; managers rarely last more than a few years. It is difficult to maintain a partnership when the identity of one of the partners is constantly changing.

Decision-making

Authority in the university is diffuse and subtle. The nature and amount of authority delegated to the faculty by the dean comes as a real shock to persons outside the system. Agency administrators take it for granted that academic deans and directors can act on behalf of their institutions. They may be surprised at the degree to which faculty can over-rule or ignore the dean. In fact, agency directors have a much higher degree of administrative authority.

Furthermore, the pace of change in academic settings can be frustrating. Co-ordinated efforts and team work are more the exception than the rule. This individualistic way of working, while it can promote some forms of scholarship, creates significant barriers to collaborative work between college faculty and practitioners.

The California Social Work Education Center

Given these barriers, how can schools and agencies develop a respect for each other's strengths and limitations and create new structures that fit organizational realities? The California Social Work Education Center (CalSWEC) illustrates a successful new structure. It emerged from four years of local and regional collaboration between county departments of social services and schools of social work on in-service training and field instruction.

The following elements are seen as crucial to the goals of change in professional education for the public social services.

A new structure with shared accountability had to be created. While CalSWEC is linked to the University of California, it is governed by a board of directors balanced between deans of social work and public agency managers. State, non-profit, and professional organizations also participate. All CalSWEC committees have co-chair teams of deans and agency managers.

A programme was required that would address the needs and limitations of both sectors and tap resources that neither could access independently.

Three crucial elements of the programme are described below.

The need to link financial aid to commitments by students to work in public agencies

This strategy helps the schools with their problems of supporting students and the agencies with their recruitment problems. Furthermore, the schools agree to give priority to returning employees (an agency need) and to under-represented ethnic groups (a common concern). Thus students receive a substantial stipend for the two-year MSW programme that must be repaid by two years of work in public child welfare agencies in California. Some employees retain their full-time salary but are allowed to work part-time. Their tuition, fees, books and travel costs are paid through CalSWEC, and they return to full-time work with their county employers upon graduation.

The source of funding for these financial aid programmes particularly illustrates the advantages of the agency–school partnership. The federal government has funds that can be used for graduate training, but there is a required state funding match of 25 per cent. Because county agencies receive federal funds, they have few sources of such matching dollars. The local match in CalSWEC is achieved without cost to the agencies by using university state funds and by forgoing overheads that universities are permitted to charge on federal funding. Overhead charges of about 40 to 50 per cent are allowed to meet the administrative costs of the universities. By claiming these charges as a match rather than collecting the funds, the universities are able to bring substantial federal monies into the state with no direct cost to the county agencies.

The creation of a competency-based curriculum to meet the needs of public child welfare workers

A collaborative process was employed to create a set of core competencies that each school would implement with the support of regional agencies and CalSWEC. Trainers from the agencies together with college faculty selected competencies vital for agency practice at the MSW level from a broad scan of potential knowledge, value and skill statements. The final list of 72 items was adopted as a set of curriculum objectives by all schools and as a standard of practice in the agencies. This mutual definition of curriculum is unique in the United States. CalSWEC supports and monitors the teaching of the required competencies and evaluates students' mastery of the material. It studies the effects of these competencies on agency practice and client outcomes. It provides faculty development workshops and supports the creation of teaching materials such as videotapes and case studies to be used in the classroom.

The facilitation of collaborative research and development (R&D) between schools and agencies

To improve agency practice and to create a climate likely to encourage new graduates to remain in the public sector, an effort was undertaken to encourage schools and agencies to conduct mutual research. Faculty often contribute research and evaluation skills, and the agencies identify crucial practice questions and make the data accessible. Students are involved in these efforts as an aspect of their research training at the university. The goal is to create new practitioners that can serve effectively as agents of change and programme development as well as effective workers in the current system. This long-range perspective can help to counter discouragement among employees and can also excite the enthusiasm of current staff about the linkage between college and agency.

CalSWEC now supports about 400 full-time and 160 part-time students throughout the state in its child welfare programme. Similar partnerships are being developed in mental health, social work in schools, ageing, and inter-disciplinary practice.

The effects of CalSWEC initiatives: A three-year comparison

As part of a continuing effort to monitor the effects of CalSWEC initiatives, a demographic and attitudinal profile is collected from all entering MSW students throughout the state of California each year. Students sampled in 1991 provide a baseline for comparison with students sampled in 1992 and 1993, when various CalSWEC initiatives began to take shape and exert an influence on student funding, graduate school recruitment and curricula throughout the state. Every entering MSW student was sampled for the purposes of this study. This represents an overall response rate varying between approximately 80 and 86 per cent for each year.

The proportion of African-American and Hispanic students increased following the implementation of CalSWEC initiatives (see Table 4.1). Based on a two-tailed test of significance for two independent proportions, the observed increase in African-American students ($p<0.05$) and Hispanic students ($p<0.01$) proved significant. This change is accompanied by a significant decrease in Caucasian students between 1991 and 1993 ($p=0.0026$).

When examining attitudes regarding the appropriate goal for the profession, a significant increase is observed each year with respect to those students who believe that social work should devote most of its attention to problems of the poor (see Table 4.2). In 1991, only 31.2 per cent of entering

Table 4.1   Ethnicity of entering MSW students in California by year (per cent)

Race/Ethnicity	1991 (n=912)	1992 (n=946)	1993 (n=917)
1 African-American/Black	9.7	8.6	12.6[1]
2 American Indian	1.6	0.7	1.9
3 Asian American	6.8	6.4	6.1
4 Caucasian	65.4	64.0	58.6[1]
5 Hispanic/Latino	11.5	12.1	15.5[2]
6 Pacific Islander	0.2	0.8	0.4
7 Filipino	2.0	1.0	2.1
8 Other	2.8	6.5	2.9

Notes:
1   Observed change between 1991 and 1993 significant p<0.05
2   Observed change between 1991 and 1993 significant p<0.01

Table 4.2   Perspective on goals for the profession of California MSW students by year

When asked to best describe their attitude toward goals for the profession of social work:

	1991	1992	1993
Percentage who said social work should devote equal attention to *all* social class groupings	68.8	62.0	59.0
Percentage who said social work should devote most of its attention to problems of the poor	31.2	38.0[1]	41.0[2]

Notes:
1   Observed change between 1991 and 1992 significant p<0.05, two-tailed test
2   Observed change between 1991 and 1993 significant p<0.01, two-tailed test

students, when asked to decide which of two statements best represented their attitude toward goals for the profession, believed the profession should devote most of its attention to the poor. This figure increased to 38 per cent (p=0.022 when compared to 1991) in 1992 and 41 per cent (p<0.01) in 1993. Thus we have seen moderate and significant increases in ethnic diversity of graduate students, coupled with an increase in perceived commitment or belief that the profession should focus or identify more profoundly with ser-vice to the poor.

These changes appear to coincide with changes in the level of appeal of various fields of practice. Table 4.3 outlines the rating of each field of practice by year according to the mean level of appeal (attraction) attributed to ten categories or listed fields of practice. A two-tailed significance test using a Wilcoxon Rank Sum Test was used to determine whether observed differ-ences between year pairs by field of practice proved significant. Although ranked in the top five fields in 1993, there has been a consistent, significant

Table 4.3   Rankings of fields of practice by mean level of appeal for California MSW students by year of admission

When asked to rate the *fields of practice* according to their *level of appeal* on a scale from 1 to 10, where the top ranking reflects the highest level of appeal, student responses were:

		1991 (n=912)		1992 (n=946)		1993 (n=917)	
1	Counselling	1	(6.06)	1	(6.00)	1	(5.92)[1]
2	Group work	2	(5.50)	2	(5.41)	3	(5.37)[1]
3	Family/marital therapy	3	(5.34)	4	(5.25)[2]	5	(5.06)[3]
4	Client advocacy	4	(5.33)	3	(5.36)	2	(5.47)
5	Casework	5	(4.96)	5	(5.02)	4	(5.12)
6	Psychotherapy	6	(4.83)	6	(4.78)	6	(4.67)
7	Programme/policy design	7	(4.58)	7	(4.59)	7	(4.64)
8	Protective services	8	(4.50)	8	(4.47)	7	(4.64)[1]
9	Community organizing	9	(4.34)	9	(4.46)	9	(4.48)
10	Administration	10	(3.86)	10	(4.04)	10	(3.99)

Notes:
1 Observed change between 1991 and 1993 significant p<0.05, two-tailed test using Wilcoxon Rank Sum Test
2 Observed change between 1991 and 1992 significant p<0.05, two-tailed test
3 Observed change between 1991 and 1993 significant p<0.01, two-tailed test

yearly decrease (when 1991–93 comparisons are made) in the level of appeal attributed to counselling (p=0.0467), group work (p=0.0250) and marital/family therapy (p=0.0015).

The drop in appeal for these fields of practice has coincided with a significant increase in level of appeal of protective services (p=0.0331), although its ranking hasn't improved dramatically (from 8 to 7 in two years). The increase in appeal of protective services has also coincided with a consistent increase in the mean level of appeal for client advocacy and casework practice, although these increases have not been statistically significant. Regardless, these findings suggest a growing (although modest) interest in fields of practice more traditionally associated with public service, as opposed to individualized approaches concurrent with private practice orientations.

These findings hold true when one observes rankings of client groups or case situations by level of appeal detailed in Table 4.4. Of those groups or situations that show consistent increases or decreases in mean appeal ratings, where differences over two years prove significant (using the Wilcoxon Rank Sum Test), there is a significant increase in the appeal of working with abused and neglected children (p=0.0468) and the poor (p=0.011). These increases are contrasted with a consistent and significant decrease in the appeal of working with people with marital and family problems (p=0.0468). Such findings are reduced in significance by the fact that all those groupings listed above originally and consistently maintained an overall ranking in the top 5 of 21 client groups or case situations rated. Still, the significance levels observed suggest a trend which, when evaluated over time, may point to a reversal of the tendency for graduate students to aspire towards private practice at the expense of the poor.

Indeed, this appears so. Students were asked to rate the degree of importance which seven factors had in their decision to enter graduate school (see Table 4.5). The desire to serve the poor increased consistently and significantly from 1991 to 1992 (p=0.012), and overall from 1991 to 1993 (p=0.0016), while the desire to enter private practice significantly decreased from 1991 to 1993 (p=0.0016). It is interesting to note that private practice has maintained a relatively low ranking in comparison to other motivating factors. While this question is not intended to detect whether students are likely to enter private practice following completion of their graduate degree, previous research has shown that education and practice experiences can affect student motivations and practice aspirations (Rubin, Johnson and DeWeaver, 1986). Therefore the intense exposure to public agency ideas and practices should have the effect of strengthening graduates' commitment to work in that sector.

Table 4.4   Rankings of client groups or case situations by mean level of appeal for California MSW students by year of admission

When asked to rate the *client groups* or *case situations* according to their level of appeal on a scale from 1 to 21, where the top ranking reflects the highest level of appeal, student responses were:

		1991 (n=912)		1992 (n=946)		1993 (n=917)	
1	Teen mothers with limited resources	1	(5.28)	1	(5.30)	2	(5.28)
2	Abused and neglected children	2	(5.25)	3	(5.27)[1]	1	(5.40)[2]
3	People with marital/family problems	3	(5.22)	2	(5.29)	4	(5.11)[2]
4	People in poverty needing resources	4	(5.09)	4	(5.21)	2	(5.28)[2]
5	Teens experiencing turbulent adolescence	5	(4.96)	5	(5.15)[1]	5	(5.04)
6	Alcohol/substance abusers	6	(4.77)	8	(4.69)	10	(4.63)
7	People who are depressed	7	(4.74)	7	(4.70)	7	(4.70)
8	Children with AIDS	8	(4.73)	6	(4.82)	6	(4.83)
9	Homeless families	9	(4.68)	9	(4.68)	8	(4.68)
10	Abusive parents	10	(4.54)	11	(4.58)	9	(4.67)
11	People wanting to adopt a child	11	(4.44)	13	(4.42)	12	(4.45)
12	Homeless adults	12	(4.41)	13	(4.42)	14	(4.40)
13	Adults with AIDS	13	(4.40)	12	(4.54)	11	(4.49)
14	College students in crisis	14	(4.35)	10	(4.63)[3]	13	(4.47)[4]
15	Juvenile status offenders	15	(4.12)	15	(4.05)	15	(4.18)
16	The aged	16	(4.03)	17	(3.92)	17	(3.93)
17	The physically disabled	17	(4.02)	18	(3.81)	18	(3.90)
18	Hospital discharge/care	18	(3.93)	16	(3.94)	16	(4.07)
19	The developmentally disabled	19	(3.74)	19	(3.59)	19	(3.58)
20	The chronically mentally ill	20	(3.45)	20	(3.51)	20	(3.43)
21	Adult criminal offenders	21	(3.32)	21	(3.30)	21	(3.41)

Notes:
1   Observed change between 1991 and 1992 significant $p<0.05$, two-tailed test using Wilcoxon Rank Sum Test
2   Observed change between 1991 and 1993 significant $p<0.05$, two-tailed test
3   Observed change between 1991 and 1992 significant $p<0.01$, two-tailed test
4   Observed change between 1992 and 1993 significant $p<0.05$, two-tailed test

Table 4.5   Rankings of motivating factors by mean importance for entering graduate school for California MSW students by year of admission

Students were asked to rate a series of statements, according to how each best represents its *degree of importance* in their decision to enter graduate school in social work, where 1 = very *un*important; 2 = *un*important; 3 = neither; 4 = important; 5 = very important:

		1991 (n=912)		1992 (n=946)		1993 (n=917)	
1	Contribute to society	1	(4.63)	1	$(4.68)^1$	1	$(4.69)^2$
2	Versatility of the MSW	2	(4.53)	2	(4.57)	2	(4.53)
3	Job promotion	3	(4.27)	3	(4.24)	4	(4.24)
4	To serve the poor	4	(4.15)	3	$(4.24)^3$	3	$(4.26)^2$
5	Personal growth	5	(4.05)	5	(4.07)	5	(4.12)
6	Private practice	6	(3.69)	6	(3.66)	6	$(3.52)^2$
7	Extension of BSW	7	(2.88)	7	$(3.08)^1$	7	$(3.07)^2$

Notes:
1   Observed change between 1991 and 1992 significant p<0.01, two-tailed test using Wilcoxon Rank Sum Test
2   Observed change between 1991 and 1993 significant p<0.01, two-tailed test
3   Observed change between 1991 and 1992 significant p<0.05, two-tailed test

Developing an engaged profession

The profession of social work in the United States has responded to the changes in the public debate about the needs and entitlements of the poor. It has shown a continuing ambivalence about its focus. As a profession serving middle-class clients through private auspices, however, it is increasingly in competition with a host of other professionals whose training is more focused on psychotherapy (including clinical psychologists, counselling psychologists, marriage, family and child counsellors and psychiatric nurses). It is only in the publicly-supported services, governmental and non-profit contractors that MSWs enjoy any cachet, but even this realm is becoming contested.

Social work in Russia can avoid these pitfalls by establishing from the outset a clear connection between practice and education. Partnerships like CalSWEC should be the norm. If leading regional agencies were active partners in the development of schools of social work, the profession might avoid a split between the practical needs of agencies for well-trained staff and the academic concerns of faculty. An early emphasis on relevant practice research and a practice curriculum based on competencies could forge a unified profession – a profession equipped to bring the best available knowledge to the design of programmes and the training of professionals to serve the neediest clients. In this way, Russia may learn from the strengths and shortcomings of social work education in the United States.

Part Two

Teaching and Learning

5 Liberated practice teaching: The experience of self-selection in finding placements

Harry Walker

The philosophy

The philosophy for encouraging self-selection in finding places is based on the application of the principles of Paulo Freire to social work education. Freire (Hope and Timmel, 1984) states that education is not neutral: it can either liberate or domesticate. He states further that the education must be relevant, must be about issues that are presently important to people, must be about the resolution of issues, must involve dialogue and must also be about reflecting and acting.

For change to come about, Freire suggests that whole communities must be involved, that action must be collective and not just an individualistic academic exercise. There is recognition that every person has a contribution to make in building a new society. People therefore have to support each other and their communities to become more capable of providing a service to the people of whom they are a part and the community from which they come, and more committed to doing so.

The other basic tenet is that we are all both teachers and learners. The word *ako* in Maori is most apt, as it describes both learning and teaching.

The focus of this chapter is the rationale in students selecting their own placements and the issues of Maori people choosing to work with their own.

The type of institution is often irrelevant as, proportionately, Maori are over-represented as users of the government agency social services. Regardless of the agency, Maori students still want to work with people of their own culture.

Placement success is dependent upon the nature of the relationship between the practice teacher and the student, and the support given by the university to the student.

This chapter is illustrated by the views of twelve students (eleven Maori and one Samoan) who selected their own placements in Maori organizations.

Significance of practice placements

The purpose of practice placements is for the student to move from an academic learning environment – where the closest they come to 'practice' are role-plays and simulated learning situations – to a situation of supervised practice, which is of central importance in the professional education of social workers. Social work requires that supervised practice is an integral part of the core curriculum. The placement offers the students opportunities to experience 'live' working situations in what should be a supportive and stimulating work environment. At the same time, they are assessed as they demonstrate the skills and knowledge necessary for social work. Practice occurs as the theory is being attended to. The theoretical paradigms to which the students have been exposed at university are tested. The practice implications of the course philosophy and the value-base of the student, while explored in a formal class setting, are also examined under the guidance of the practice teacher in a practice setting.

The *applied* nature of the course has advantages, as the application of theories has to be demonstrated by those lecturers who have a practice focus. All lecturers are practitioners in their subject area. For example, social work practice lecturers are currently practising; social policy lecturers are still involved in policy formulation, development or analysis; lecturers in research are themselves involved in ongoing research.

The integration of the course curriculum extends to the relationship between economic theory, social policy and their impact on social work practice.

Selection in practice placements

For most students, the placement period provokes anxiety. This varies according to the maturity of the student and the social work experience prior to entry to the course. Students will often opt for safety or comfort zones in terms of the desired practice placement.

The process begins before the students arrive, as the application form and interview for entry to the course raise the issue of placements. Discussions on placements occur from the first week of the course and assist students in clarifying their practice learning needs and where they can possibly best be met. The practice placement occurs eight weeks into the period of study at the university. All lectures during this period are focused on preparing for practice.

The self-selection of practice placements is most effective when students honestly assess their strengths and skills and identify the strengths and skills which they need to develop further. A range of possible placements is then sought; indeed, the student may already have identified a placement.

Each lecturer, who has responsibility for ten to twelve students, will also assist with their knowledge of the placement opportunities, at both a local and national level. It is important for the lecturers to be familiar with the agencies and ethnic groups who are offering practice placement opportunities. Many of the students are from other parts of Aotearoa (New Zealand), and are therefore often not familiar with what is available.

The lecturer must also be committed to the notion that the positive life experiences of the student are relevant bases from which they can integrate their institutional learning into the 'live' placement experience being presented. The recognition and accreditation of relevant early life experiences are considered.

The principles of self-selection are based on the belief that, as adults, students are capable of assessing and identifying the nature of the practice placement which would maximize both their learning and the benefits to the agency and the service-user. The ability to self-select depends very much on the relationship between the lecturer and the student. The position adopted by lecturers is to be clear on how all parties involved in the placement can benefit from the relationship.

The Maori and Samoan students whose views are discussed in this chapter were all positive about working with their own people, whether the institution they worked in was a Western-style bureaucracy managed by *Pakeha* (white) people or an urban or rural tribal organization. This included two Maori students who were not happy with their relationship with their placement teacher but who maximized positive learning from a negative situation.

The views of Maori students who worked in government departments and were supervised by *Pakeha* practice teachers will also be reflected.

Students chose placements based on:

- what they perceived they needed to learn;
- the opportunity to work in an area of social work in which they had minimal experience;
- the desire to work in an organization run by their own people;
- the desire to contribute their skills and experiences to benefit their own people;
- the desire to learn about the processes of healing and conflict resolution of their own Maori people – to learn about the tribal traditions and history of their tribe;
- the desire to work in an environment they believed to be supportive;
- the desire to be with Maori organizations which they believed were better than the 'official' agencies in providing culturally appropriate services to Maori people;

- the opportunity to work in a government bureaucracy with a practice teacher of the same culture;
- the opportunity to impress prospective employers.

For Maori students, selection of the placement is always discussed and debated with the lecturer, who is also Maori.

Following the student's choice of placement, contact is made with the agency, and a pre-placement visit is arranged. The purpose of this visit is for the student and the placement agency to assess each other's suitability. The length of the visit with Maori organizations is determined by the factors each sees as relevant for a decision to be made. The visits to non-Maori organizations usually last an hour.

To date, no Maori student has been refused a placement in a Maori organization; neither has any student declined to take the opportunity to join such an organization. Maori, on the other hand, have declined some offers for placement in non-Maori agencies and, like other students, have not been accepted by these agencies.

The type of Maori organization varies from the multi-tribal, urban organization to the single-tribe, urban or rural organization. Where a sole tribal organization is the focus, only members of that tribe choose and are referred for that placement. This position is determined by the philosophy of the course, which supports the social structure of tribes and student awareness of the independence of each tribe.

In the early part of the placement, a contract is drawn up between the student and the agency, each identifying the expectations they have of the other. Much of this would have been discussed in the pre-placement visit.

The experience

Of the twelve students who discussed self-selection in some depth (eleven Maori and one Samoan), the majority felt they were treated as equals; indeed, one indicated that she believed that the Maori organization with which she worked elevated her. Five students felt they were treated as subordinates by the practice teachers and other staff; two of these students worked for a Maori organization and two for a government department.

Most of the students who worked for Maori organizations or who were supervised by someone from their own culture felt they were respected for the knowledge they brought with them. They also observed that users of the agency were treated as guests and were respected on that basis. The respect was demonstrated by the offering of food and drink, which is a tradition demonstrating respect for visitors by Maori people. Some of the students working in the government organizations did not feel as comfortable and did not believe people were treated as guests.

The students who had previously worked for government agencies began to see their own people differently. Their prior view was strongly influenced by the culture of the government agency and its employees, who were the majority *Pakeha* people. This view was a negative one of their own people. These students have stated the importance of being decolonized from the prevailing Western social work values to which they had succumbed.

For example, many Maori workers ignore the circular process of discussion which leads to reconciliation and healing. In one *hui* (meeting), for example, the process of discussion is that words are addressed to the middle of the room. People are not referred to directly, and people are never interrupted when speaking. What each speaker has to offer is metaphorically placed in the middle of the room, and anyone can take what they choose from the wisdom in the middle. They leave what they do not want. Western social work encourages people to address each other directly.

The word 'I' is not used; the word 'we' is. 'I' excludes others and is individualistic; 'we' includes the 'I' and is group-oriented. Maori believe that what 'I' does has implications for 'us', my *whanau* (extended family), *hapu* (sub-tribe) and *iwi* (tribe).

The Western paradigm of social work encourages people to make 'I' statements. While many Maori social workers have difficulty with this concept, many are increasingly individualizing people by overtly encouraging the use of 'I'. One tribe has a saying that goes: *'ko te kawau anake te mea e korero ana i tona ake ingoa, ko au, ko au, ko au'* ('the shag is the only thing that says "it is I; it is I; it is I'''). Maori do not use 'I' statements; the group takes responsibility, and all individuals are part of the group. Moving away from group responsibility, which in the process individualizes people, is, in the Maori view, a colonized position. Ignoring the traditional, circular communication processes of the *hui* – which emphasize group responsibility and which are known to be successful at resolving issues with the absence of punishment – is also a colonized position.

Positive aspects of the Maori placements

The positive aspects of the placements with Maori organizations were:

- Students felt culturally safe, in that their views from their own ethnic/ cultural perspectives were acknowledged and appreciated. Most of the practice teachers were of the same culture/ethnic group.
- Students found it was much easier to work with their own people – both as supervisor/co-worker and with those who visited the agency to address their concerns.
- Students learned new skills to 'take back home to my people'.

- The focus was not on pathology.
- Lateral thinking and creativity were encouraged to resolve issues of concern. Government economic and social policies did not affect the social work relationship between the people and the worker.
- There were fewer administrative restrictions.
- There was a cohesion and unity of purpose amongst the workers. The motivating force for the workers was that 'we are providing a service and working for our own people'. This also became the *raison d'être* for the students.
- Discussion was open and respectful. Discussions were often undertaken with the appropriate rituals setting the parameters.
- The organizations insisted on providing the best service they were capable of delivering.
- The workers were committed to working hard, and they acted as good role models for the student group.
- Students commented on the ability of their supervisors to manage stress. Humour was an excellent mechanism.
- Responsibility was shared, with no one solely responsible.
- Students learned how to put limited resources to good use.
- Theories, practices and processes were Maori, and clearly did not belong to the Western colonizing power.
- The power relationship between the student, the practice teacher and the people seeking the service was generally not apparent and certainly not abusive, at either a worker level or an institutional level.
- The workers were extremely non-judgemental, as the possibility always existed that the person or persons using the agency might be related to the worker or one of his or her colleagues.
- People were respected.

The twelve students felt strongest about the first four of these points.

Issues of concern about the Maori placements

The issues students believed needed to be addressed related to:

1 Philosophy and practice were inconsistent. The philosophy was one of liberation, the practice was still that of the colonizing Western oppressor. Students believed that this organization had not completed the process of decolonization from Western thinking and behaviour.
2 Workers exercised power over people using the service in quite an overt way, particularly when challenged.
3 Students were treated as subordinates, and the student label was continually affirmed.

4   The organization still adhered to the *Pakeha* government agenda, mores and rules.
5   Distance from the university and the cost of visiting prohibited the three intended support visits by the lecturers during the fourteen-week practice placement.
6   The distance also placed these students at a disadvantage, as they were denied the opportunity to attend a two-hour practice seminar every second week, when practice issues and case studies were discussed with the tutorial group and lecturer.
7   Workers had a multiplicity of roles as a result of a lack of cash to resource the service properly. This is common with the indigenous organizations.

The first four points came from two Maori students who had a placement in the same agency, points 5 and 6 related to placements more than 250 miles from the university, and the last point applied to all Maori organizations.

The major differences between placement with a Maori organization and a *Pakeha* organization relate to culture. Maori organizations exist to cater for a distinct ethnic group who relate to each other on the basis of their genealogical links and common history as a significant, colonized minority in a country which was once theirs. The same group are now reclaiming their history, as they are also challenging the state for resources of which they were illegally deprived. This means that students are likely to become involved in political activism along with their people. They are likely to be involved in preparing compensation claims against the state.

The workers and the students in such organizations are more than likely to be working with people with whom they are genealogically linked, and who have suffered the same levels of oppression from a majority, colonizing culture. There is also dissatisfaction with the services offered by *Pakeha* organizations and *Pakeha* people.

Maori working in the state organizations also have the desire to work with their own people as an incentive, but the difference with a placement in a *Pakeha* organization is that the culture and values are Anglo-Saxon and originate from a distant land. The *Pakeha* workers, who are in the majority, are generally not from the same class as the users of the service. The odds of these workers coming across their own relatives or friends are not great. The motive of working with those to whom they are genealogically linked does not exist. Many *Pakeha* women, however, work in the social services in order to support women and children with whom they identify, but with whom they are unlikely to have genealogical or class links.

Very few Maori are supervisors or practice teachers in the *Pakeha* organizations, despite having 'Pakeha' qualifications, and those who do become supervisors do not last very long. The perception many *Pakeha* people and *Pakeha* organizations have of their cultural superiority and knowledge of what is the 'truth' hinders the advancement of Maori in such organizations. This perception also calls into question the quality of the service Maori people receive through such organizations. Ironically, this is the very reason for the growth of numerous Maori groups delivering services to their own people.

The benefits of self-selection can be summarized as:

- respecting that students are capable of making informed choices, following dialogue and debate within tutorial groups;
- a greater motivation for the student to perform in the practice placement;
- the elimination of students' feelings that they have been forced into a placement against their will.

The only difficulty experienced with self-selection to date has been conflict between a student and a tutor who had advised the student that she did not think what the student had identified as a placement was appropriate. The student was successful in requesting a change to a tutor who encouraged self-selection; the student competed with other students for the placement of her choice and was successful.

No evaluative study has been undertaken to compare self-selection with overt direction by lecturers. Anecdotal evidence suggests that self-selection is the preferred option for both Maori and *Pakeha* students. The limiting factors are availability of placements, distance from university and cost of moving to another area.

Practice teachers support self-selection and see it as preferable to students being assigned on the basis of a shortage of placement opportunities or direction from lecturers.

Is placement with Maori groups an easy option for Maori?

Maori students believe that they are put under closer scrutiny than *Pakeha* students, and that it is not an easy option. The demands put on them are greater, especially when working with Maori organizations. They believe that, regardless of the placement, not only are they expected to know their own language, processes and customs, they are also expected to know the language, theories and social work processes of *Pakeha*.

They also believe that not only are they as individuals under scrutiny but also their *whanau* and tribe, and – if in a *Pakeha* agency – their race. This has parallels with the experiences of black social work students in the UK. *Pakeha* students do not have the same demands placed on them, because the individual is judged, not their race. Maori students perceive that *Pakeha* students get an easier deal. Indeed, in the last two years, four Maori students have had to repeat their practice placement (none of these were included in the sample of twelve discussed earlier). One assessed her own performance as unsatisfactory, two had their performances assessed as unsatisfactory by the agency, and one performance was assessed as unsatisfactory by the university, although the tribal group had rated the performance as satisfactory. All these placements were with Maori organizations, with Maori practice teachers and Maori tutors.

An empowered Maori social work community?

Maori tribal and non-tribal organizations are now actively recommending and supporting tribal members in enrolling on the course. It is impossible to tell whether the process of self-selection has empowered the Maori social work community or whether the empowerment has been as a result of more Maori students gaining entry to the course, and therefore becoming more visible to the Maori social work community as a result of the university encouraging placements with tribal groups and pro-active advertising of the social work course amongst Maori organizations. One of the major tribal groups in the country is designing a social work course comparable to those being offered in universities at present.

With Maori organizations, care has to be taken in that the organization, while espousing an adherence to Maori custom and tradition, may in fact be a colonized version of a *Pakeha* agency. Disillusionment sets in very quickly with Maori students who enter into these types of placement with a lot of positive energy and enthusiasm. Students often have to be cautioned that the very high expectations they have may be unrealistic, as the indigenous organizations function with a large number of volunteers and are woefully under-resourced. Many of these organizations are coming to terms with reclaiming indigenous processes, subsumed under the colonial yoke.

It is important for the tutors to be conversant with the language and understand tribal nuances and protocols. Above all, a prerequisite is to demonstrate humility and respect. One of the greatest differences regarding professional ethics in social work relates to the question of working with one's own *whanau*. Some practice teachers do not support this, whereas in the Maori organizations, there is an expectation that the students will work with their own.

Conclusion

Self-selection of practice placements is but one component of a liberated approach to social work education. The employment of Maori lecturers with practice experience by the university and the placement of Maori students with tribal organizations have challenged Western paradigms of social work education and practice. The healing practices and processes of *hui*, the exposure of students to traditional healers and healing processes, the questioning of the origins of the value-base for Western social work theory, the challenging of Western social science research design, methodology and ethos, and the desire for self-determination by the tribes have added an exciting dimension to social work in Aotearoa.

The lessons learned are also being taught by indigenous people throughout the world. The reference point for Maori in social work comes immediately from the indigenous people of Australia, our relatives in the Pacific Ocean and the indigenous peoples of both North and South America. What we have is not new, it is merely the reclamation of our humanness. It is the reclaiming of our perception of the world. It is the removal of the word 'problem', and its replacement with 'issues of concern'. It is no longer to dehumanize by using the word 'client'. It is to replace 'client' with 'person', 'people' or 'families we work with'. It is to trust that we can use our culture, our philosophies and our own theories and language to address the issues of concern.

A continuing issue for all indigenous peoples – and in this instance, Maori – is the insidious nature of racism which permeates the structures of the system, whether it be the non-Maori institutions which employ social workers or the institutions in which social work education is carried out. Maori social work educators, social workers and practice teachers have to be very clear that what the recipients of the service deserve is the best that is available. It is also incumbent upon them to support the indigenous social structures which have survived, despite colonization.

To succeed in liberating social work education, one must celebrate difference, one must acknowledge one's cultural eyes, one must recognize the imbalance of power, and one must trust and embrace the people.

Na te hinengaro ko te mahara, na te mahara ko te whakaaro, na te whakaaro ko te korero, ma te korero ka tu he tikanga. He taonga nui te wareware. I hara mai tatau i roto i o tatau matua, kai mua i a tatau ko te mate, ara te tuturutanga o te ora.

From the source of emotions comes the memory, from the memory come the thoughts, from the thoughts come the words, words create customs, forgetfulness is to be treasured. We descend from our ancestors, we exist in another world, before us lies death, the ultimate achievement of life. (Tibble, 1984)

Acknowledgements

I would like to thank the following:

Current students who contributed their thoughts, ideas and reflections on their experience, particularly Gerard Boot, Claire Te Rina Brown, Hinga Daymond-Smith, Dawn Glen, Nan Henry, Te Aroha Karaitiana, Tania Mohi, Soraya Stone, William Te Kira, Betty Whakatau, Maria Wilson and Roimata Wilson.

Former students whose experiences I have reflected on in the writing of this chapter: Toa Afele, Lee Cooke, Tuck Gardiner, Mal Hack, Aroha Harris, Ani Henry, Rawiri Hillman, Larry Monu, Mere Pahau, Adrianne Panoho, Tamati Parore, Te Paea Peehi-Barlow, Mihi Pickering, Sonia Rimene, John Simon, Mate Waiwai and Grace Wilkinson.

Practice teachers: Dorothy McArthur and Patricia Walker.

Colleagues: Riripeti Reedy and Caren Wickliffe.

6   The practice curriculum and methods of practice teaching

Mark Doel and Steven Shardlow

Introduction

In this chapter, we begin by looking at the content of the student's learning on placement in the practice agency. More specifically, we review the ways in which this content can be made systematic, and the development of the notion of an explicit practice curriculum in the United Kingdom. An analogy using the notion of a map is presented to help to conceptualize the 'practice curriculum' and to consider it in detail.

We also look at the methods which practice teachers can use in order to enable students to learn about social work practice on placements. The value of simulations is discussed, using a specific example. There is a brief consideration of the significance of learning sequences, the pace of learning and some of the issues around assessment in relation to our idea of the curriculum. The reality of the 'hidden' curriculum is also described.

Finally, we review the tensions between 'education' and 'training' in social work and present a tentative hypothesis about the pattern of development of practice curricula.

Constructing a practice curriculum

Let us look at the question of how to build a curriculum for learning practice on a placement in an agency (the *practicum*) by using an analogy. Imagine a new country, which we will call 'The Land of Social Work Practice' – or Socialworkland for short. We could begin to map out the territory of this country by describing some of its key features: the 'mountains', 'plains', 'forests', 'rivers', 'roads', 'towns', etc. of Socialworkland. By naming these features and locating them on a map, we make them explicit and known, we give them a location in relation to each other, and we can invite others to see if their view of the topography of Socialworkland corresponds to ours (see Figure 6.1).

Indeed, we can contemplate a meeting of all the people who have an interest in social work education (the 'stakeholders'), drawing a composite map of Socialworkland. This would be made up of the different perspectives of practice teachers, students, college tutors and agency managers. Eventually, after much debate and negotiation, a map of Socialworkland would emerge, with features recognizable to all the persons inhabiting it.

What these people have been doing is, in effect, to map out a curriculum for social work practice. They have begun to identify and to name what had been only implicitly understood; they have begun to give weight and significance to some topographical features in relation to others, and they have started to negotiate with different stakeholders about the appearance of this map, rather than impose their own or submit to another's.

A similar process of curriculum-building has been operating in the South Yorkshire Diploma in Social Work Programme since the late 1980s. This programme brings together two universities, several public welfare agencies (social services departments), a probation service (correctional service) and a number of voluntary, non-profit organizations. Together, they provide the social work education programme for the region around Sheffield in England.

The model of curriculum-building was developed from Doel (1987). Doel (1988) describes three categories of curriculum construction – paradigm, broad framework and empirical – and the Sheffield curriculum is an example of the third kind. Representatives of the various stakeholders were involved in constructing a practice curriculum which would be used by all 150 students and their practice teachers in the programme; in effect, they were mapping out *what a student needs to learn on placement,* like the people we imagined drawing the map of Socialworkland.[1] There are parallels with the mutual definition of curriculum described by Grossman and Perry in Chapter 4.

After the first run of this curriculum, a large feedback forum was organized for all the practice teachers, students and tutors in the programme. A questionnaire was also used to elicit the opinions of the participants in this first pilot. The results were encouraging, with nine out of ten respondents being generally or very satisfied with the curriculum; the 10 per cent who expressed some degree of dissatisfaction were practice teachers who were unhappy about the idea of *any* explicit curriculum, not specifically this one. In subsequent years, the curriculum gained even more acceptance, with only minor modifications made to the basic 'map'.

The advantages of involving all the interested parties in mapping the curriculum are evident:

- It is a visible expression of mutual respect by the people who are engaged in helping students to learn social work practice. The very act of meeting together to decide what goes on the map is significant and leads to negotiation and collaboration.
- It begins to address power differentials between various stakeholders and organizational interests; too often, the curriculum has been seen as the college's territory, and the process we have described opens this to broader groups. Others whose perspectives have often been excluded, such as black social workers, residential and day care workers, etc., can be included as map-drawers, too.
- This approach to curriculum mapping is more likely to result in one which is practice-led (Phillipson, Richards and Sawdon, 1988). Let us be clear that 'practice' is *not* synonymous with 'social work employing agency'; there is no implication that the practice curriculum should be driven by the agencies, any more than it should be instigated by colleges. Of course, it is shaped by the college and the agency, but social work practice is not equivalent to what goes on in a social work agency, nor what is taught at a school of social work. It transcends setting, institution and stakeholder. A curriculum which arises out of different perspectives can help to ensure that it is practice-led.

Implicit and explicit practice curricula

Let us return to Socialworkland, but this time we will also imagine ourselves travelling back in time – to 1980, when practice teachers in the UK were called 'student supervisors' (field instructors), and there was no such thing as a practice curriculum.

Socialworkland existed then just as it exists now. Its features were different in some respects; for example, there are at least three 'ghost towns' on the 1996 map which in the UK in 1980 would have been thriving communities: these locations are Neighbourhood Social Work, Localization of Services and Patchwork. Conversely, the huge River of Anti-oppressive Practice, which flows right through the 1996 map, would perhaps be recognizable only as a small stream called Clients' Rights in 1980. Looking to the future, we see some possible changes to Socialworkland, as the CCETSW (1995) Review of the Diploma in Social Work has every appearance of damming the River of Anti-oppressive Practice, with fears that it may begin to run dry.

We can see that Socialworkland in the UK in 1980 had some features that were similar and some different to the 1990s map. However, the biggest difference then was the lack of *any* map. The experience for student supervisors and students was like being blindfolded and taken by plane to parachute into *terra incognita*; who knows where they landed, who knows how they would

Figure 6.1 Socialworkland (as seen from the UK in 1996)

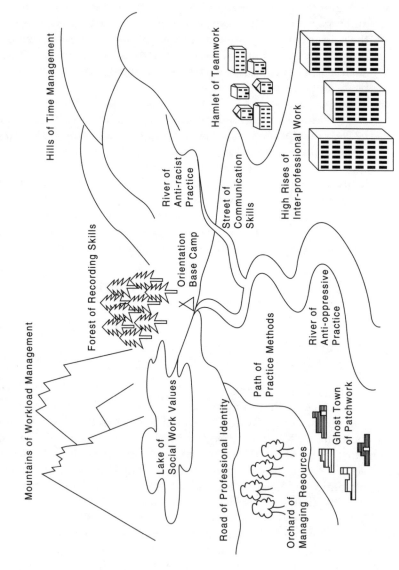

find their way around? For some (perhaps the 10 per cent in the survey mentioned earlier) the adventure of discovery was the main point, but for most it was a bewildering and time-consuming effort to find their bearings.

The practice curriculum is therefore an attempt to make explicit what has often been implicit. A map of the terrain means that the practice teacher and the student have some foreknowledge of the key features, a general understanding of how they relate to each other, the opportunity to make choices about how they will visit this land, and an overall sense of fairness, because they know that other practice teachers and students are starting off with the same map of the same terrain.

Methods of learning

We have been discussing the *content* of practice learning by using a territorial analogy. However, this is only one aspect of a practice curriculum. We also need to consider the *methods* by which the territory is going to be explored.

With the map, the practice teacher and the student no longer have to do the initial exploratory work to discover the basic features of Socialworkland. This gives them more time and opportunity to consider *how* they are going to visit this land. To extend the analogy, *how* are they going to climb the Mountains of Workload Management, travel the Road of Professional Identity, cycle the Path of Social Work Practice Methods, backpack into the Forest of Recording Skills? Are they going to swim or boat the River of Anti-oppressive Practice? And, in this particular agency, will this be swimming against the current, or will the student be able to go with the flow?

There are also decisions to be made about which features students will be expected to explore in the company of the practice teacher or other colleagues, and which ones they will investigate alone. The student will also need to know how to make use of unexpected opportunities, and the practice teacher will need to find out what experiences of other lands students bring with them. Experienced orienteerers, like experienced learners, will quickly adapt to the task of discovering Socialworkland; others will need to acquire these skills. In social work terms, they need to learn how to learn.

What is interesting for practice teachers is the difference between living in a land and visiting it. In other words, experienced practitioners might know Socialworkland all too well, but this does not help them to look at it as a newcomer; indeed, the very familiarity can be a hindrance.

Action techniques

Nowhere is the transition from 'student supervisor' to 'practice teacher' more dramatic than in the range of teaching methods which has opened up for social workers to use with students.

Sawdon (1985) has called these methods *action techniques*, as opposed to *interactional techniques*, such as accurate listening, summarizing, etc. She has also categorized the available teaching methods in social work (see Figure 6.2).

Structural arrangements

In addition to the five categories of methods in Figure 6.2, we need to consider the arrangements for using these methods (see Payne and Scott, 1982, for more discussion of these arrangements):

- 1-to-1;
- tandem;
- peer;
- group;
- pair(s);
- co-work;
- joint work;
- live teaching;
- tag;
- long-arm;
- outreach;
- periodic on-site;
- observed;
- team;
- direct evidence;
- linked.

Another useful way of categorizing teaching methods in social work is to consider activities which are *live* and those which are *simulated*. Simulations have been discussed in relation to social work for at least twenty years, when Meinert (1972) explored the relevance of simulation technology as a potential tool for social work education. There is a tendency to consider simulations as formal, relying either on sophisticated technology (such as interactional video), or requiring faithful replications of reality (such as flight simulators). However, there is considerable scope for the use of informal simulations, which require only creativity and imagination. We have discussed the uses of live and simulated methods in practice teaching in more detail elsewhere (Doel and Shardlow, 1993; Doel and Shardlow, 1996). In addition, Evans (1987) has a good example of how practice teachers can use live teaching with a student and a client in the same room.

Figure 6.2   Action techniques (adapted from Sawdon, 1985)

I   HARDWARE

- Audio
- Tape
- Film
- One-way screens
- CD-TV (interactional video)

- Video
- Slide
- Computer
- Internet

II   WRITTEN

- Practice folder
- Logs
- Summaries
- Case records
- Task analysis
- Letters
- Critical incident analysis
- Individual care plans

- Minutes
- Reports
- Day books
- Resource file
- Questionnaires
- Contracts
- Evaluation sheets
- Recorded, timed observations

III   EXPERIENTIAL

- Exercises
- Games
- Rehearsal
- Sculpting
- Discussions
- Court appearances
- Tribunals

- Activities
- Role-play
- Simulations
- Drama
- Meetings
- Ward rounds
- Project development

IV   GRAPHIC

- OHP
- Plans
- Charts
- Cartoons
- Diagrams

- Flipcharts
- Photographs
- Drawings
- Sketches

V   PRINTED

- Articles
- Books
- Texts
- Newspaper items
- Statistics
- Policy documents

- Handouts
- Novels
- Reports
- Journals
- Official document analysis
- Procedure manuals

Informal simulations

The power of simulations lies in their ability to capture an essence of reality rather than necessarily faithfully replicating it. A good simulation is one which is neutral enough to have an impact on a broad range of people with different life experiences. It is paradoxical that this neutrality allows differences to shine through, assumptions to become transparent and values to take shape.

The example in Figure 6.3 is taken from a book of exercises and activities for social work practice learning (Doel and Shardlow, 1993: 159). Unlike a formal simulation, such as one which reproduces procedures in a court room or ward-round practices in a hospital, the relevance of this informal simulation to social work practice is not immediately obvious. However, it is a powerful trigger to help students (and practice teachers) to consider issues of socially-structured difference (Thompson, 1993). In working through this simulation, participants begin to challenge assumptions about themselves and other people, to understand how their experience of the world colours their present vision, and the effects of differences in power (associated, for example, with race, gender and class). The simulation also helps participants to learn about self-disclosure, as well as providing an opportunity to consider interactional skills.

All of these elements are of considerable significance to social work practice. It is especially important that this kind of learning is included in the curriculum to counteract any tendency to see practice solely in terms of skills reduced to task-based competences. The value-base of social work practice is what makes it distinct from other professions, and if this is diluted beyond recognition, there will be nothing to prevent the tasks which are at present performed by social workers from being split off for others to do.

Confining discussions about social work values to college-based learning is not effective, because the chasm between what is learned in college and what is done in agencies becomes too great. Practice teachers are experienced practitioners working within the agency, and it brings the teaching of values deep into the heart of the agency when they use these kinds of informal simulation. There is a chance that this will act as a counter-weight to the focus on technical skills and abilities to follow procedures.[2]

Sequence and assessment

We have explored two aspects of the practice curriculum – content and methods – and there are two others which are essential to complete the idea of curriculum. The first of these is *sequence and pace*. Returning to Socialworkland,

Figure 6.3   An informal simulation to look at personal biographies, the influence of culture and issues of diversity (taken from Doel and Shardlow, 1993)

YOU ARE WHAT YOU EAT

To prepare for this activity, put these meals in order for a typical day – and add any meals which are not named (for example, some people in South Wales eat *tea-tea*, a meal of cold, sweet foods, in the late afternoon):

DINNER BRUNCH TEA BREAKFAST LUNCH ELEVENSES SUPPER

- As a child, which of these meals did you eat?
- What image does the word used to describe each meal bring to mind?
- We only need to eat two meals a day, so why so many possible meals?
- Were there any periods of fasting in your family?
- What was the main meal of the day in your family; who was present?
- On weekdays, was your main meal of the day at school or at home?
- Was there any special day of the week with different meal patterns?

Smells

- What are your earliest memories of food smells?
- What, if any, smells greeted you as you came home from school?
- Are there any smells which have special memories for you?

Tastes

- What was your favourite-tasting food; was it associated with a family meal?
- Did your family encourage you to try unfamiliar foods and tastes?
- If you didn't like the taste of something on your plate, what happened?

Touch

- Did you have to wash your hands before coming to the table?
- What foods could you eat by hand at the main family meal?
- Were you ever hit for misbehaviour at the table? If so, what had you done?

Sounds

- Did your family make any blessing before eating?
- Were family meals time for conversation or silence?
- If conversational, were these happy, argumentative or a mix?

Figure 6.3　continued

Sights

- Who prepared the meal, set the table and served the food?
- How was the table set – did you have a tablecloth, napkins, etc.?
- Would you often or seldom see guests eating with you at the family table?

How have the habits of your childhood meals influenced your adult meals?

If you share meal-times with a partner, what similarities and differences did you notice in your meal-time behaviours?

Have other cultures influenced the way you take the main meal of the day now, or is it very similar to your childhood experience?

---

the practice teacher and the student need to ask themselves if there are any special sequences in which the locations on the map need to be visited.

A practice teacher who is experienced at showing students around Socialworkland may have learned patterns of discovery which are especially effective, starting out from Orientation Base Camp. These patterns would need to respect differences between students, with the understanding that what worked for one student might not necessarily work for another. Nevertheless, any short cuts are welcome, because the student's time to explore Socialworkland is brief – only as long as the placement. Practice teachers must also be prepared to depart from their usual pace, in response to each student's capacity; what has become familiar and commonplace to the practitioner who is resident in Socialworkland may entice the visiting student to linger.

The fourth element in the practice curriculum is *assessment*. It is not the purpose of this chapter to explore issues of assessment in great detail (see Hughes and Heycox in Chapter 7 of this book for three perspectives on assessment in practice learning, and Rogers in Chapter 2 for a review of issues surrounding assessment criteria and methods). However, practice teachers need to consider how they are going to gather evidence that the student has made successful visits to the key features of Socialworkland. They should develop criteria which spell out what 'successful' means. For example:

- *climbed unaided to the very top of the Mountains of Workload Management* (in other words, the student can work independently);

or

- *made it when allowed to drop the load* (the student can work independently as long as she or he does not have a full workload);

or
- *got a good view of it from the observation point on the road* (the student can discuss what it is like to do this work, but has not actually done it);

or
- *allegedly gave a good account of the view to a colleague* (you have second-hand evidence about the student's work).

Other considerations are:

- Who is responsible for gathering the evidence?
- What are the most appropriate types of evidence?
- What effect does the process of being assessed have on the learning?

Students are not tourists enjoying a carefree holiday in Socialworkland; at the end of their stay, like London taxi-drivers, they are expected to have 'the knowledge' (that is, the ability to find their way around and to take others).

The hidden curriculum

So far, we have been discussing the visible landscape of the curriculum. We have described the value of an explicit curriculum, shared by all the students and teachers in a programme, rather than several implicit ones. In an ideal world, this would be the end of the matter. However, most practitioners are aware that there are other aspects of the work in their organization which are not written down or codified in any explicit policy document but are nevertheless essential to understanding how the organization works. For example, the culture in any organization has unique features, intangible and mysterious – a truly hidden part of the curriculum. Students will have no success in working in the agency if they fail to understand it.

If we think back to Socialworkland, this hidden curriculum is like the sub-terranean landscape – the caves, potholes and labyrinths which connect the various visible features. In terms of sequence, it is likely that a student will get to know more about the surface curriculum before getting to grips with any more complex underground chambers. Nevertheless, at some point the student will need to become acquainted with these other parts of the curriculum.

Education or training?

There is a tension inherent in the enterprise of teaching students to become social workers. This is the tension between the desire to develop reflective, critical professionals and the need to fashion skilled, competent staff to do the agency job. These are not mutually exclusive aims, but neither are they free from conflict.

In the UK, this equation is becoming increasingly unbalanced as the job of social work becomes prescribed by procedures and routines. This is probably the result of social work's difficulty in articulating what it does and why it is worth doing it, and also the consequence of a broad ideological onslaught on professions in general. There is genuine concern that social work's position as a single, identifiable profession is precarious, and that it could be broken into various parts, thus revisiting the question first posed by Brewer and Lait (1980) – *Can social work survive?*

The notion of a curriculum for practice learning is extremely important in the struggle between the education of reflective practitioners and the training of competent operators. The content of that curriculum indicates the direction for the next generation of social workers, so it is significant how this landscape is described.

We suggest two indicators to gauge the developmental stage of professional education programmes for social workers:

- To what extent is the curriculum for practice learning (the practice curriculum or practicum) *explicit*? It is our hypothesis that in the early stages, the practice curriculum in social work education and training programmes has been relatively implicit, individual and *ad hoc*. Often, the notion of a curriculum has been entirely absent from the learning taking place during the placement.
- Once the curriculum does become explicit, *where is the power located* to decide what the content of the curriculum is? Again, we hypothesize that in the early stages of curriculum development, this power tends to be located in the educational establishments – colleges and universities. As the familiarity with a practice curriculum develops, practice teachers are likely to gain more confidence, and the content of the curriculum becomes a collaboration between educational institutions and practice agencies. This requires considerable negotiation and a commitment to social work practice as something that *transcends* setting – educational or employment.

In seeking to describe and define your own local Socialworkland, we believe that the desire to balance educational and training requirements, professional and employers' needs, is best met by a collaborative 'map', drawn by all parties engaged in the challenging work of preparing students for professional social work practice.

Notes

1   For other examples of curriculum-building see Butler and Elliot (1985) and Richards (1988). Also, in Chapter 4 of this book, Grossman and Perry make reference to how the curriculum in their project was developed around competencies.
2   Simulations can trigger powerful emotions. This is no different from the powerful feelings which live practice with clients can evoke. In most cases, it is appropriate that students know that they can choose how much they wish to disclose about themselves. Occasionally, exercises such as the one reproduced in Figure 6.3 can have painful associations for students, and they need to know that they are not obliged to take part.

7 Three perspectives on assessment in practice learning

Lesley Hughes and Karen Heycox

Introduction

Ultimately, social work education has a responsibility to the profession and the people it serves, to ensure that graduates can perform competently and in an ethical manner. To be an effective social worker, one obviously needs to be able to perform well both in classroom subjects and in practice learning in the field setting. While students may perform well in work at university, there is no guarantee that this level of performance will be matched in practice learning. It is therefore essential that there is careful assessment of student performance in the practice setting before graduation and admission to the profession.

In writing this chapter, we are proceeding on the basis of certain assumptions about the nature and place of practice learning in social work education. From our experience and reading of the literature, we believe that:

- Practice learning is important but sometimes neglected, and is often seen as having lower academic status than classroom subjects (Duncan et al., 1990).
- Practice learning is the 'real' testing-ground for social work knowledge and skills (Rosenblum and Raphael, 1987; Vayda and Bogo, 1991).
- Assessment of practice learning is much more complex than in other subjects in the curriculum, in terms of what is assessed and how, as well as the number of persons involved in the assessment (Kimber, 1982; Wilson and Moore, 1989).
- Any difficulties that are highlighted or arise during the assessment of student performance in practice learning inevitably have an impact on all parties in a way that is personally stressful (Gitterman and Gitterman, 1979; Rosenblum and Raphael, 1987).
- Practice learning particularly highlights issues concerning the relationship between the university and social workers in the field.

We know from our experience and that of colleagues elsewhere that while the above beliefs are commonly held, they have not always been addressed adequately in the literature. This is of concern in itself, but also because of the role social work courses play as gatekeepers to the profession (Moore and Urwin, 1991; Cole and Lewis, 1993). The authors' own experience as educators concerned with practice teaching and learning concurs with suggestions in the literature that fewer students than expected fail this part of their social work courses (Brandon and Davies, 1979; Coulshed, 1980). In order to change this situation, we need to understand why it comes about. Part of the answer lies, of course, in the nature of practice learning and the way it is assessed.

As discussed elsewhere in this book, practice learning is an essential aspect of social work education (Dore, Newman Epstein and Herrerias, 1992). The importance of practice learning is reflected in the fact that a social work qualification cannot be obtained without a substantial period of practice learning in the field. In Australia, for example, a minimum of 140 days in at least two settings is required (Duncan et al., 1990). This is equivalent to a full year of full-time university study. It is also a distinctive, indeed unique, component of social work education. Not only are students able to learn about social work from observing and analysing the practice of experienced workers 'in the real world', they must develop *in situ* the myriad skills required. In doing this, they are expected to draw upon and integrate learning from numerous, diverse university subjects.

At the same time, students come to the practice learning situation with their own individual packages of values, beliefs, ways of seeing the world, personality and communication styles. Students also enter the practice learning situation with their own individual learning style, which may or may not be compatible with the teaching style of the practice teacher (Gardiner, 1989). All of these are often challenged in practice learning. In addition, the other two parties in the practice learning situation – practice teacher (field teacher/supervisor) and university staff – also have their own individual 'packages' which affect practice learning. Further, one of the distinctive features of practice teaching and learning is that it occurs in the context of a relationship between student and practice teacher, with the university staff member being involved at significant points. Therefore, as practice teaching and learning is a complex process and as it operates at a number of levels for the individuals involved, it is not surprising that the assessment of student competence in practice learning can be difficult.

In this chapter, we hope to explore factors which impinge on the assessment process, particularly when there are concerns about student competence. Factors affecting the student, the practice teacher and particularly the university staff will be addressed through the authors' research and the relevant literature.

Social work education in Australia and New Zealand

Before discussing the research, it is necessary to describe social work education in Australia and New Zealand. For example, practice learning is commonly known as 'field education', 'fieldwork' or 'prac' (practicum), and Australian social work courses are accredited by the professional body, the Australian Association of Social Workers. In Australia, all social work courses require the equivalent of four years' full-time study at a university, leading to the awarding of a Bachelor's degree. There are also three-year degree courses in social and community welfare at several universities, and a larger number of associate diploma and advanced certificate courses at colleges of further education. The New Zealand picture is less clear-cut, as there are no welfare courses *per se*, and social work courses are located in polytechnics as well as universities, ranging from two-year undergraduate qualifications to four-year degrees. In order to practise as a social worker in New Zealand, individuals must apply to the professional association for accreditation, which is then reviewed every five years.

In Australian social work courses, there is some variation in the mix of liberal arts subjects and professionally-focused subjects. Courses also vary in terms of the point in the course at which students begin the professional social work component and practice learning. As stated earlier, the minimum required period of practice learning in Australia is 140 days (980 hours), and in New Zealand the minimum is 120 days. In Australia, practice learning must include a range of practice methods in at least two agency settings. Practice learning subjects are graded on a 'pass/fail' or 'satisfactory/unsatisfactory' basis.

Practice teachers who supervise students make a recommendation to the subject co-ordinator at the university, who consults with the university staff member who visited the placement before awarding the final grade. Satisfactory performance in each practice learning subject is a prerequisite for progression to the next field subject. Mid-placement and final placement assessments provide the formal feedback to the university on student progress. Often, students are expected to keep journals and complete written assignments for each practice learning subject. Visits by the university staff provide an avenue for assessment and support to the student and practice teacher.

It is important to note that there seem to be major differences in cultural background between social work students in Australia and New Zealand. This is largely due to differences in the composition and cultural backgrounds of the Australian and New Zealand populations (see Harry Walker's Chapter 5 for more details). New Zealand has a significant indigenous population (approximately 10 per cent), with the majority of the remainder being of Anglo-Celtic background. Those of non-English-speaking background tend to be South Pacific islanders. This situation is reflected in a bi-cultural approach to social work education. In Australia, however, the indigenous population is much smaller (approximately 1 per cent), and there is a significant population from non-English-speaking backgrounds, originating from most parts of the world. In Australia, the rhetoric speaks of a cross-cultural or multi-cultural approach.

While the difference in the composition of the populations of the two countries is reflected in the respective social work student populations, indigenous people are still under-represented in Australian social work courses. There are issues of access and equity for indigenous students in both countries. Aboriginal (Koori) students in Australia tend to be better represented in the social and community welfare courses at diploma and certificate level, compared to the social work degree courses. In New Zealand, as there is no differentiation between social welfare and social work courses, indigenous students are more visible in the social work student population.

By way of further illustration, in the last eight years only six Koori students have undertaken practice learning in the authors' school. Two other students left the course during this period, and five more have yet to attempt the practice learning component.

Background to the research

One impetus for the authors' research stemmed from our awareness that in the past, few of our students had failed practice learning subjects. Also, within our school's student culture, it was commonly believed that it was almost impossible to fail a practice learning subject. However, in each practice learning subject, there were students whose practice had been of concern and for whom failure had been a possibility. In addition to the need to examine standards of student performance, there was the need to demonstrate accountability of practice learning subjects and enhance their credibility within the course.

Our research was conducted in four parts from mid-1991 to mid-1994. First, we reviewed student placements at our school in the preceding two-and-a-half years in order to obtain a picture of marginal performance in practice learning, both in terms of numbers of students where there was concern and the reasons for concern. Second, we surveyed all social workers who had acted as practice teachers (field teachers) for student practice learning placements in this two-and-a-half-year period, focusing on their experiences of assessing student performance but covering other areas as well – for example, a personal and professional profile. Then we asked students about their experiences of the assessment process by means of a questionnaire.

Finally, we interviewed university staff in Australia and New Zealand who were involved in practice learning subjects about their concerns regarding student performance and how these are handled. Findings from this latter stage of the research were discussed at an international social work educators' forum in Amsterdam (1994) to begin to explore commonalities and differences in university staffs' experiences of assessment.

Review of placements

To obtain a picture of marginal student performance in practice learning, we reviewed all practice learning situations in the Bachelor of Social Work (BSW) course at the authors' school over 1989, 1990 and the first half of 1991. The identification of students about whom there had been concerns was made retrospectively. The criterion used was whether the practice teacher or the university staff had raised any concerns about a student's performance with the subject co-ordinator. The reasons for concern about each student's performance were tabulated and then collated by category. This method is clearly open to the criticism of being both retrospective and subjective. The criticism of subjectivity has been made regarding the very process of assessment in practice learning (Kimber, 1982). Since our aim in this regard was exploratory rather than to test hypotheses, the present methodology seems acceptable. As a counter to criticisms of inaccuracy due to the retrospective identification of concerns, it must be stated that university staff remember particularly well the students who occasion them anguish and extra work!

Concerns about student performance

Our review showed that in 9 per cent of practice learning situations, concerns about students' performance were expressed by practice teachers and/or university staff. Of these, 19 per cent of students ultimately failed. Therefore, the overall failure rate was 2 per cent. This percentage falls at the lower end of the range of 'fail' grades recommended by the authors' faculty (0–20 per cent). It also confirms the authors' suspicion that too few students were failing practice learning.

For some students, there was more than one aspect of their practice which caused concern (the areas of student performance which were of concern are ranked in order from most frequently occurring to least frequently occurring):

- generally poor inter-personal and communication skills;
- lack of self-awareness/lack of awareness of impact on others;

- poor professional skills (for example, assessment, referral, report writing);
- lack of interest, initiative;
- poor work organization;
- laziness;
- role boundary issues, unprofessional behaviour;
- values issues;
- lack of confidence.

The most frequently occurring reasons related to what could be called students' *use of self*. This is in keeping with the findings of other researchers, such as Brandon and Davies (1979).

Having obtained a picture of the number and nature of concerns about marginal practice learning, the authors then surveyed practice teachers.

The survey of practice teachers

Aims

The survey was based on questions raised in the literature about the 'what' and 'how' of assessment in practice learning and the experience of university staff in dealing with marginal students. There were two broad aims:

- to describe practice teachers' experience of the assessment process, particularly the criteria they used to reach a decision about the final grade to be recommended;
- to construct a personal and professional profile of our practice teachers which might have implications for the supervisory relationship and assessment.

Methodology

The study, carried out by a mailed questionnaire, focused on practice teachers who supervised practice learning placements for the authors' school in 1989, 1990 and the first half of 1991.

We asked practice teachers about the criteria they used to assess student performance; their attitudes towards failing a student; what action they had taken when they did have concerns about student performance, and what action they had taken when failure was a possibility. Other questions in the survey related to satisfaction with their relationship with the university, and questions which enabled us to compile a personal and professional profile of practice teachers; 125 (out of 421) practice teachers returned the question-naires, a response rate of 30 per cent.

Results

Assessment criteria

Table 7.1 How practice teachers assess student performance on placement: Criteria found useful by practice teachers

Criteria	
University expectations	84%
Personal standards	86%
Agency guidelines	67%
Other standards (e.g. professional code of ethics, students' own goals, standards and opinions of colleagues)	25%

From Table 7.1, it would seem that although the provision of specific guidelines by the university is useful, assessment involves the application of other criteria as well, such as personal standards and agency guidelines. Moreover, this appears to be the case for the vast majority of those surveyed.

Practice teachers were also asked about the importance of students' personal characteristics in assessing their competence. Not surprisingly, most practice teachers (78 per cent) placed 'much' to 'very much' importance on students' personal characteristics. The reasons given for the importance of personal characteristics essentially focused on the view that social work is about inter-personal relations and skills *vis-á-vis* the client and co-workers – that is, social work is essentially about the use of self. As one practice teacher put it, 'These characteristics are the vehicle through which social work skills are expressed.' This is consistent with the reasons why students caused concern in the earlier review of placements. Of all the reasons for concern about student performance, 'poor inter-personal and communication skills' and 'lack of self-awareness/awareness of impact on others' were frequently given.

Practice teachers' attitudes towards failing a student

Most practice teachers (91 per cent) said they would fail a student if it was necessary, but many indicated that this would be a last resort 'only if all else failed'. The typical reasons why practice teachers would fail a student included comments such as 'It's one's professional responsibility.'

It is of some concern that 9 per cent of our practice teachers stated that they would never fail a student. This last point could be related to the fact that each of these respondents was fairly inexperienced as a practice teacher, and half of them had never taught a student about whom they had concerns.

We also asked practice teachers whether the level of placement made a difference to their willingness to fail a student. The majority (59 per cent) said that it would make a difference. Typical comments included: 'With a first placement there's time to learn and rectify'; 'It is a more important decision regarding final placement, because the student is about to go into the world.'

Among those who said their decision was not affected by the level of placement, comments included: 'There are standards regardless of which placement it is'; 'Failure is based on the student not reaching the standard set for that particular placement.'

Dealing with concerns about student performance

Interestingly, 55 per cent of the practice teachers said they had experienced concerns about student competence. Of those who had experienced concerns, most (89 per cent) had involved the university staff in some way in an attempt to resolve the situation. Most respondents did not indicate in what order actions were taken – whether the concerns were first discussed with the student, with the university staff or with a colleague.

Those practice teachers who had dealt with concerns about their student's performance without recourse to the university staff generally resolved the issues by: raising the problem with the student; working out ways of tackling the problem, and/or altering the intensity or focus of supervision. One practice teacher even stated that the student was given 'counselling and support to examine and review their career choice'.

Those practice teachers who had involved the university when they had concerns about student competence also usually raised the issues with the student, and stated that one common way of dealing with the problem was in a three-way meeting with the university staff. Practice teachers said that the most frequent actions of the university staff included: clarifying the situation; facilitating problem-solving; setting standards to be achieved by the end of placement; supporting the practice teacher; acting as mediator, and/or supporting the student.

Action taken in cases of possible failure

Twelve per cent of practice teachers said that they had at some stage thought of failing a student but had not gone on to do so.

When asked what would have made it possible for them to fail the student, answers could be divided into practice teacher and agency factors on the one hand and university factors on the other. Among the former, practice teachers most commonly mentioned that they should have acted earlier in raising their concerns. A typical comment was: 'In future, I would raise issues with the university as soon as they're not resolved between the student and myself, so there's more time and room for an objective and more positive examination of the subject.'

Another issue for practice teachers concerned the conflicts which can arise in the educator role: 'There is a dilemma for social workers in the role of educator, as they are not geared to "fail" clients/students.'

The other commonly mentioned practice teacher factor was lack of confidence in their judgement of the student's performance or in their ability to handle the consequences of recommending a 'fail' grade. This can possibly be related to the degree and type of support provided by the university and the employing agency (Bogo and Power, 1992). For example, in responding to the question about what would have made it possible to fail a student, one practice teacher said: 'more confidence in support from the university staff, and less pressure of work within my agency allowing time for the process'. In dealing with situations in which student performance was considered marginal, practice teachers suggested that ongoing contact and support from university liaison staff helps the assessment process. This is in line with literature which suggests that a pro-active stance by university liaison staff is necessary in the assessment of marginal students (Rosenblum and Raphael, 1987).

Personal and professional profile of practice teachers

Analysis of responses to a number of items in the survey enabled us to construct the following profile. The typical practice teacher:

- is *female* and under 40 years old (66 per cent);
- is relatively *new* in the position (50 per cent had been in their position less than three years) and relatively inexperienced as a practice teacher (just under 60 per cent had been supervising students for five years or less);
- does *not* receive supervision within her own agency (65 per cent);
- is fairly likely *not* to have a colleague who also supervises social work students (just under 50 per cent);
- is very likely *not* to have their job description include supervision of students (only 20 per cent of the sample had this included).

All the results of the survey of practice teachers suggest possible reasons why 'fail' grades are rarely recommended to the university.

Implications of the practice teachers' survey

As a result of this research and review of the literature, we concluded that there were four areas, or clusters of factors, which made it difficult for practice teachers to recommend a 'fail' grade for marginal performance in practice learning. These factors have been explored in more detail elsewhere by the authors (Hughes, Heycox and Eisenberg, 1994). These are:

- *Difficulty in articulating and applying assessment criteria* – while practice teachers are at some level aware that they use criteria in addition to those provided by the university, the latter appear to be inadequate, while the former are not explicitly recognized in the assessment process.
- *The multiple and often conflicting roles of practice teachers* – there is a potential conflict between the traditional nurturer/facilitator role of social workers and the assessment role, which requires making judgements about student performance and confronting the student with these (Rosenblum and Raphael, 1987).
- *Practice teachers' lack of experience and confidence in their role as educator* – it is likely that the more students one has supervised, the greater the probability that one has had to deal with marginal performance and gained increased experience in the assessment process. This is in keeping with Coulshed's (1980) finding in her survey of British practice teachers.
- *The organizational contexts of practice learning* – both in the practice teacher's own agency and the university, there is insufficient recognition for practice learning. A constellation of organizational factors may add up to practice teachers being unsupported in carrying out the various tasks of their role, including assessment.

Having gained some understanding of the practice teachers' perspective of the range of factors which can affect their ability to recommend a 'fail' where there is marginal performance, we decided to seek the students' perspective.

The survey of students

Aims

- To ascertain students' experience of the assessment process in practice learning, particularly where practice teachers or university staff had concerns about the student's performance.

- To find out whether the students themselves had concerns about their own performance or concerns about other aspects of practice learning. We also sought information on various aspects of their relationship with practice teachers, particularly details of student supervision.

Methodology

For the study of student views of placement, we chose students and former students who took part in practice learning between 1989 and 1991 (the same period used in the survey of practice teachers). Half were chosen on the basis that staff had concerns about their performance in practice learning, and half were randomly selected from students where concerns had not been identified. A questionnaire covering the areas listed above under 'Aims' was developed and mailed out to 135 students. The results are based on analysis of the 48 questionnaires returned (a response rate of 35 per cent); half of these were from students about whom there had been concern. We do not know how many students received the questionnaire, but the response rate was probably affected by factors such as change of address and the fact that some students who were still doing their practice learning may have been concerned about how the assessment of their current performance would be affected.

Results

Student concerns about practice learning

The majority of students did have concerns about their own performance and about other aspects of practice learning. Almost half the students thought that their practice teachers had concerns about their performance (this last point reflects the way the sample was constructed). While students' concerns about their performance were most frequently related to confidence, the second most common concern was related to inter-personal skills. Practice teachers identified the latter as the main area of concern about student performance.

Action taken by students about concerns

Where students had concerns about their own performance, their most common course of action was to speak to the practice teacher. The next most common courses of action were speaking with students or staff at university and speaking with family or friends. When students were concerned about other aspects of practice learning, the most common action was to talk to university staff, followed closely by discussion with the practice teacher.

Characteristics of supervision

We asked students a number of questions about their experience of supervision over their practice learning placements, both on the practice learning they were 'most satisfied' with and on the one they were 'least satisfied' with. We did this for two reasons: to establish a baseline with which to compare the supervision experiences of students about whom there were concerns and/or who failed placement, and to use in developing training and support structures for practice teachers.

The results are not surprising, but interesting nevertheless. It seems that in the 'typical' practice learning placement with which students were 'most satisfied', supervision sessions were weekly or more frequent; of one to two hours' duration; had an agenda set by both student and practice teacher, and used to discuss student performance and progress. This is in keeping with what has been described elsewhere as 'effective supervision' (Cimino et al., 1985; Gardiner, 1989). Also, in such practice learning placements, field teachers were unlikely to be absent on leave.

The 'typical' placement with which students were 'least satisfied' was a mirror opposite of this scenario.

Significant points from the student survey

Regarding the student survey, the following points seem to be significant in understanding the assessment process when there are concerns about student performance:

- There is a high number of students whose performance is of concern to themselves.
- The main areas of student concern about their own performance relate to levels of confidence and inter-personal skills.
- Most students have concerns about other aspects of their placement, especially the relationship with their practice teacher and the structure of supervision.

After surveying practice teachers and students, the perspective of the third party to the practice situation – the university staff – needed to be explored.

The survey of university staff (Australia and New Zealand)

So far, the research confirmed the complexity of the assessment process, particularly where there was marginal performance, and we wished to explore the views of the third party – the university staff. We had begun to examine our own perspectives as staff, but we also wanted to explore the situation and experiences of university staff elsewhere. We hoped to identify the nature and extent of student difficulties in practice learning, and the processes and procedures followed in dealing with these difficulties. Structured interviews were conducted with university staff from six New Zealand and thirteen Australian schools of social work.

Reasons for concern

It is interesting to note that the reasons for concern about student performance in practice learning which were given by staff of these nineteen schools of social work were similar to those we identified in our own review of students. The most commonly identified concerns were:

- *learning difficulties* – for example, slowness to learn; not learning from mistakes; lack of adaptability; not leaving previous training behind, such as teaching, nursing;
- *inability to conceptualize* – for example, relating theory to practice;
- *poor communication and inter-personal skills* – this included poor command of English in some students of non-English-speaking background;
- *lack of awareness of impact on others;*
- *personal issues that interfere with learning.*

Staff also discussed situations which were problematic for assessment, which involved differences in religious beliefs and/or cultural backgrounds; issues to do with gender differences between student and practice teacher, and situations which were complicated by mental health issues for the student.

It is interesting to note that the staff mentioned concerns about 'mature' (older) students as much as they mentioned younger students. While older students may have life experience, age alone does not guarantee they will not have difficulties on placement. No matter what age, it is the student's openness to learning and degree of resolution of personal issues that can facilitate their progress in practice learning situations.

When these findings were presented at an international conference (Amsterdam, 1994), university staff from seven countries identified a similar range of concerns. There was also consistency across the Australian and New Zealand schools in how these concerns were handled.

Action taken by university staff

In all Australasian institutions, one or two students (at most) failed per year.

In fact, one institution could only recall two or three failures in the last decade. This is consistent with the low failure rate at the authors' school.

The most commonly mentioned ways of handling difficulties in student performance on practice learning (in order of frequency) were:

- withdrawal/counselling out/transfer;
- extension of placement;
- action plan/re-contract/extra support;
- outside help for personal crisis;
- diverting students from starting placement;
- moving student to another agency;
- placement terminated.

Most of the schools of social work interviewed had established mechanisms through which students could appeal against 'fail' decisions in practice learning subjects. In a few institutions, the appeal process is part of an automatic review of overall progress of each student. For the majority of schools, there was either a similar appeal procedure for all individual subjects or a separate process for the practice learning subjects.

Factors affecting university staff in the assessment process

Some of the factors which affect practice teachers in assessing student performance also impinge on university staff. These are:

- *Difficulty in interpreting and applying assessment criteria* – these criteria may be too general or vague (Coulshed, 1980) or alternatively, detailed but cumbersome. It must also be recognized that university staff, like practice teachers, may have their own standards, previous practice experience, and idiosyncratic approaches to assessment.
- *The multiple roles, and potential conflict between these roles* – the university staff act as support for both the student and the practice teacher, alongside acting as a resource person and consultant to the placement. There is also a direct teaching role as well as the assessment role, of which the latter has an inherent potential for confrontation (Faria, Brownstein and Smith, 1988).

Moreover, in common with the practice teachers, staff experience factors which stem from the organizational context. These include:

- The existence and nature of prerequisites for student entry to practice learning. For example, prior to starting the first practice learning subject, some institutions may not have any preconditions, while others may have quite a rigorous assessment of communication and analytical skills.

- In some instances of student difficulties in practice learning, particularly when there are personal crises for the student, the university staff may want to encourage the student to withdraw from the placement rather than receive a 'fail' grade. This may not be an option, depending on the particular university regulations governing withdrawal without penalty.
- There may be other university regulations affecting assessment and appeals, sometimes not as appropriate to practice learning subjects as to classroom subjects. For example, lack of understanding about practice learning in relation to progression standards may result in other university staff rejecting the recommendation of a 'fail' grade for practice learning.
- Limited time, energy and other resources sometimes result in issues about student performance not being recognized and dealt with appropriately. University staff involved in practice learning have a workload which is heavy, diverse and stressful (Lindsay and Fook, 1994). Most university staff involved in practice learning also have responsibility for classroom subjects, research, committee work and fundraising. This means that the seriousness of concerns about student performance in practice learning may go unrecognized, and the student goes on to pass.

Thus, dealing with student difficulties in practice learning is inherently stressful for all parties, including university staff, who – like practice teachers – may not be adequately supported in their employing organizations.

University staff, and indeed all involved in social work training, require the support of health and welfare agencies to provide practice learning opportunities for students. The relationship between such agencies and the university has to be maintained and nurtured (Slocombe, 1991). This is especially true of schools located in regions where there is a limited pool of agencies. In such a situation, it may be difficult for university staff not to use all agencies, including those where they believe the learning opportunities are insufficient and/or inappropriate. This may also hinder university staff's ability to negotiate when issues related to the agency and/or practice teacher arise. When there are too few practice learning opportunities available, any confrontation by university staff risks a possible long-term loss of such opportunities.

There are, of course, a number of other factors besides those named above. First, with inadequate knowledge of students and practice teachers – with changes in agencies, turnover of staff and practitioners new to student supervision – it can be difficult to have adequate knowledge of practice teachers' abilities. Also, particularly where there are large numbers of students, it may be difficult to know all students well enough. The lack of such knowledge may detract from establishing an appropriate learning experience and can complicate the assessment of the student's achievements. For example, while there may be concerns about a student's performance, the student is likely to be less harshly judged when there are also problems with the quality of the placement itself (Brandon and Davies, 1979).

Another factor involving university staff knowledge of the practice learning situation may stem from reluctance by the student or practice teacher to inform the university of any concerns. The practice teacher may feel lack of appreciation of the seriousness of concerns, or not want to damage the relationship with the student. For the student, while there may be fears about damaging the relationship, there can also be issues related to the power differential in this relationship (Raphael and Rosenblum, 1989). In addition, in the light of other commitments, there can be a reluctance to risk the possibility of having to extend the period of practice learning.

A final factor which impinges on university staff in the assessment process concerns students with special needs, such as students with a disability (Reeser, 1992) or who do not have an English-speaking background (McRoy et al., 1986). The problem here for assessment is how to assess student performance with rigour but without discrimination. It is often difficult to know whether difficulties in the practice learning situation stem from issues of competence or from 'difference' related to particular cultural backgrounds or disabilities.

Implications of the research

We see a number of implications for social work educators arising from this research:

- developing strategies to monitor what is happening in practice learning situations;
- developing support systems for students;
- assisting university staff and practice teachers to delineate and understand their various roles;
- training for practice teachers;
- training for university staff involved in practice learning/teaching;
- addressing barriers within tertiary institutions which affect students' abilities to transfer out of social work courses.

As practice learning is part of a course provided by tertiary institutions, any changes thought desirable should be instigated by educators in these institutions.

Focusing in the first instance on students, educators need to recognize that students may often have concerns about their own performance as well as about other aspects of practice learning, such as supervision arrangements. In addition, students may be reluctant to inform university staff of their concerns. Therefore, in order to address these issues, staff need to develop strategies to monitor what is happening in the practice learning situation. Such strategies could include regular classes to discuss the process and content of practice learning, submission of student journals and designing student assignments to elicit student concerns. It needs to be noted that practice learning itself may trigger or re-activate personal issues. Tutors therefore need to have knowledge both of their students and of the pool of resources to which students can be referred. University staff and practice teachers must also respect the boundaries of their roles as educators and not become therapists to such students (Rosenblatt and Mayer, 1975; Gardiner, 1989).

Regarding practice teachers, they would benefit from both formal training and continuing dialogue with university staff. This would enhance their confidence in carrying out the various and sometimes conflicting roles for them as educators. Such training, similar to that outlined by Fernandez (1994), could also provide input on the characteristics of effective supervision and help them to identify and articulate any implicit criteria they are using apart from those provided by the university. While these criteria need to be comprehensive, they must also be accessible to practice teachers in jargon-free language, with specific examples. We hope that one outcome of these actions would be that practice teachers are more able to recognize and deal with marginal performance by students. This might also be aided by university staff alerting practice teachers to any issues of competence likely to arise for particular students. This has to be considered alongside issues of confidentiality for the student and the need to be as objective as possible in the assessment process.

While recognizing that practice teachers require training, schools of social work should also address the need for training of university staff who assess students' practice learning (Gardiner, 1989). For example, training could focus on the multiple roles of university staff, as well as the application of the various assessment criteria used in practice learning situations. Such training should also include input on the needs of students with disabilities or students from other cultures, as well as basic knowledge about how to use resource people with specialist knowledge of these areas in order to carry out a full but fair assessment.

Another action which may be necessary to enhance university staff's abilities to deal with marginal performance of students may be the changing of school or university structures and processes which currently act against students' transferring out of social work courses (Cobb and Jordan, 1989). Action at school and university level might also incorporate working alongside professional associations and unions to secure employer recognition of the value of the practice teaching role for social workers.

Even though we are proposing a range of strategies which follow on from an examination of these three perspectives on assessment, each school must review their own situation to devise an appropriate plan of action, in consultation with their students and practice learning teachers. As Kimber (1982: 101) concludes: 'performance in fieldwork (practice learning) must be valued highly and much care taken in choosing the priorities in social work education'. We also think that effective assessment in practice learning is a universal priority.

8 Training, education and networking for practice teachers

Marion Bogo

Introduction

Most social work students and alumni consider the practicum to be the core of their educational preparation for professional practice and personal development as a social worker. The field practicum provides authentic practice situations which require knowledgeable and effective actions on the part of the practitioner or student. This context provides the data, internal motivation and opportunity for cognitive, affective and behavioural learning. Students learn to integrate theory and practice, to examine, critique and test out in action the knowledge, concepts and principles they have studied in academic courses. In the practicum, students are exposed to a wide range of intervention approaches and can learn to use practice techniques skilfully and with regard to the unique dynamics of particular situations. Confronted with potent and urgent social issues and human situations, students wrestle with ethical and value dilemmas, developing an understanding of their own idiosyncratic thoughts and reactions and the effect these have on their professional practice. Ultimately, they construct a practice approach which is congruent with a personal set of values and beliefs.

Field education takes place in a practice setting, and field instructors are those persons who are selected to guide students through the practicum. In most instances, field educators are employees of the service-delivery organization. Recent empirical studies confirm the importance of the field instructor as pivotal in promoting student learning and satisfaction in the field (Fortune et al., 1985; Tolson and Kopp, 1988). Hence, the competence of the field instructor as a social work practice educator is crucial to ensuring the success of the practicum. Therefore, the recruitment, development and retention of highly competent and knowledgeable, independent field instructors is a goal for all schools of social work who aim for excellence in professional education. An intensive training programme for new instructors is likely to be the most important component required to achieve this goal.

The academic component and the field component of social work education programmes ideally complement each other. Universities in Canada are
increasingly concerned with the teaching effectiveness of their faculty members and are including criteria and processes in hiring, tenure and promotion
decisions to assess and enhance excellence in academic courses. If field education is to occupy a place of equivalent standing and respect, accountability
procedures to ensure the teaching effectiveness of field educators need to be
in place. This chapter will discuss the recruitment, training and continuing
educational programmes and procedures used at the Faculty of Social Work,
University of Toronto, Canada, to advance the excellence of field educators.

The practicum provides graduate education for over 220 students a year in
approximately sixty field settings located in a large, urban, multi-racial and
multi-cultural centre. The educational programmes for field instructors were
developed over the past fifteen years and represent the efforts and commitment of numerous field instructors, faculty members and students to innovative approaches and the continuous refinement of the programme. In many
instances, programme components are similar to those used in other schools
and countries throughout the world. In designing their field education component, schools of social work take into account a multitude of variables
which will affect the scope of their programme and the resources that can be
allocated. Of crucial importance are the service organizations in their locality, the linkages established with the school, the opportunities for collaboration in education and research to develop and enhance social work and
social welfare, and the service settings' commitment to practicum education.
Effective practicum programmes are designed in close conjunction with
senior administrators in these settings, since their willingness to allocate
resources to the field programme is a significant determinant of the success
of the field programme.

Recruitment of field instructors

Since the field practicum takes place in a service setting, recruitment and
training of field instructors are by-products of the agency context and the
collaborative relationship between the school and agency. Schools of social
work dedicated to excellence in the field programme must commit themselves to strong partnerships with a range of service organizations. There is a
dearth of literature on school–agency relationships; however, it appears that
in most countries, the social work field practicum is carried out in service
organizations that voluntarily offer education that prepares social work students for professional practice. In some situations, the university pays the
practice setting for providing education. This may be done at the local level

or, in publicly-funded systems, through grants between the respective government ministries. In some cases, schools employ field instructors and organize independent field projects or develop a collaborative arrangement with a setting that is willing to incorporate the field instructor and a student unit into their organization.

The mission of agencies is to provide service. Many service-delivery systems have committed themselves, in their mission statements, to education and research as well. For example, in the health field, university teaching hospitals are linked with university faculties and departments and offer education for health science professionals such as doctors, nurses, physiotherapists, occupational therapists and pharmacists as well as for social workers. Social work departments in such settings are likely to contribute to the institutional commitment to education. In settings that do not have a formal mandate for education, schools of social work find it useful to consider what benefits might accrue to these agencies if they commit themselves to student education and to the allocation of resources to field instruction. Resources include time for agency staff to provide educational inputs in field instruction, in team and staff meetings, and through practice and learning assignments with other social workers in the setting. Resources also include release time for new field instructor training. Agencies value field instructor training as professional development for their workers and preparation for potential roles for these individuals as staff supervisors in the agency. Agencies often hire students who have completed their practicum education in the setting, since these new social workers can immediately begin to offer service to the agency's clients and consumers. Schools of social work can consider other resources that might be exchanged with practice settings, such as continuing education and research consultation.

Schools and agencies will produce procedures to determine together what criteria will be used in selecting new field instructors. Generally, a social work degree and a minimum number of years of practice are required. In countries where professional social work is newly developed, the requirement of a social work degree may be unrealistic. Similarly, new service organizations targeting emerging social issues or offering innovative programmes may not necessarily employ professional social workers. Schools that value student practicum in such settings make exceptions to the degree requirement. In contracting with these settings, it is important to clarify expectations for learning and assignments. While recognizing that field learning takes place through the medium of service delivery, the primacy of the practicum as an educational experience for students must be upheld by the setting and the instructor.

Schools seek to recruit as field instructors competent practitioners who are committed to learning and teaching as a life-long process – they recognize that effective social workers must always learn and grow. They believe that education is stimulating, creative and never-ending. These social workers approach their own learning as new field instructors with enthusiasm and energy and provide a valuable role model for students. In a study of factors affecting field instructor continuance in the role, Bogo and Power (1992) found that instructors who intend to continue are those persons who enjoy teaching and who value contributing to the profession and sharpening their practice skills. They also found that realistic expectations about the increased workload of field instruction was an important predictive factor and recommended that schools be clear about the time expectation involved when recruiting new field instructors. As discussed above, in working with agencies as partners in field education, resource allocation and resource exchange need to be addressed at the institutional level, so that time accommodation does not become the burden of the individual social worker.

Training new field instructors

The effective training of new field instructors is likely to be one of the most critical factors in enabling competent and committed social workers to become excellent field teachers. Social work practitioners who agree to take on the new role of field instructor report that they need the following institutional inputs from the school:

- education about the theory, process and skill of field instruction;
- information about the school's social work programme, the objectives of the practicum component, and specific administrative procedures related to various phases – for example, the nature and number of practice assignments, the learning contract, mid-term review, recording and final evaluation;
- consultation and support.

New field instructors have commented on the sense of isolation they have, especially when they are the only instructor in a setting. Many schools assign a faculty member, called a 'field liaison' or 'advisor', to meet with the student and field instructor periodically through the year to review student learning and progress. In addition, the instructor can consult the liaison as needed. Feedback from new field instructors indicated that this individual model did not sufficiently meet their preference for more intense and regular discussion and reflection with other field instructors about their common and specific experiences.

At the Faculty of Social Work, University of Toronto, a training programme for new field instructors was designed to respond to these three identified needs. Feedback gained from instructors and leaders was used to refine the programme over time. A unique feature of the model is that it combines training and field liaison for new instructors.

The programme consists of small groups of new field instructors led by a faculty member who functions as group leader and facilitator, as well as faculty field liaison. Each group consists of twelve to fifteen new instructors and meets throughout the field practicum term, every second week, for approximately twelve sessions. This structure enables new instructors to learn and use relevant content in relation to the students' stage in the field (Bogo, 1981). The aim of the group training programme is to develop competent field instructors who can apply educational theory to their current experiences as first-time field instructors with graduate social work students. The goals are to teach instructors the theory and practice of field instruction, to strengthen the linkages between the academic curriculum and practicum and to provide consultation and support to new instructors through a group learning model that emphasizes problem-solving, networking and mutual aid (Bogo, 1981). Educational methodologies include:

- structured presentations and discussion of concepts, issues and examples;
- review of students' work and review of field instructors' work with students, through videotape, audiotape and/or process recordings;
- use of exercises and role-plays.

Field instruction literature is offered in a systematic manner relating to current issues under discussion. Sections of the text *The Practice of Field Instruction in Social Work: Theory and process* (Bogo and Vayda, 1987) are suggested, or photocopies of specific readings are distributed to the participants.

An evaluation of the training model found that instructors valued group processes that included sharing with students accounts of successes and struggles, presentation of problems and working for solutions (Bogo and Power, 1994). A supportive learning group composed of peers confronted with similar issues who understood and accepted the unique features of each member's agency context was an important factor in producing satisfaction with the training. Seminar leaders who were skilled group educators were able to sustain a highly productive learning environment. Clearly, a well-functioning group results in valuable learning and provides opportunities for mutual aid and networking among the participants.

Educational theory

Educational theorists have produced an enormous body of literature about how adults learn and how teachers teach to best facilitate the achievement of educational goals (Brundage and MacKeracher, 1980; Hunt, 1987; Kolb, Rubin and McIntyre, 1984; Knowles, 1972). Four major concepts have proven useful in the design, implementation and refinement of the training programme.

The nature of the adult's self-concept

Adults enter learning activities with an organized set of descriptions and feelings about themselves. 'Descriptions' refers to self-concept and includes assumptions, beliefs and a world-view. 'Feelings' refers to self-esteem, how individuals feel about themselves in comparison with others and with some ideal (Brundage and MacKeracher, 1980). Any new learning experience poses a challenge to our self-concept and our sense of competence and self-esteem.

Concerns about success or failure have an impact on our involvement in learning. Social workers who begin field instructor training are likely to have mixed feelings as they approach this new role. On the one hand, they have opinions about who they are as professionals, what they expect students to learn and what they have to offer in a teaching role. On the other hand, they may also wonder whether they can be effective teachers, and to what extent this particular group learning experience will validate their self-esteem and provide useful and supportive learning. Therefore, in designing a training approach, attention needs to be paid to creating a learning environment which takes into account issues of self-esteem. An atmosphere that is supportive, promotes openness, risk-taking and diversity of opinion and respects each individual's perspective has been found to promote participation and learning.

The role of experience

Adults have an expanding reservoir of experience that is a rich and meaningful resource for learning (Knowles, 1972). Research on learning styles reveals a range of individual preferences; however, recent studies suggest that social workers prefer learning approaches which are concrete and experiential (Kolb, Rubin and McIntyre, 1984; Kruzich, Friesen and Van Soest, 1986). This research refers to approaches that draw on one's own personal experiences, feelings, and issues, and that provide learning outcomes that are practical and can be useful in current situations.

Training needs to provide the opportunity for using the social workers' experiences as learners: for example, when they were students, in situations where they are supervisees, and, currently, as new field instructors in the learning group. These experiences contribute important data to their personal knowledge, assumptions and beliefs about what constitutes the conditions for effective teaching and learning. 'Beginning with ourselves' (Hunt, 1987) is a useful principle in learning as well as in social work practice.

The adult's readiness to learn

Adults tend to learn readily those things that are most relevant to the needs of their social roles. They will be motivated to learn if they perceive that the new knowledge and skill will help them in the performance of important tasks in a current problem-solving activity.

The challenge for field instructor training is to organize education about the theory, process and technique of field instruction so that pragmatic approaches are learned which can be transferred to the immediate tasks and issues confronted in their current teaching roles with their students. A training programme which is offered while the student is working in the field provides the opportunity for dealing with the phases of field instruction concurrently in the training group.

The integration of theory and practice

Bogo and Vayda (1987) designed a model for field instructors to use with students to assist in the integration of theory and practice in field education. The model is a process guide and emphasizes an interactive educational process. This process model is applicable to the training of new field instructors as well.

The process begins with the retrieval of the factual elements of a learning situation. The next step, reflection, focuses on the effectiveness of the retrieved interaction as well as the identification of personal values, attitudes and assumptions which modify the retrieved facts. These processes are then linked to professional knowledge about field education that can explain or account for the findings of the preceding steps. This leads directly to the selection of a professional response to the initial action that began the sequence.

A concurrent structure of field instructor training allows for both advance and *post hoc* discussions and analysis of field instructor and student work and provides the data for the integration of field instruction theory and practice. Discussion of each phase and its accompanying tasks in advance of working with the student helps instructors to examine and critically analyse their own experiences and current assumptions. Through presentation and readings, instructors are exposed to the field instruction literature, and they can consider and learn alternative approaches and plan how they will use these ideas with their student in practice. Sharing experiences after the interaction leads to reflection about the effectiveness of the approach used and identification of facilitating factors and constraining issues which can be addressed in future interactions with the student. In group presentation and discussion, instructors compare their approaches with those of others and can learn alternative ways of conceptualizing and intervening.

This process of moving from concrete to abstract, active to reflective, represents points in a cyclical loop which promotes the integration of theory and practice. Learning is ongoing, cumulative and multi-dimensional. Each experience builds on learning from previous interactions and also provides the stimulus for acquiring and integrating further new knowledge.

Using these educational concepts and principles, the training programme interweaves instructors' learning needs with the various stages of field instruction and the educational and administrative tasks associated with each phase. The group learning approach is structured so that participants have ample opportunity to work intensively with data derived from their current educational practice with their students, relate those experiences to the concepts presented and studied, and ultimately integrate their new learning in future interactions with their students in the practicum. In this way, the learning process in the seminar models and replicates the students' learning process in the field.

The curriculum content of the training programme

Schools of social work will, in conjunction with their field settings and field instructors, develop the curriculum content deemed necessary for effective training. The following topics represent a typical curriculum for the training programme and form a basis from which a training programme could be developed to fit the needs of a particular school and its field settings.

Preparing for the student

Conducting one or more sessions before the student arrives in the setting is very important in helping new instructors in the transition from practitioner to teacher. Using the 'integration of theory and practice' model, exercises are used to help the instructors reflect on their own experiences, identify positive and negative elements, examine these factors in relation to knowledge about effective field teaching, develop objectivity and distance from these experiences, and move forward to plan their work with students (Bogo and Vayda, 1993).

Practitioners, as they become educators, must be able to articulate the knowledge and value-base which undergirds their practice and will be likely to serve as a frame of reference in the learning and teaching enterprise with students. Experienced social workers report that the exercise of analysing and identifying the underpinnings of their 'integrated knowledge' is complex; however, this is a necessary step which assists instructors in communication with students and replicates the process that the instructor and student will undertake together to help students build their own practice approach which is consistent with a professional knowledge and value-base and which results in practice competence. Instructors are encouraged to prepare a short bibliography of readings relevant to their practice.

Preparation also involves preparing the setting, so that students will be welcome in the organization. It includes the pragmatics of obtaining space and materials for the students, as well as gaining the collaboration of staff members to contribute to the education of the student.

Schools of social work will have an array of written materials which they can introduce to new instructors before the practicum begins, and which they can use in greater depth at specific times through the term. These include the Field Practicum Manual, the School Calendar and course outlines and bibliographies. If a school uses a specific practice approach which it expects to be taught in the practicum, it will need to take this requirement into account in recruiting new field instructors and assessing the social worker's knowledge of and commitment to this approach; or it may develop one or more modules to train field instructors who are interested in using this approach. Given the presence of a multitude of practice approaches, most schools identify practice learning objectives at a level of abstraction which allows for the inclusion of a wide range of models. The specific practice content – and hence, learning objectives – of each student's practicum reflects the approaches used in the setting.

Beginning the practicum

Beginnings are critical in creating a productive educational experience. Early training sessions help instructors develop plans for the students' first few days in the setting, with attention paid to:

- orientating students to the organization and introducing them to the setting, the formal and informal structure, the key personnel, policies and written material;
- creating a productive working relationship between students and instructors;
- identifying principles for selecting learning assignments.

Training sessions for field instructors at this stage help them examine the most salient issues that they need to attend to with their students and provide them with perspectives and techniques. Clarification of expectations of the roles and responsibilities of the student and the instructor in the practicum and in the specific setting is an ongoing process. However, early on, it is important to introduce and discuss the notion of mutuality and the expectation that both parties will strive for openness and feedback so that practicum learning goals may be achieved. Expectations will also be discussed with regard to the specific learning experiences in the setting, the student's practice and the structure and educational methods for the field instruction conference. The question of how to build on the experience, knowledge and skill of the student to meet learning goals may also be considered.

Educational theory

Concepts derived from educational theory will be used throughout the entire training programme to illuminate the issues discussed; hence, this topic will not be introduced at one time. The following have proven useful in field instruction:

- principles of adult learning;
- experiential education;
- learning/teaching styles;
- assessment of styles;
- creating an educational environment conducive to learning-style needs.

Literature is offered in a systematic manner and is related to current issues under discussion. Sections of the text *The Practice of Field Instruction in Social Work: Theory and process* (Bogo and Vayda, 1987) are suggested, or photocopies of specific readings are distributed to the participants.

The educational contract

A learning contract or agreement is an effective tool to promote a joint process between student and instructor. While the agreement is framed by the school's general learning objectives or practice competencies for the field component, it individualizes a particular student's learning in a specific setting. It represents the specific learning activities and educational methods available in the setting, the individual interests and needs of the student, and the specific approaches of the instructor. In the training sessions, instructors learn about the purposes, content and structure of the contract, and processes for its development.

Relationship

The critical nature of the student–field instructor relationship in promoting student learning and satisfaction in the practicum has been demonstrated (Fortune and Abramson, 1993). Training focuses on developing the necessary ingredients: in particular, providing emotional support, encouraging autonomy, integrating theory and practice, and giving ongoing feedback and evaluation. Attitudes and behaviours that facilitate a collaborative partnership are emphasized, as well as identifying barriers, responding to difficulties and developing joint problem-solving strategies. Attention is also paid to the context within which educational relationships occur, both the practice organization and the new field instructors' training seminar.

Anti-oppressive practice

Issues of power and exploitation are examined in respect to the student–field instructor relationship. This micro focus provides the springboard for examining anti-racist issues at structural, organizational and service levels. Instructors are helped to work with students to identify and respond to racist attitudes and behaviours, as well as to develop inter-cultural practice competence.

Methods of teaching

A wide range of methods exist for use in field education. Instructors learn to use the following techniques and consider the strengths, limitations and purpose of each: audio- and videotape and analysis; direct observation and discussion of others' practice; one-way mirrors; co-leadership; process recordings, and role-plays. Conditions and skills of effective feedback and processes for the integration of theory and practice using these technologies are emphasized.

Dealing with problems and blocks in learning

It is likely that students' problems in learning will emerge as instructors work together in the training group and present actual situations to illustrate the topics presented earlier. At some point, the participants should cover the following:

- identifying problems or blocks in learning, communicating concerns to the student and clarifying expectations;
- working with the student and the school to develop approaches to facilitate learning and deal with continuing poor performance.

Evaluation

Throughout the training, instructors learn about ongoing evaluation, the relationship of the learning agreement to this process, and methods to ensure the active participation of the student in self-evaluation and evaluation of the educational work with the instructor; however, there are some important issues unique to the final evaluation. Unlike academic courses where classroom instructors evaluate substantial numbers of students each semester, it is typical for field instructors to have responsibility for only one student at a time. New field instructors are uneasy about the responsibility of evaluation, and welcome help in understanding and operationalizing the school's educational objectives for the practicum. They especially value 'developing a sense' of the school's criteria for rating performance. In training sessions, instructors rate written or taped examples of actual student performance and discuss these ratings with other instructors and the faculty leaders so that a common interpretation of performance standards emerges. Other issues connected to final evaluation are: preparation for the conference; the evaluation report; readiness to practise and developing new learning goals for the student's ongoing education; evaluation of the student–instructor relationship, and termination.

Continuing education

Opportunities for ongoing and continuing education for field instructors allow them to keep abreast of new knowledge and approaches to field education. Field agencies which are highly committed to student education and offer practicum to substantial numbers of students often hold regular meetings of all field instructors in the setting. The purpose of these meetings is:

- to provide ongoing and advanced education to their field educators;
- to provide an opportunity for consultation, support and networking;
- to monitor and refine the overall student educational programme in that setting.

As with the training programme for new field instructors, these sessions are structured in tandem with the students' education in the field. This structure enhances the integration of concepts of teaching and learning with the instructors' current educational practices with students. Since these groups consist of both new and experienced instructors, peer learning, networking and mutual support is high. Colleagues learn from each other as they focus on a variety of common issues related to student learning and progress, and offer educational strategies for dealing with difficulties. These on-site seminars greatly contribute to the formation of a consistent, committed and expert cohort of field teachers.

Schools are highly committed to the continuing education of their instructors. It is critical that field instructors be actively involved in identifying the issues and topics that they believe are important to build their competence. A variety of organizational structures can be used to ensure a partnership between agencies and their field instructors and schools and faculty that will give leadership to educational planning. Student input should also be sought to identify issues that need further attention. Some schools have established advisory committees or boards to assist with this task, others have governance structures that include field instructors and a field committee, others have associations of field educators with elected representatives to policy and planning committees. Continuing education takes many forms, including guest lectures, workshops on specific topics, a series of seminars or an advanced course. Again, in evaluating these experiences, it was found that those methods which provided the opportunity for instructors to relate new knowledge to their current experiences, through discussion or role-play, were perceived as the most useful.

Recently, there has been a growing interest in scholarship in field education and the development of empirical studies to build the knowledge base. Symposia and field education conferences have been held at local and national levels. Papers covering a wide range of topics have presented new concepts, educational innovations and empirical studies. These conferences have contributed to networking and camaraderie in advancing the commonly shared challenges of assuring quality field education in schools of social work, especially for faculty members with an interest in the field. Increasingly, presenters are field instructors employed in social service settings, committed to contributing to the conceptualization as well as implementation of the practicum. This is an important development, and one that should be fully supported by the schools. As field instructors commit themselves to the development of the knowledge base of field education and articulate their expertise as social work practice educators, they take their place as colleagues with university-based teaching faculty in social work education. The evolution of field education is progressing rapidly, and social work educators can be increasingly confident that this component of the programme is based on a well-articulated and tested knowledge base.

The following guidelines may be useful to social work educators interested in developing approaches for training new field instructors:

- Schools will work with the service organizations in their locality to establish linkages for collaboration in education and research in order to develop and enhance social work and social welfare and to secure the commitment of these service organizations to practicum education. Effective practicum programmes are designed in close conjunction with senior administrators in these settings, since the willingness of these administrators to allocate resources to the field programme is a significant determinant of the success of the field programme. Resource allocation and resource exchange need to be negotiated at the institutional level.

- The primacy of the practicum as an educational experience for students must be upheld by the setting and the instructor. This principle is useful in developing locally relevant criteria for use in selection of settings and personnel for field education.
- An effective programme design for new field instructors takes into account questions such as: what identified needs will the programme respond to; what educational concepts will underpin the programme, and what empirically-tested knowledge and approaches will be used. Programme design consists of two components: first, curriculum content to be covered is articulated; and second, educational methodologies are chosen to match particular curriculum units employing a range of techniques.
- Group training programmes will be led by faculty members or experienced field educators who themselves are trained and skilled in group educational approaches. In setting up training programmes, new trainers will benefit from intensive collaboration in programme development and refinement.
- Training prior to the beginning of the student practicum is important and covers preparation for the instructor role, preparation of the setting, planning for the student, distribution of written materials, communication of school expectations and specific models or concepts to be mastered by students.
- A comprehensive training programme will cover the following content areas as well as any other topics deemed important for the particular school: beginnings; educational theory; learning contracts; student–instructor relationship; anti-oppressive practice; methods of teaching; problems in learning, and evaluation.
- Continuing education activities are best planned jointly by faculty members and by field instructors who have completed the training.

9 The experiences of students and practice teachers: Factors influencing students' practice learning

Svein Bøe

Introduction

There are two parallel processes going on simultaneously in the education of social workers. In the first place, one can look upon college learning as an academic way of learning – from theory to practice. On the other hand, there is an experiential way of learning which takes place in the agency – from practice to theory. Practice and theory make a dialectical unity, and both processes need to be considered in order to educate reflective social workers. What affects the student's learning of practice?

This chapter is based on a study undertaken in nine different practice placements, where both practice teachers and students were interviewed. The study was carried out in southern Norway during December 1992 and January 1993 (Bøe, Haarberg-Aas and Sundt-Rasmussen, 1993). The practice teachers were well trained and experienced, and the students were in the last year of their college education, undergoing their second twelve-week placement.

Finally, the chapter will consider how to explain the learning processes using perspectives drawn from social learning theory, construct theory and critical theory.

A qualitative study of practice teachers' and students' learning in practice agencies

The practice teachers' point of view

What practice teachers think they can teach the student

We found that practice teachers were using two forms of teaching:

Figure 9.1   What influences the processes of the student's practice learning?

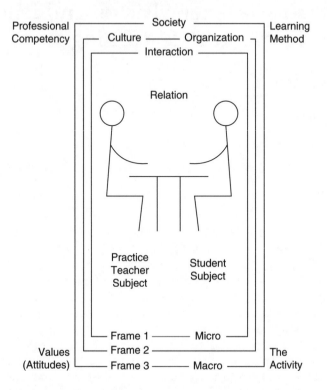

- *Modelling*, which usually occurs in the first period of the placement – the students observe the practice teacher in action, then they are given tasks adjusted to their ability where they imitate the practice teacher.
- *Experiential learning* usually starts with an observation of a situation or a client – this is analysed, reflected upon and generalized together with the practice teacher. The learning goes from practice to theory. A practice teacher summarized this process: 'First the student observes, then participates under the supervision of the practice teacher, and finally operates on their own.'

What are valid knowledge, skills and attitudes within the field of social work, and what do practice teachers think they can teach the student?

First, with regard to knowledge, the practice teacher looks upon the agency as a sort of training centre for students, where they can practise the theories learned in college.

Second, the practice teacher teaches the student to look at the client in a holistic way – the student has to learn something about the client's setting and context.

Third, they believe they can teach the student to develop the professional skills of a social worker – for instance, communicative, technical and analytic competencies:

- *Communicative competency* is the ability to establish contact with the client and to communicate, implying the development of professional attitudes, such as respect, loyalty and empathy.
- *Technical competency* is mastering written and oral tasks to advocate for the client.
- *Analytic competency* is the ability to summarize, identify the problem, make a hypothesis, collect relevant information, carry out a plan and, finally, evaluate it. One practice teacher stated: 'You have an idea of what's going to happen. Suddenly something unexpected occurs so you quickly have to change your plan.' This analytic competency, this flexibility at work, is also called *reflection on reflection-in-action* (Schön, 1987).

Fourth, practice teachers emphasized that a *professional identity* implies a professional role that is a clear and distinct adult role towards the client, emphasizing that an adult role should not be built upon power, but rather reflect a secure and safe attitude.

Practice teachers stated that it is important that students are allowed to be students, to ask questions and to show uncertainty. At the same time, students must be confronted with the demands and expectations of the role of the professional social worker. A practice teacher summarized professional identity thus:

> Identity is how the professional understands his or her own role ... I want them to be proud and efficient in performing the profession, a person who is able to associate with other professions and clients.

What the practice teacher thinks the student can learn from the agency

How did the practice teachers look upon the significance of the whole agency in the student's practice learning?

First is the student's opportunity to learn daily routines, the rules and the different functions of the employees in the agency: in other words, the culture of the organization.

Second, students can learn something about co-operation by learning on placement: co-operation not just within the agency, but also with external partners, such as families, schools, social security offices, psychiatric clinics, etc. The student is taught about the different settings in which clients are found and sees them in a more holistic way. The client is not just a case, but a human being.

Third, practice teachers pointed out that the agency allows the student the opportunity of direct work with the client, learning by observing a practitioner and by discussing this with the practice teacher. Then students get the opportunity to perform work on their own analysis, making reflections and generalizations, but now with the agency as a reference.

Fourth, practice teachers were aware that they are not the only model; colleagues also provide models for students to learn from.

What practice teachers believed helps or hinders the student's practice learning

Practice teachers pointed out eight different factors affecting the learning process of the student:

1   The *context* of the student's learning – at the beginning of the placement, before practice begins, it is necessary to discover what kind of working experiences the student has had, what they know about the practice field, and what kind of theoretical knowledge they have. Is this the kind of practice the student expected, and what is their motivation for the work?
2   The *working arrangements* – there has to be sufficient space and time to supervise the student, without interruption from other duties.
3   The organization of the *daily activities* – practice teachers reported that the daily routines in the agency play an important role in the student's learning, either promoting or inhibiting the learning process. This includes both formal and informal structures in the agency.
4   The *objectives* of the agency – both the agency and the student have objectives for their learning. Practice teachers stated that clear and explicit objectives made the student's practice learning easier.
5   The *practice methods* – practice teachers pointed out that clear methods of practice help the student's learning.
6   The *evaluation* of the supervision – planning, preparing, performing and evaluating are necessary if the student is going to learn. It is perhaps obvious, but nevertheless, it is significant to evaluate how the plan was carried out and what was the outcome.
7   *Roles* – the role of the practice teacher in relation to the student should be clear and obvious, so that there are no confusions.
8   *Relationship* – practice teachers were fully aware of being a model for the student and that the quality of the relationship enhanced or inhibited the strength of the role-modelling. This relationship is an essential basis for all practice learning to occur.

The students' point of view

What students believed they can learn most from the practice teachers

Students identified the practice teacher's position as a *role model* as the most important factor in their learning: the practice teacher is the most significant influence on the student.

Second, students saw the practice teacher as a *guide*: someone to distinguish the essential from the less essential, to distinguish the problems of the client from the problems of the student, and finally, to summarize the experiences of the practice learning. This is what is called *knowing in action* (Schön, 1987) or what was earlier called *experiential learning* (Moxness, 1981). This is the process of moving from practice to theory. What constitute valid knowledge, skills and attitudes in social work, according to students? They emphasized that knowledge learned in college can be tested in practice, and it can become more integrated as a result. Students are given the opportunity to pick up what they take to be valid knowledge in social work.

Third, students thought practice teachers can help them to develop *professional skills*, for instance communication, technical and analytical competencies. Practice teachers are of special significance in teaching technical and analytical competency, according to students. They receive continuous feedback about the student's practical work, with the opportunity to reflect and discuss these in supervision.

Fourth, students pointed to *attitudes* to be developed. These can be seen in relation to the clients, the students themselves and the profession.

In relation to the client, students said that practice teachers can teach them what respect and open-mindedness mean in practice. 'Respect' refers here to the perspective of each human being as unique and equal, with the right to be treated respectfully, in spite of their problems. Students emphasized that the practice teacher can help the student to identify the client's own resources. Students pointed out the necessity of being aware of what provokes them when they are working with clients – what causes strong emotional reactions or prejudices? The practice teacher is of great help in confronting these emotions.

The students also thought that the practice teacher can help to develop a more professional attitude in work: it is very important that the practice teacher makes the practice situation as secure as possible.

What students believe they can learn from the agency setting

The students' responses can be summarized thus:

● *The agency's respect for the client* – the way in which clients are received and worked with demonstrates the agency's respect, or otherwise, for clients.

- *Agency culture* – students said they can learn about the functions which the agency employees have in relation to the clients, and policies affecting the work. Students gain a rounded picture of the agency and learn something about organizing and structuring the work.
- *The causes of social problems* – students learn different theories which explain social problems and what the agency can offer in order to help the client.
- *Observing other colleagues* – the practice teacher is not the only model for students, who stated that they pick up what they consider to be good practice and drop poor practices.
- *Developing different perspectives* – learning in agencies enables students to 'look at and interpret situations in different ways'. Usually, there is not only one answer to a given question in social work, so it is necessary for students to test out and develop their own methods and practices.
- *Developing professional attitudes* – this is particularly the case in relation to working with clients of the agency.

What students believe helps and hinders their practice learning

Students identified the following aspects, which can either help or hinder their learning:

- *The context of the learning*
  - Students mentioned their motivation. Are they interested in this kind of practice, is this what they originally wanted, and are they curious to learn more about this agency?
  - Students focused on the importance of their own *activity*. If the student is passive, this will inhibit learning; if active, this will promote learning.
  - Students mentioned personal characteristics: sense of self-esteem influences the learning, so students should be honest and admit uncertainties.
  - Life situations have a big impact, so that personal poverty or hardship which requires a job to finance studying can affect students' concentration and awareness.

- *The working arrangements*
  - Students pointed out the disadvantage of not having a regular workplace in the agency; some students were seated at different places in the agency every day.

   – It is necessary to have space and time to analyse and summarize discussions with the practice teacher. Time pressures and deadlines may sometimes be a problem, inhibiting the practice learning.

   – There needs to be the opportunity to understand and use computer equipment in the agency.

● *Activities and routines*

   – A well-organized agency with rational procedures may make it easier for the student to understand what is going on.

● *The aims of the student's learning*

   – Students stated that clear and realistic objectives drawn up together with the practice teacher are significant in the learning process. They identified a learning contract as a great help in this respect.

● *Practice methods*

   – What opportunity does the student have to apply methods which have been learned in the college setting? A student briefly summarized this in the following manner: 'The student is seeing theories tested in a practice context. A direct experience is important in learning, but reflections afterwards are also important. Making hypotheses and reflections is of great importance. It promotes the learning process.'

● *Evaluation*

   – The practice teachers and the students evaluated the practice learning mid-way and at the end of the placement. The way in which this evaluation is conducted is significant in helping or hindering the student's learning. Students' comments on the significance of the evaluation in this manner included: 'Evaluation is of great importance in order to summarize what happens in practice'; 'It is important to get feedback on what you are doing well and what you ought to work on'; 'It is necessary to elicit emotions, especially unpleasant emotions experienced in practice.' The last statement refers particularly to situations with aggressive clients that have obviously frightened the student.

● *Organizational culture*

   – Students said that the way the agency receives them influences the quality of the learning. Are the workers prepared for them, and are they interested in having students?

   – Students suggested that it helps if the agency is 'clear' and

'predictable', so that it is easy to understand what is happening, which gives the student a sense of security.
- Students paid attention to the working conditions in the agency: 'Are they tolerant, and am I allowed to ask questions?' This reflects on the confidence of those employed in the agency, and the climate for learning there.

● *The relationship with the practice teacher*

- Some of the students' comments demonstrated their view of the significance of the relationship in learning: 'The relationship between the student and the practice teacher is extremely important'; 'The relation is a condition for growth and development'; 'It is important in practice that there are two human beings (practice teacher and student) who match each other'; 'It is important for the learning process that I dare to be open-minded with the practice teacher if I am to develop a personal and professional attitude.' The practice teacher must be a good practitioner, somebody whose skills the student can respect, but also somebody who acts in a democratic fashion with the student.

Theoretical perspectives on the study

Learning theory as a reference in order to understand practice learning

Can learning theory explain what is going on in the interaction between the practice teacher and the student, and do the data from our interviews verify or falsify this kind of understanding? Social learning theory uses terms like 'stimulus', 'response', 'reinforcement', and so on, but the theory disagrees with classical behaviourism (Skinner, 1974). It is essential in social learning theory that human behaviour be understood not only as a result of external influences but also in the context of cognitive processes.

Behaviour is not only a result of learning through direct experience but also a result of observing *significant others*. Thus social models are of importance, because the behaviour of the significant others is imitated. Albert Bandura (1969) pays much attention to the mediating processes going on between the stimulus and the responses – emotions, motivation and reflections are important.

If we transfer this theory into the practice field, we would explain the student's learning as the result of imitating the practice teacher's behaviours. Is there evidence of this in our study?

We found that both the practice teacher and the student are aware of the significance of having good models in the learning process:

First, I observe the practice teacher, then I do tasks of my own, and finally the practice teacher observes me.

However, there is usually more than one model to imitate on placements, and it is even possible to learn from a poor model:

This is, however, not the way I am going to do it.

This shows that there are reflections going on in the mind of the student at the same time as he or she is observing the model; a reflection on reflection-in-action (Schön, 1987). Our study shows that learning is not a mechanical process, but rather that it is dialectical.

Construct theory as a reference in order to understand practice learning

Students are going through a process of professional socialization during the placement. How is this professional identity developed?

According to Berger and Luckmann (1967) and Vygotskij (1971), the student is constructing his or her own reality. There is an institutionalized process, where the student is both adapting to the social circumstance and also creating it. This happens in the interaction between student and surroundings in a dialectical way; society is here represented through the practice agency. What are the mechanisms by which this socialization occurs in the agency?

Wadel (1990) separates three forms of interaction:

- *The trade perspective:* 'If you give me something, I will give you something.' When practice teachers say that both they and the agency get something in return for having a student, this is an example of this perspective.
- *The power/dependency perspective:* 'If you don't do what I tell you to do, you will regret it.' Being in a position of power, the practice teacher can fail the student's practice, and therefore the action of the student must adapt to the demands of the teacher rather than the practice situation.
- *The incorporation perspective:* 'You do me a favour, because I am what I am and you are what you are.' This sort of interaction implies a clarification of the roles of the practice teacher and the student. What expectations are to be met by the roles of the student and practice teacher? The roles have to be complementary.

Few interactions are purely relations of trade, power or incorporation. Most of them contain elements from all these sorts of interactions.

Critical theory as a reference in order to understand practice learning

Students assert that developing professional attitudes towards clients is something that is important and can be developed in practice learning. Skjervheim (1974) thinks it is necessary to pay attention to the ethical and philosophical foundations of human behaviour. Similarly, Habermas (1975) underlines the necessity of competency in communication. He asserts that science can be divided into three categories that have different objectives:

1   positivism that has a technical objective;
2   humanism that has a practical objective;
3   critical theory that has an objective of emancipation.

Therefore the obligation of every democratic person is to study and discuss matters of relevance to social development, the scientist in particular. This can be achieved through a dialogue in which the participants are obliged to be led by the best arguments. The good argument challenges the poorer one, the ethical argument challenges the less ethical, the truth challenges the lie, the aesthetic argument against the less aesthetic, and so on. This is what Habermas (1975) calls 'the discourse'.

This way of thinking is relevant in clarifying the foundation of the action in social work learning and practice. Students in our study also agreed that reflections are particularly important in developing both analytical and communicative competency.

The practice learning must try to develop the student's sense of critical socialization; this is particularly important if students are to develop their practice. If we do not succeed in this, we will be educating technocrats and bureaucrats rather than professional thinkers and activists.

Summary

This chapter has focused on what influences the learning process in practice. My conclusion is that there are at least five factors involved:

1   Practice teachers and students identified the significance of *interaction*. The learning should be characterized by dialogue: a democratic, not didactic, practice.
2   The *professional competency* of the practice teacher is essential if the student is going to develop valid knowledge, skills and values in practice.
3   The practice teacher is the most significant *role model* for the student in practice, though there are other models in practice as well.

4   The *context* of the learning process needs to be considered if the outcome is to be good.
5   The *attitudes and values* of the student are a necessary part of the teaching and learning, in order to develop a more professional practice.

Finally, I have reflected on the study by using three different theoretical references: a social learning theory, construct theory and critical theory. All of these perspectives – and others – throw some light on the transactions between students, practice teachers and agencies.

Note

This is a qualitative study, so I have not given numbers of practice teachers or students who identified particular factors. Where a response was atypical, this has been noted in the text.

The quotations are taken from an unpublished study carried out by S. Bøe, K. Haarberg-Aas and S. Sundt-Rasmussen (1993) *Praksistedet som læringsarena* (The agency as learning seat), Oslo, Norwegian State College of Public Administration and Social Work.

Part Three

Case Studies

10 Developing placements and opportunities for practice learning in the Czech Republic

Ivo Reznicek

Introduction: The legacy of the Communist regime

After the fall of the Communist regime in the Czech Republic in 1989, the previously suppressed profession of social work began to look forward to new, emerging opportunities that the old system simply did not offer. Czech observers who were either trained in the pre-war or early post-war schools of social work, or who had an opportunity to see social work in Western countries, complained bitterly about the degradation that social work suffered at the hands of the Communists. Politically, in the period prior to 1989, social problems were seen as 'relics of capitalism' that would vanish with the 'abolition of exploitation'. In terms of expertise and qualification, social care was merely a tolerated adjunct of grandiose social engineering; it was work that could be done easily by people with secondary education, in the employ of the state (Schimmerlingová, 1992).

This ideological conception of social problems, and their solution, left little room for social casework and group work, that is to say a social work practice encompassing client-oriented, personally engaged, expert intervention based on problem-solving relationships. The role of social workers under the supposed 'really existing socialism' was diminished to that of benefit eligibility assessors, home environment inspectors and providers of financial benefits. Social work education was adjusted to reflect these ideological arrangements. Under the Communist regime, social work education was abolished at the university level and re-organized as post-secondary training. New graduates mostly assumed roles as office workers in state and local bureaucracies, because private charities were also abolished.

Excluded from this professional decline were social workers from three specialized professional areas:

- The so-called *social nurses* – medical personnel who underwent specialized courses in social medicine and social policy, or social workers who took specialized pre-medical training. They were able to assert their professional identity in their own educational system and organizations. Most of them worked in hospitals, where they served as liaisons between patients, their families and communities.

- *Residential social workers* in facilities for children and young people, disabled persons and pensioners also had an opportunity to undertake individualized client work if they were so inclined. Most of their duties, however, involved gathering of information for other personnel in these homes (mainly educators or nurses), for courts where decisions were made about their clients, or organizations to which their clients were subsequently referred. These social workers were also expected to provide general custodial care for their clients.

- Finally, *social curators* for youth and adults, primarily those who had problems with the law. These were perhaps the only types of social workers, under the previous regime, who practised as case workers or group workers. Their duties included providing support and assistance to persons without natural social networks of families and friends. They sought to intervene in the lives of their clients in a curative or supportive manner. This was perhaps the area of expertise where genuine social work had managed best to survive.

It is worth noting that these positions as educators and social curators were often given to sociologists, psychologists, lawyers, pedagogues or other university graduates, rather than social workers, as social workers were then educated only at secondary or post-secondary schools. It was also these university-trained professionals who worked as therapists, counsellors or educators in other facilities, such as hospitals, clinics and enterprises. They often developed social programmes within the framework of their professions to pave the way for client-oriented intervention beyond medical or custodial care and benefit determination. During this period, social work in clients' homes or other natural environments was almost unknown.

Developments after 1989

At the beginning of the 1990s, there were approximately 1,500 social workers in Czechoslovakia, 500 of whom were members of the Society of Social Workers in the Czech Republic (there was no counterpart in the Slovak Republic), and 400 of whom were members of the Federal Union of Social Nurses. There were about 16,000,000 inhabitants in Czechoslovakia, 5,000,000 of whom lived in the Slovak Republic. One social worker thus had, on average, a potential clientele of 10,000 people – substantially more than in the West. However, social workers as well as social nurses were concentrated in cities and towns, and the practice of rural social work was almost unknown.

Clients have sometimes been seen as intruders or potential manipulators intent on creating undue problems for social workers. Respect for clients' human rights, such as the preservation of their dignity, privacy and confidentiality of information, was often not strictly observed. Fieldwork had been virtually reduced to mere inspections of the material and hygienic conditions of clients' homes; usually, these inspections were conducted without much human warmth.

This institutional degradation and neglect was, perhaps understandably, reflected in the low status of social work *vis-à-vis* other professions and with the population at large. Only senior citizens seemed to have understood the role of social work and embraced its utility. Even then, the recognition of the value of social work was only partial: only somewhere between half and two-thirds of pensioners surveyed in the 1970s and 1980s were able to identify the functions of social workers. Moreover, the quality of care provided by social workers was thought to be poor or very poor by the majority of people (see, for instance, Schimmerlingová, 1992; Slavíková, 1992).

The bureaucratized forms of social work still surviving from the previous period have been tolerated by the clientele only under duress. Czech social workers have a lot of power over their clients by virtue of making decisions concerning clients' eligibility for financial benefits, parental rights, housing allocation, and in similar other matters. Uncooperative clients are not always given prompt, courteous or standard treatment, and sometimes they are deliberately misinformed or mistreated. Visits by social workers to clients in their homes and visits by clients to 'social offices' therefore carry a certain stigma. Naturally, clients of social workers display resistance to being perceived as 'problem people' by their neighbours, peers and 'nosy bureaucrats'. In contrast, social work as 'client work' – legitimate helping – has been accepted and appreciated by a number of people in need, mainly the aged and the disabled. It is precisely in these relatively neglected client circles that a re-oriented social work can again find its relevant mission in the Czech Republic.

Improvement is clearly needed, and the profession works hard at it. A broadly-based coalition of social workers, social educators and ministry representatives has established a Co-ordinating Council for Social Work Standards in order to give a clear impetus for the re-professionalization of social work. After several unsuccessful attempts, the Society of Social Workers has gained partial support in the most important government ministries and has lobbied hard for recognition of two job categories with different job descriptions: 'specialists for benefit determination' and 'specialists for work with clients'. If these distinct roles are accepted, the stage will be set for recognition of casework as a legitimate social work function within the public sector of national and local government.

In addition, help for a variety of clients has begun to be provided by many newly-arising non-profit and for-profit non-governmental organizations, mainly churches and foundations. By 1993, more than 120 social service non-profit and client interest groups and over 20 large foundations had been established in the Czech Republic. The Catholic and the Reformed Churches and also the Jewish communities have made inroads into the provision of services in the health and human service sectors. However, these secular and religious groups have recognized – just as in the governmental sector, and perhaps more so – that the educational backgrounds and professional experience of their personnel have been simply inadequate to deal with the enormity of the demands made of them. Re-training courses have been organized with the assistance of various governmental ministries and the co-operation of university departments and post-secondary institutes. However, these have been rather uncertain beginnings to the development of a new social work education.

When I came to Czechoslovakia in 1991 as a US-trained teacher of social work, I was already aware of the issues that we were going to encounter thanks to my previous brief visits to Belorussia and Hungary, where similar efforts to develop social work were under way. Social work education had, of course, existed in many of the Soviet Bloc countries, sometimes before the arrival of Communism, sometimes during the Communist period. However, compared to Western practices, its focus, content and connections with the real world were diminished. In the Czech Republic, there was a broken tradition of social work with roots in the inter-war period. This tradition could be drawn upon, but only to a limited extent, to reconstruct social work education (see, for instance, Reznicek, 1994; Kanerova, 1992).

By 1991, there were five departments of sociology or pedagogy at Czech universities that had developed social work education at Bachelor level (first university qualification) or which had envisioned its expansion to the Masters level. However, only three of these universities – Palacky University in Olomouc, Charles University in Prague and Masaryk University in Brno – were actively developing seminal practice placements and case analysis seminars for their students, while other departments were only at the curriculum development stage. At a pre-university level, there were the surviving social work schools from the previous period. One independent social work academy was providing three-year education at the post-secondary level in Prague, and two Czech and two Moravian social/legal work programmes of study were available at two-year business academies.

At the university level, Czech social work programmes have mostly arisen in departments of sociology. This was a natural development, because sociologists have been the professionals most interested and involved in the identification and research of social problems in the Czech Republic. In consequence, social work education has been grafted on to, and also supported by, sociological and educational research and theory. Comparatively speaking, psychological, legal, ethical, economic and administrative contents have not been as strongly represented in the curriculum. Many of the teachers of these disciplines have been visiting personnel. Perhaps the weakest component of the curriculum was field practice and the related theory for practice. If students conducted visits to various social service agencies and municipal departments or were at all engaged in their work, they did not practise under the supervision of field instructors. In fact, there are no field instructors as such. Theory for practice was available from domestic and foreign sources, but it proved to be rather unrelated to the real work content of most social workers in the field (Reznicek, 1991; also personal communications to the author from Pavel Vozábal, Magdaléna Barèiaková and Kateøina Kupèová, representatives of social work academies in Prague, Dolny Kubín and Ostrava, respectively).

In this situation, in 1991, the Department of Sociology in Brno, where I was to teach, made the decision to develop quickly regular, week-by-week placements (a placement for a part of the week – sometimes called a concurrent placement, because the placement and academic work occur *concurrently* in the same week) for students and to teach jointly a practice course with a methods seminar based on the American tradition. It was intended as the best possible compromise between a Western approach and the Czech reality, because we knew that the students would have to bear the burden of experimenting with what was possible to accomplish and what was not.

Development of practice placements

By contrast with Prague (a magnet for talented Czech professionals and foreign visitors eager to help), Brno does not have as much breadth and depth in its social service network. However, there are sufficient placement opportunities for the body of about forty students per year. Brno, a city of 400,000 inhabitants, possesses a large municipal system of social security offices, social service department facilities, about a dozen homes for aged and disabled people, several special education schools, two shelters for the homeless, one for single mothers and one for those who are drug-dependent, centres for in-home services for aged people, one psychiatric hospital and one psychiatric clinic, about ten general hospitals, a home for infants at risk and several counselling facilities. Only the shelters and some of the counselling facilities belong to private charities, while the rest are governmental bodies.

Most of these institutions, including the municipal social department, were to some extent accustomed to having students practise on their premises. Prior to 1991, these were mostly post-secondary school students who were placed there towards the end of their studies for a period of two or three weeks. The personnel of these facilities were also accustomed to seeing university sociology students on half-day-per-year orientation visits. Similarly, special schools provided limited teaching opportunities for students of pedagogy, and psychiatric hospitals, clinics and counselling centres offered a short-term training stay for students of psychology. The idea of the regular, week-to-week, year-round presence of students was new to most of them, and our first goal was to convince them of the meaningfulness of this approach to student learning.

To help achieve acceptance of placements, members of the Department of Sociology have drawn on the help of past acquaintances. My practice teaching[1] colleague (a psychologist by training) and the Head of the Sociology Department used to work as marital counsellors during the difficult political period when they were not allowed to teach. They were both familiar with the counselling network. Also, I discovered four of my former classmates from Masaryk University in Brno in various administrative positions in the municipal bureaucracy. When they found out that I had come back to the Czech Republic with so-called 'American' know-how, they were willing to help. As soon as the Salvation Army established itself in Brno, the Department of Sociology made contact. In addition, we pleaded with the newly-installed Director of the Brno City Social Department to open its offices to our students, which he did after much hesitation.

My colleague also quickly renewed contacts with the places previously visited by sociology students, and then we decided simply to call other potential sites of practice placements, explain our intentions to them and invite ourselves for a friendly visit. This did not always work, but generally speaking, we have met with respect and co-operation. Within a period of three weeks, we were able to obtain statements of intent to collaborate from fourteen different organizations. In total, they could potentially cater for about thirty student placements.

At this point, the value of personal contacts must be emphasized. Brno, a medium-sized town, and the surrounding region encompass relatively small professional networks. Because Brno is also an educational centre for Southern Moravia, the acquaintances developed during studies and early work life are both personally close and long-lasting. These acquaintances have been very helpful. Once we established that the department wanted to be an active centre of hands-on professional learning, our task of finding suitable placements was simplified thanks to the assistance of our friends and interested colleagues. This is an important lesson for others seeking to develop a network of placements where little has existed previously.

From the very beginning of our recruitment exercise, we were worried about the response of social workers in the field. The problem, as we saw it, was that most of the social workers in the field possessed only post-secondary education and might feel threatened by the presence of possibly strongly-opinionated university students with what might seem to be far-fetched ideas about how to practise social work. Another difficulty was that our colleagues in the field had no formal supervisory training, and their connection to our department was tenuous at best. We were also concerned that our students might present an additional burden to the workers already besieged by clients.

The head of the department was willing to accept as students any interested social workers from the field, under the usual admission procedures and slightly relaxed full-time study regulations. However, he wanted to avoid repeating the previous practice of 'distance education' that helped Communist Party members gain university degrees under lowered admission and performance criteria than those applied to regular students. Only two of our colleagues from the field expressed interest in studying at the department. Nevertheless, the Educational Section at the Czech Ministry of Labour and Social Affairs gave us a small grant to develop supervisory training courses. These were attended by fifteen to twenty field workers from the city of Brno and helped the department to forge stronger relationships with them and their agencies. Our field supervisors were slightly uncomfortable at the beginning, before we got to know one another and until we, the practice teachers,[2] gained a realistic idea about the workings of their organizations.

In particular, we realized that the traditional work approach, and indeed the very work ethic of Czech social workers, presented a complicated picture in which the 'workers' comforts' have to be balanced with the levels of pay and the degree of difficulties experienced in work with clients. Fridays, for instance, were not feasible for student practice placements, because many workers used to leave their workplace early. On the other hand, observational visits by students were welcome, because they relieved social workers of some of their more routine burdens. The introduction of innovative strategies by students into governmental organizations was difficult, if achievable at all, but innovation was more acceptable in non-governmental facilities. Placements in the non-governmental organizations were often less structured and less reliable: for example, sometimes students could not easily define their function in these organizations.

We had to be reasonably flexible. Together with four colleagues from the municipal social service structure, we have contributed to the founding of a regional branch office of the Society of Social Workers. This society, based in the Brno University Sociology Department premises, has organized a series of lectures by nationally-known practitioners, policy-makers and researchers. These lectures have been widely attended by both professionals and students. This gave the department the necessary reputation to consolidate a network of friendly collaborators.

For the benefit of agencies, students and the Department of Sociology, we established a formal evaluation procedure for students' placements. To our dissatisfaction, this has remained a rather rigid and formal exercise. Much more meaningful, and rewarding, have been the semi-formal contacts we have developed in the course of our mutual collaboration. Over cups of coffee and mugs of beer, we have learned about the field, our students, professional concerns, city politics and developed initial strategies for the enhancement of social work in Southern Moravia. One such event, for instance, brought agency staff and faculty together over the issue of achieving neighbourhood support for locating a shelter in an available building despite organized local opposition. The department provided an impromptu research analysis of the situation for the leadership of the municipal social department. This eventually motivated the social department to improve public safety and recreational opportunities in the part of the city in question, in exchange for having the shelter in the area. We included our students in these activities as well, and their involvement became a part of their learning process.

Gradually, over the two-year period, we developed an almost all-inclusive list of placements in Brno agencies. At the beginning of the second year, when we were certain that our students had performed reasonably well in the city, we encouraged them to identify and create their own placements, if they so desired. About half of our students were from the outlying regions, and some preferred to practise in or near their own communities. After two school years of experimenting with this procedure, we could call on over thirty agencies in Southern and Central Moravia to provide opportunities for our students to do their regular field practice. Since then, the number of agencies involved has steadily increased.

Because standards of supervision and practice content were very varied, or supervision sometimes was non-existent, our strategy was to use the practice seminar as a means of identifying, analysing, clarifying and possibly defining with students what would be their approach to social work practice in a way that might be acceptable to all involved.

Practice course and seminar

An integral part of field practice was a taught course in the theory of social work and a related seminar. The traditional Czech teaching approach, dating back to the times of the Austro-Hungarian Empire, was to study a rather dry, not particularly inspiring text, whose presentation in the class had to be endured by teachers and students alike. Such texts as were available (including those by some Western authors) usually included relevant theoretical information but were not necessarily related to actual practice outside academia. We looked at the available texts and found some of them useful as recommended reading – particularly because they were written in Czech (Novotná and Schimmerlingová, 1992; Charvátová, 1990; Nerudová, 1980).

However, we were very tentative about introducing a social work methodology from abroad, so we carefully examined some twenty American and German textbooks on social work practice and settled on two volumes that offered the most in terms of practical problem-solving in the widest possible range of situations, professional settings and with a variety of clients (Sheafor, Horejsi and Horejsi, 1991; Pippin, 1980). From these two texts, we have prepared lectures, assignments and seminar topics for the weekly course on social work theory. Learning from our mistakes and from the practice experiences of students, we made necessary adjustments as the course progressed.

The results of this *ad hoc* approach have been uneven. First, students had to struggle with the idea of direct intervention in both learning and practice, whereas in the other subjects taught at the department, they were expected to maintain the stance of objective observers. Second, there was a clear and wide gap between what we taught them about the 'social work mission' (the purpose, direction and function of social work) and the surviving conception of social work from the times of 'really existing socialism'. Third, at some placement locations, there was still strong resistance to the innovative ideas of treating clients as service customers and of social workers behaving as service-providers.

A variety of factors had much to do with the changing idea of what the content of social work could be. The Czech Republic seemed to be at a similar historical threshold to that of the Western industrialized countries at the beginning of the 1960s, prior to the expansion of the welfare state, with an increasingly tolerant approach towards non-traditional social behaviour, and before the development of numerous service approaches for persons outside the mainstream of society. Notions of what is right and wrong are still relatively strong in the Czech Republic – although these norms are not always observed in private and public life. Personal responsibility is considered a virtue in the essentially middle-class Czech society, and the social work profession, together with the social policy establishment, is unabashedly middle-class-oriented.

Moreover, occasional encounters with Western social work practices and knowledge of the limitations and failures of the welfare state had not convinced Czech representatives of helping professions that permissive and apologetic social work is the answer to social problems. Czech social workers, however sympathetic they may be to their clients' plight, want them to uphold the notions and habits of a responsible way of life. The family is still considered the mainstay of one's well-being and an institution that can and should be expected to provide essential support to its members; this is the case to a much greater degree than in the urbanized and supposedly anonymous Western societies. Because most of the citizens of the Czech Republic are neither poor nor very well off, only those incapable of work and those without families to support them can expect to be supported fully by the rest of society.

However, as our students often noted in the seminars, social problems have been on the rise as a result of the large number of upheavals that Czech society has experienced. Unemployment, criminality, drug abuse and disabilities have all been increasing. The students were not interested in the theoretical explications of the 'American' social work that appeared to them strongly Marxist-oriented and, given the Czech experience, misguided. They knew they needed theories from their teachers of sociology and psychology, and the Western social work theory appeared watered-down and simplistic in comparison with other disciplines. If they wanted the Western know-how, it would have to be task-oriented, methodical, verifiable, common-sensical and potentially effective.

We accommodated their wishes primarily by concentrating on client problem diagnostics (working with clients to identify their problems). In this respect, the task-oriented methodology proved particularly useful in organizing clients' problems hierarchically, ordering them logically and establishing possible priorities for solutions. We had also required that students quickly identify their agency purviews, learn from available documents about successful interventions and enquire widely about various approaches that were being used. They were also asked to grasp a basic knowledge of essential legislation and working regulations, and in addition, to learn the legal and practical limits to their involvement.

Then they were expected to concentrate on one particular client or family, follow their history of involvement with the agency and other governmental facilities and, where possible, become actively involved in actual social work with the client or family. In some cases, the last task was impossible to pursue, but instead, students had the freedom to request analogous assignments from their supervisors. We have required written documentation of their practicum work, and students have periodically presented these in seminars for critique and advice. We also tried an American-style assignment, in which the students were to suggest possible improvements in services of their agencies, but these remained in the realm of the theoretical.

In contrast, a particularly attractive form of instruction for the students were exercises in various diagnostic, communication and intervention techniques which we adapted from the American textbooks. At times, students were able to replicate them in their agencies. More often than not, however, students had to adhere to the customs and practices of their host institutions, and to the apparent limitations of these agencies. The idea of strong personal intervention by a social worker who assists clients in the restructuring of their lifestyles, habits and practices has only limited application in current Czech society, where public and private finances are relatively restricted. The explicitly defined role of the redesigned welfare state is to guarantee basic means for survival, to organize social insurance and leave the rest to the initiative and effort of its citizens. In other words, the state prefers paying means-tested public assistance grants rather than developing extensive social services. It is the families, not the state, who are expected to give most support to the needy (Pachl et al., 1991).

As teachers, we had accepted these shortcomings in the hope that, over time, the representatives of the profession, the administrative bodies in cities and communities, pressures from other professionals and the students themselves after their graduation would gradually raise standards of social work practice and extend its scope. On the whole, and to our satisfaction, colleagues in the field have informally expressed their high regard for our students, their preparedness, flexibility and strong efforts in developing social work practice. Three of our students were asked to work in their placement agencies part-time, soon after they finished their practice learning there. Several others have used the contacts for the development of their Bachelors' theses. Many have participated in various research projects into social problems undertaken by the department for the local and national governments. It appears that the experiment has worked, although its results were more modest than we had originally expected.

As a postscript, it should be noted that when the two (faculty-based) practice instructors left the department, the head could not fill these positions with full-time, in-house faculty. During the two subsequent school years, external teachers gave the lectures a different, more psychologically-oriented direction, and the seminar was abandoned. Nevertheless, field placements have remained a staple of the curriculum and have, in fact, expanded. To us, this proves their viability, attractiveness and usefulness to the students. Developments in home-grown Czech social work theory, the content of Czech social work, and indeed the content of practice learning, can take their time, and can be flexible.

Notes

1 A faculty member who teaches a course in social work practice. In this chapter, the term 'practice teacher' follows the North American usage. See the glossary.
2 Faculty-based teachers of social work practice.

11 Developing practice learning at a school of social work: Process, perspective and outcome

R.R. Singh

The context of social work practice

When the first Indian graduate school of social work was started in 1936 by the House of Tatas at Bombay (now known as the Tata Institute of Social Sciences), the people of India were engaged in their struggle for independence. Earlier, in the second decade of this century, community development programmes for co-operation, increased productivity and rural education at the local levels in the then states of Madras, Punjab and Bengal had also been initiated under different auspices. The Royal Commission on Labour had submitted its report in 1931. The adverse working conditions of industrial labour and unhygienic living conditions in urban slums had already attracted the attention of nationalist political leaders who were sympathetic to the cause of workers.

The corollaries of industrialization – such social problems as prostitution, abuse of drugs, gambling and drunkenness – were manifesting themselves. The rate of morbidity and mortality was high. In the early 1930s, the number of mothers who died during childbirth surpassed the number of dead due to the plague, cholera and smallpox. The Nagpada neighbourhood in Bombay was no exception to this trend. This depressed neighbourhood was the first location chosen to start welfare work through a community centre, which continued for almost a decade before the first graduate school of social work was established there. Thus the school was born out of practice, and reflected a concern to ameliorate human misery through practice.

The rising political consciousness of the time; the increase in social problems; growth in urban slums; isolated grass-roots-level experiments in community development; welfare work of the missionaries and others, enactment of social legislation; establishment of ashrams (social settlements) by Gandhi for constructive work; the rich experience of the community centre at Nagpada, and the intellectuals' concern for the study of social problems in order to find solutions through action programmes all provided (among other factors) the ideal context for 'pioneering on social frontiers in India' (Manshardt, 1967).

The second school of social work, which was founded by the Young Women's Christian Association (YWCA) in 1946, lived a peripatetic existence until it was sheltered in the abandoned military barracks by the University of Delhi. These barracks had been leased to the university by the government. While the new school had yet to organize itself properly on its new site, the partition of the country brought in its wake communal riots and consequent influx and population movements. Thus the practice learning of the teachers and students of this school began with relief work. While providing relief to the victims of riots, social workers in Delhi did not disclose their identities to warring groups at this time for fear of reprisals.

Much later, the school set up the Urban Welfare Centre (Kalyan Kendra) which was subsequently converted into the Child Guidance Centre. The Gram Mahila Kendra (Rural Women's Centre) was also established. These two units still provide direct services through their own full-time social workers as well as practice learning opportunities to students. In collaboration with the Indian Association of Trained Social Workers and the Association of Schools of Social Work in India, during the 1960s the Delhi School of Social Work (DSSW) also participated in the development of social work practice and relief work for the victims of Bihar famine. By then, it had already demonstrated the effectiveness of medical and psychiatric social work in some of the local hospitals, which led to the appointment of professional social workers.

Issues in developing practice learning for students in India

Education for social work – and education itself, for that manner – is not an autonomous process in any society. In order to be relevant, education ought to relate simultaneously to the historical context; contemporary and emerging needs; evolved methodologies of social intervention; findings of research from socio-behavioural and allied sciences; policies, plans and programmes of economic and social development; social movements; geo-political and global changes, and also concern for human development and security. These issues are both local and global, and they also affect practice learning at the micro level. These dimensions are incorporated in the descriptions that follow.

Developing practice learning at an Indian school of social work

For nearly five decades now, the DSSW has organized its practicum under the headship (now directorship) of a senior member of the academic staff. This responsibility has rotated subsequently every two or three years. The change of director invariably results in a shift of focus in its administration within the overall policy framework. This occurs in terms of pattern maintenance, routine administration of practice learning, inclusion or exclusion of certain agencies and communities for the placement of students, innovations in practicum and alliances with local service institutions. At times, the director of fieldwork also acts as honorary director of the Child Guidance Centre or Rural Women's Centre. Also, the interest of the head of the institution in the practicum facilitates innovations in practice learning, or at least prevents the routinization of the practicum, thus avoiding the practicum being provided in a stereotyped manner. For nearly four decades now, the school has operated a grading system for evaluating the practicum of its students, replacing the earlier 'no grade system'.

The school instituted specialization courses for each field of practice for the second-year students, and demonstrations were undertaken by the staff in industrial social work, medical and psychiatric social work and rural welfare to strengthen practice learning. Later, school social work was also promoted.

In terms of practice learning, the period between 1946 and 1965 may be regarded as one of welfare, relief and clinical orientation. By the mid-1960s, this model of social work education began to be questioned in favour of a developmental model, but practice learning continued to be organized according to the earlier pattern. In 1969, the school was awarded a specialized unit by the government of India, to organize training programmes for university teachers to provide guidance to youth for work on national projects. The University of Delhi asked the school to run the youth programme on its behalf. This continued until 1987. As a result of this development, some of the youth projects also became fieldwork centres for social work students. These 'floating' placements could at best be regarded as accretive rather than integrative opportunities for practice learning.

Following the generic pattern of education in the 1970s, even though the honorary directorship of the psychiatrist at the Child Guidance Centre ended, its clinical orientation continued as usual, with an adjunct of a community outreach programme which links the primary schools of the neighbourhood with the Child Guidance Centre. With special financial assistance from the University Grants Commission (UGC) in the mid-1980s and early 1990s, a social developmental thrust is being provided through additional staff, and a community profile is under preparation for both the Child Guidance Centre and Rural Women's Centre. The team of the Child Guidance Centre still consists of a full-time social worker, an honorary psychiatrist, psychologist and speech therapist. The specialists from disciplines other than social work still favour a centre-based approach over the community-based one.

The team of the Rural Women's Centre previously consisted of an honorary director, a social worker, a pre-school teacher and a craft teacher. After the latter's retirement in the late 1980s, the post of craft teacher was upgraded to that of a social worker in order to respond to emerging issues related to women. This marks a shift from sole concentration on the provision of welfare to a developmental orientation at the organizational level. The field action project in social development, which focused on street children for three years, with financial assistance from the UGC, is continuing in a different form (described later in this chapter).

While the integration of methods of social work is appreciated by the school, and the course titles of social casework and group work have been changed to Working With Individuals and Groups, teaching of these courses is still done by different teachers, with the result that an integrated approach has not been formally and effectively developed.

This demonstrates that a shift in perspective at the formal level may not result in changes to practice teaching and learning, as a result of the different orientations of functionaries; conflict between the old and the new orientation (with only intellectual acceptance of the latter, and even that, rather half-heartedly); use of teaching materials; style of supervision; mode of evaluation, and the overall functioning of the school, which reflects the importance or otherwise attached to practice learning. The descriptions of three practice learning programmes run by the school that follow should therefore be seen in this light.

The Child Guidance Centre

The school has preferred the use of the term 'centre' to 'clinic' in order to stress the preventive aspects of social work practice since 1971 – although a psychiatrist was its honorary director. The change of director, after some years, from the honorary psychiatrist to a social work educator marked a shift from a clinical to a social orientation, although practice has still veered towards the clinical mode. The Child Guidance Centre serves the twin purpose of training students and providing services to the neighbourhood. Apart from its usual functions, the centre, under a former social worker and an honorary director, had, for some time, also carried out recreational and non-formal educational programmes for the children of school employees living on the campus and in its vicinity. During this period, a new institution for mentally retarded children in the voluntary sector, of which the honorary director was the vice-president, was fostered for a couple of years before its formal registration. This was done with the help of volunteer social work students.

From 1960 to 1971, the erstwhile welfare centre catered for the needs of the women and children of the neighbouring community before it was converted into a child guidance centre. Counselling, referral and group work services continue to be provided by the centre. Problems referred to the centre relate to scholastic backwardness; mental sub-normality; delayed speech and speech defects. Children come from lower-class and lower-middle-class families.

Apart from counselling, the full-time social worker attends to various activities which result in a scattering of energies along several lines (Taber, 1994). The social worker and the students placed at the Child Guidance Centre have attempted to initiate activities for pre-school children and have also made visits to schools in order to sensitize teachers towards the behaviour problems of children. However, these efforts have not yielded the desired results so far. Three or four sites have been identified and negotiated for play centres as part of the outreach programme, without any success to date. The invitation to parents to visit the Child Guidance Centre has also met with indifference. Parents usually refer learning problems rather than behavioural problems, and the social worker thus finds it difficult to get 'the right kind of cases' (Taber, 1994).

Initiatives for community-based work along with the counselling service may, in a way, be characterized as a return to the original functions identified in the 1960s, and these initiatives will need to establish a proper balance between counselling and community development. The latter assumes importance for two reasons. First, the problems that disadvantaged children of the slum area face include: lack of space for them to play; absence of organized recreation; school drop-out and its prevalence and acceptance in the community; under-employment and unemployment among parents, and rag-picking by children. These problems cannot be overlooked by a service centre in its programmes. Second, the thrust of practice, which has been social development since the mid-1980s, and the developmental social work approach formally adopted by the school since the early 1970s point clearly to this group as a priority in spite of the frustrating experiences of the staff so far. The centre has tried to effect partnerships with the paediatric department of the local general hospital, primary schools, college of education and a few nursery schools. However, these links remain tenuous. Efforts to secure a grant to run a pre-school for such children have also not borne fruit. The preparation of a community profile is under way – this will constitute the basis for introducing innovations in practice and also practice learning, including the organization of health and awareness camps on the hospital and primary school premises.

The experience of the Child Guidance Centre clearly illustrates that change in nomenclature or perspective alone is not sufficient to re-orient a service programme – even though it may be under one's own control. Appreciation of such a change by the professionals, their preparation and willingness to effect change by re-allocation of responsibilities and budgeting of time, experimentation with innovative approaches and comparison of results for further action are all needed. Moreover, a change of workers (and also in the social ecology of the neighbourhood) may bring about change in the focus of practice learning. Progression and regression in the life-cycle of an institution may also expand or limit its possibilities, in that the same aspects of work may be perceived differently by two different social workers.

The Rural Women's Centre

The Rural Women's Centre was established in 1957, before the Child Guidance Centre, in order to provide training and services, with a special focus on rural women. It ran centres for pre-school children and craft, through a *balwadi* (pre-school) and a craft teacher respectively, under the guidance of a professional social worker. Depending upon the availability of physical space – free of charge or at modest rent – these centres occasionally used to shift from one village to another. In this sense, the Rural Women's Centre has been truly peripatetic, and the present cluster of villages chosen for its work is only a continuation of the earlier tradition. Selection of the area has depended upon: the willingness of a village council; availability of space; visibility of unmet social needs; initial acceptance and co-operation by the potential beneficiary group(s) in the village(s), and also the changing caste, communal and party politics of the area.

When the Rural Women's Centre was established, the Union Territory of Delhi – which is also the nation's capital – possessed the characteristics of a rural area beyond the immediate urban environment. In the programmes of national development, and especially the grant-in-aid programmes of the Central Social Welfare Board (an autonomous national organization established in 1953 to promote women's and children's welfare in the voluntary sector), special emphasis was laid on education, vocational training, income supplementation and craft work.

The approach adopted then was welfarist and clinical. Issues which began to occupy the global and national consciousness during the International Year of Women in 1975 and thereafter – development, participation, patriarchy, gender justice, women's representation in decision-making, empowerment, special programmes for female children, etc. – had not yet surfaced in social welfare. The extent of urbanization (and the pressure of the capital's pull) was not so high. In fact, the present trend of urbanization has led a social scientist to remark that there is no 'villageness' in the villages of Delhi.[1] Most villages are awaiting urban status, which will increase the value of property. Thus the macro process of urbanization is accelerating the process of de-villagization. Therefore, any examination of practice learning opportunities cannot ignore this changed context, including the increased politicization of welfare.

The upgrading of the post of craft teacher to that of a social worker referred to earlier was done in recognition of this changed context, which coincided with the retirement of the social worker at the Rural Women's Centre and the appointment of a new one. The newly-appointed worker was a participant in the exploration of the present site. However, this upgraded position of social worker has sometimes remained vacant due to delays in appointments and the lack of suitable candidates.

The present centre is located about 11 kilometres from the School of Social Work. In addition to Burari village, there are five other locations where the Rural Women's Centre is running activities. The total population of the area is 40,000, which consists of scheduled castes, scheduled tribes, dominant castes, professional beggars, multi-religious groups and new migrants who encroach on government land. According to the present honorary director, one of the localities is most difficult to deal with due to social groupings, resistance and high expectations. Incidentally, the present director, who had been exposed to practice learning at the Rural Women's Centre as a student in the late 1950s, recalls that no welfare work was in evidence then. Transport was a serious constraint; tasks were non-specific; students were required to go to fieldwork six days a week, and they used to return only at night. The demands of practice made some students drop out of the programme for ever, and visibility of women workers in the villages was rare.[2]

Any visitor to the new location cannot fail to notice a sizeable number of children out of school and such problems as illiteracy, drinking and gambling. In fact, adults and youths play cards in front of a pre-school centre, quite unmindful of its impact on the young minds! The new director who took over in 1988 therefore took some time to re-formulate the objectives of the Rural Women's Centre in terms of community organization and family welfare rather than clinical service and welfare work. Thus it was a case of goal redefinition, goal replacement and also goal enlargement. Apart from the regular staff and trainee students of social work, both material and human resources were mobilized through networking in order to initiate programmes which reflected new goals. (Networking had not been attempted in the pre-1988 period of the Rural Women's Centre's existence.) For fund-raising, a village fair was organized which raised 20,000 rupees. This resulted in the establishment of five pre-school centres, five adult education centres and a programme of health check-ups with the assistance of the National Council of Educational Research and Training; the State Resources Centre for Continuing Education (Jamia Millia Islamia); the Centre for Continuing and Adult Education (University of Delhi); the Nehru Yuvak Kendra, Ankur (meaning 'sprout'); Helpage India; the Rotary Club; the National Service Scheme; the Central Social Welfare Board; the International Youth Centre, and Delhi School of Social Work Society, among others.[3]

The new role for professional social work was envisioned as: 'strengthening the capabilities of families, promoting the use of community resources and those of civic bodies, securing community participation, developing family support systems and networking, training for skill development, and monitoring evaluation and research' (Verma, 1994). It is clear that these goals mark a significant departure from the routinization of programmes over thirty years, as evidenced by a lack of creativity in the structure, form and content of many programmes. The new programmes include health and medical services, supplementary nutrition, sanitation and environmental improvement, pre-school and non-formal education, vocational training, recreation programmes for women, welfare of older people, referral services for handicapped people, social awareness and programmes for youth. Questions of caste, marriage and dowry, however, have been left untouched (Verma, 1994). From the perspective of practice learning, therefore, these omissions are strategic, on account of the complexity of initiating structural change through a service-cum-training unit unless it is deeply entrenched within an area. In other words, a period of six years in a new location is too short even to touch on these problems! The question is not only confined to the capacity for community-building but also concerns the service organization itself. This is an important lesson on the dialectic of any practice learning and the process and the outcome of developing it.

While the above programmes were continuing, additional resources were transferred to the School of Social Work by the UGC under its programme of special assistance for introducing innovations in its practice learning programme. In 1993, the new programme personnel began to look at the rural community and the Rural Women's Centre from its own angle. They have now begun the preparation of a community profile. In addition, the Delhi School of Social Work Society has obtained funds from the Central Social Welfare Board to start a family counselling centre in the same area. The new team, funded by the UGC, proposes to organize a women's health council, and for this purpose they have sought the assistance of the Voluntary Health Association of India to train nine women health workers. These trained voluntary workers have already started health education work. With this, the Rural Women's Centre seems to have entered a phase of resource convergence and its attendant problem of proper utilization through co-ordination, team work and specification of jobs of the core staff, the new staff and also of students under training.

As it stands, the demands on the core staff have certainly increased. This has resulted in the division of their time and also overlaps in work.[4] According to Taber, the Rural Women's Centre presently finds itself in a situation of 'complicated inter-organisational and service relationships' (Taber, 1994). Therefore it is only natural that students in practice learning will be hard put to find a focus for themselves under the different programmes, and plan their work from a social development perspective about which they have yet to gain clarity. It is likely that their participation itself would clarify their own perceptions and also assist the Rural Women's Centre in developing an appropriate design for practice learning.

One thing which is quite obvious, though, is that the project (or programme) development may not *ipso facto* result in people's development or social development under any set-up. At present, there is a plan to develop the Rural Women's Centre as a non-governmental organization in order to undertake the programme of community development, with the support of the core staff initially, but with its subsequent use for innovative and pioneering work in other areas. With such a development, the Rural Women's Centre, its service partners and the School of Social Work will enter into a new phase of relationship. The present Rural Women's Centre may thus 'individuate' (Erikson, 1963: 35) to assume altogether a new identity and may also undertake responsibility for fieldwork for the undergraduate social work students of the University of Delhi. Thus, it may choose to 'die' – in its present form – in order to live and serve creatively!

Prayas: The project for street children

Reference to migration in Delhi has already been made in the context of the Rural Women's Centre. The same process is exerting enormous pressures on all the urban services: civic, social and developmental. The newcomers' struggle for survival is marked by: the strangeness of the place; being duped by the privileged as well as anti-social groups; their short stays with friends and relations; unstable work and wages; pressure on children to work; unauthorized encroachments; political exploitation, and years of social and psychological deprivation (and even depravity) before they become eligible for regular ration cards, shelter and jobs. Against this background, the school proposed a field action project in social development to the UGC for funding. After the sanction of a grant during 1987–88, the school decided to locate the new project in a large resettlement colony, Jahangirpuri, where placement of students in the open community setting had been practised since the late 1970s.

During their re-exploration of the area for the new project, the two workers and the then director of fieldwork identified a building where the Delhi police's Juvenile Aid Centre was working. Since the new project required accommodation, the workers contacted the police officer concerned, who was more than willing to collaborate.

Once the non-formal education programme was introduced, the need for vocational training was felt, because working children used to earn, on average, 40 rupees per day from rag-picking. The organizers contacted the Shramik Vidyapith (Directorate of Workers' Education) for vocational training. Their collaboration marked the second phase of partnership. Since rag-picking is a hazardous occupation, and children were showing symptoms of malnutrition, skin diseases, etc., the Rotary Club of the nearby district, and also others, when contacted, came forward with the services of an honorary physician for regular health check-ups, etc.

The questions relating to practice learning in this project concern: the phe-nomenal expansion of the organization and beneficiary groups (its coverage increasing from 25 children to 2,000 over a period of six years); the per capita cost of the service; a welfarist versus developmental thrust; the integration of its own goals and the contributions of partner organizations; differences in their perceptions; the method of service delivery; the changing psycho-social profile of children and families; the adverse staff/beneficiary ratio and the quality of service; the impact of the project on social and urban development policy, etc., and the distinct contribution of professional social work in the development of the people and also the project.

Apart from placing students in the hospitals, social and public welfare insti-tutions and its own projects, the school has selected different communities (called 'resettlement colonies') for students' practice learning placements since 1976. This is intended to expose them to the practice of developmental social work after the shift in the School of Social Work's educational policy from specialization to a generic programme. The question which has been raised time and again is whether holistic, integrated and developmental social work is being practised in the communities by students, or does their work amount to the practice of the traditional methods of social work, sever-ally or in combination? Due to limitations of space, this issue will not be pur-sued here at length.

The above account of the Child Guidance Centre, the Rural Women's Centre, Prayas and the resettlements explains clearly the area of partnership, its advantages and also limitations. Contrasts between the orientations of the Rural Women's Centre and Prayas are striking indeed. Since a school has to identify situations (agencies, communities or institutional networks) for practice learning, the onus for securing any partnership rests with it. Such a partnership depends upon the goal(s) of professional education that the school has chosen to pursue over time, the focus of the practicum, the ex-istence and availability of resource networks, the reputation of the school, congruence between the interests of the partner organizations, the socio-economic characteristics of the area, the composition of its staff and student body, the impulse of an institution for outreach in order to enrich its educa-tional programme, and its possible contribution to the programme of its partner.

The pattern of growth of the Rural Women's Centre shows that until 1988, it functioned as a free-standing unit before it began to forge new links. This was necessitated by the changing perspective on women and child welfare and the orientation of the new honorary director. Although women's issues had surfaced on the national agenda in the mid-1970s, it was only after a decade that the Rural Women's Centre thought of securing partnerships. This has resulted in 'a complicated inter-organisational and service relationship' (Taber, 1994). Through these partnerships, the Rural Women's Centre has made its presence visible in the new location and has exposed students to a variety of programmes which provide opportunities for interaction. However, the need to provide clear guidance on the structure of practice learning and its process in the new context has yet to be addressed at the institutional level. And if the Rural Women's Centre emerges as a non-governmental organization, as is being planned, its new and independent identity will call for the re-negotiation of partnership. Although it is unlikely, the Rural Women's Centre may well decide not to enter into any partnership with the parent institution, or the partnership may remain confined to referral services only and not extend to participation in organizational and direct service programmes.

In the case of the Child Guidance Centre, the experience in the area of partnership has been very different. Some of the schools, hospitals and clinics are collaborating with it only in a formal way. Efforts have been made to build partnerships, but without demonstrable and sustained results. It is likely that the demands on a community-oriented service-cum-training centre for partnerships are greater than those on a centre which is providing services on an individual basis, but the pre-1988 phase of the Rural Women's Centre challenges this assumption. The outreach programme of the Child Guidance Centre needs to develop more fully before other factors relating to partnership, including the role of social worker, can be examined.

The story of Prayas is quite different. No sooner had the organization started than networking and partnership was sought and found. However, each partner was focusing on a particular programme of the project. This partnership was both organizational and programmatic. The increase in the number of partners – organizational, programmatic and financial, with different goals, priorities and projects – has created a new situation necessitating review of such questions as co-presence, joint organization, co-operation, collaboration (sponsorship) and also professional education.

In the case of community-based practice learning, the situation is indeed unique. Students are expected to secure collaboration on the basis of their assignments, and select these assignments keeping in view the programmes and needs of agencies. The agencies too, in turn, wish to utilize students' services to strengthen their programmes. Depending upon the interest of students (and also the fieldwork supervisor), these partnerships are renewed every year. In all the settings mentioned above, and also through them, the role model of the school and its distinct mission of practice-led education ought to determine the choice of a partner. Just as a teaching hospital is organized differently from a general one, the Child Guidance Centre or Rural Women's Centre should similarly reflect their distinctiveness. The question of partnership therefore calls for a perspective to determine its form and direction in order to make practice learning effective.

Training opportunities for practice teachers

The best training opportunity for practice teachers can be provided by their participation in the programmes of their *own* institution – if this provides a positive role model for practice learning. This role model is reflected in a variety of different ways, such as: in the general administration; remarks made by the staff and students in meetings; informal comments and jokes; the seriousness with which the organization approaches practice learning; the manner in which the time for coursework and fieldwork is utilized or individual and group supervision is provided to learners; the percentage of organizational time which is devoted to practice learning; the nature of the partnerships sought and secured for practicum; the organization of practice learning seminars and their themes; recognition of practice teachers; group conferences of teachers and students on practice learning; the types of training programmes undertaken for professionals and non-governmental organizations; the priorities accorded to practice-based research by the faculty and students; relevant collections in libraries, and the work of the institution in producing indigenous materials for practice teaching and learning. In addition, individual teachers, motivated students, creative and innovative field project staff, satisfied beneficiaries and partners provide opportunities for the non-formal and continuing education of teachers.

The formal forums for the training of teachers are: the advanced institutes; faculty development seminars; in-house and in-service development programmes; practice laboratories of their own or other institutions; inter-disciplinary dialogues; sabbatical projects; field visits, camps and study tours; fieldwork evaluation by a group of local and outside examiners; training programmes of the local/national/international organizations, and consultancy and collaboration. Practice-based research projects of the teacher's own or other institutions, demonstrations of practice and the preparation and the use of bibliographies all provide opportunities for the learning of practice teachers.

Resources for practice teaching

The schools of social work which had come into existence before 1950 made special efforts to develop indigenous teaching materials in the form of mono-graphs and case records for teaching courses in social casework, group work and community organization. Since field placements also emphasized the practice of these methods in the agencies and communities, these materials were used to guide the practice learning of students.

However, although there is a prescribed list of required and recom-mended readings for different theory courses, the schools of social work have published no specific reading list on fieldwork or practice learning. Perhaps the assumption is made that readings prescribed for coursework will automatically find application in the field. This seems to be the case, in spite of the fact that the prospectuses of all the schools of social work men-tion practicum as a 'core' programme.

If one looks at the contributions made by social work educators, mainly on fieldwork (as distinct from those on methods of social work), the number of published and unpublished usable texts would be less than ten (UGC, 1990). The question arises as to how instruction in a core programme should be imparted. Obviously, the resources would include materials borrowed (or adapted) from art, literature, history, philosophy, religion, biographies of social reformers and social activists, case records, court cases, social and behavioural sciences, reports of relevant research and evaluations of social programmes, posters, news clippings, films, serials, occasional series on the work of the non-governmental organizations, case studies, documents on economic and social development planning, relevant literature in the life and environment sciences, educational methods and technology and diaries of social workers. But selection of material from such a vast corpus is indeed exacting, though self-educating. While *individual* teachers and fieldwork supervisors may be making use of diverse sources, this approach should be made an integral part of an institution's work in order to strengthen practice learning.

Even the records of the group conferences of students and teachers at the DSSW could be developed into resource materials. This would require plan-ning of these conferences, which reflect progression in practice learning. A student following these arrangements would present relevant experiences of the practicum at the beginning, ongoing or ending phases of learning, as far as possible. This would demonstrate the learner's initial or greater degree of involvement in practice and the application of skills. These presentations would also show greater complexity – requiring a still higher degree of skills, knowledge and analysis from advanced students. At present, it is entirely left to students to choose a topic and make a presentation with the approval of their supervisor; students rarely ask to write on the neglected aspects of practice. Thus students, even at the end of a term, make presentations which are rudimentary.

The present orientation programme for the first- and second-year students could also be prepared in such a manner that demands made of the second-year students are more exacting, so that students are expected to demonstrate their knowledge of the organizational processes and dynamics rather than just the structure or programmes. The general orientation of students in the two years (including visits) may be so differentially structured that it responds to the growing learning needs and demands of field placement. These changes do not require additional financial resources, but undoubtedly they will provide better training opportunities and resource material updates for practice learning. The same approach can be followed for the preparation of bibliographies (Kalra and Singh, 1987: 53, 58 and 65). Thus the boundaries of practice learning expand or contract, and they are determined by the manner in which the educational task is approached and attempted.

Recapitulation

This chapter has discussed the context of social work education; issues and experiences of developing practice learning in a school of social work; partnership in practice learning; training opportunities for practice teachers, and resources for practice training. The approach has considered context, process and perspective.

The present phase of globalization of the economy and new economic policies are generating diverse socio-political forces which have begun to make an impact on social services. The emerging ethos is one of uncertainty. The question is: how can a developing society effectively balance social development with market development (or equity with efficiency), re-orient education and practice of professional social work, identify new social spaces and methods to respond to human needs and social deprivations in a situation of growing competitiveness and consumerism, and also contribute to the shaping of social policy through practice and action research? The profession's response to these issues, in turn, has implications for developing practice learning as well as the resource materials.

Participation in any social programme may, of course, provide experience to a motivated worker, but it should not be confused with practice learning for professional social work, as the latter is also designed to produce individual change in the learner – attitudinal and affective – which cannot be achieved through either didactic or distance modes of education (Singh, 1994). Practice learning is a process of viewing and re-viewing one's self in relation to others and situations in harmony through doing purposeful and supervised activities. Such a *doing* is felt, owned, tasted, tested and made part of one's growing self. In a period of proliferation of training models and modules, the danger of relegating such a programme of learning to secondary importance, in favour of a student's contrived and floating exposure to a variety of practice situations and settings, is indeed real.

A perspective-based approach to practice learning, in contrast with an academic or assorted one, is a consciously designed and nurtured programme which is reflective, participatory and evolving. Since it keeps unfolding itself and also the self of the learner, it is involving, enabling, and even ennobling. Continuing participation, reflection and contextualization suggest themselves as preconditions for its development. These also impose limits on its replication. Viewed thus, a school of social work in any location must authentically assume a practice role model in order to experience the joy of developing practice learning and educationally mediate the dialectic which is inherent in it.

Notes

1 This expression was used by Dr Rajendra Singh about the Rural Women's Centre's work and goals in an informal discussion.
2 Based on an interview with Dr Ratna Verma, Honorary Director, Rural Women's Centre, held on 29 November 1994.
3 Based on an interview with Dr Ratna Verma, Honorary Director, Rural Women's Centre, held on 29 November 1994.
4 Comment made by Dr Ratna Verma in an interview on 29 November 1994.

12 Practice teachers' training in Hong Kong and the People's Republic of China

Iris Shuk-fong Ng-Wan

Introduction

In social work education programmes, fieldwork practice is a vital part of the curriculum. Fieldwork provides an opportunity for students to go into real-life social work settings, where they are able to develop an understanding of clients, the type of problems confronting the agency, and constraints and opportunities in providing services. They also have opportunities to try out theories and skills learned in school, to acquire an understanding of the formal and informal structure of organizations and to promote self-understanding through practice.

It has been found that many social work students highly prize the fieldwork experience. Fieldwork practice is often seen as the doorway to the 'real' world of social work. The learning that takes place in college – through reading, thinking, observing, questioning and carrying out critical discussions in classes, or through experiential learning and simulation exercises – requires students to acquire a wide range of intellectual knowledge and to assimilate it within a coherent framework (Butler, 1983). While in fieldwork practice, students start to utilize this acquired knowledge in real contacts with clients – where professional values are reflected and internalized in real-life situations, and skills are tried and refined. The down-to-earth task of integrating theory with practice has to be achieved through fieldwork practice. Hence fieldwork practice is the most exciting and challenging, yet anxiety-provoking, aspect of social work learning (Wan, 1990).

With the recognition of the importance of fieldwork practice in the social work curriculum, there is a growing concern about the quality of teaching and learning that occurs during fieldwork. In the UK, attempts have been made to improve the quality of practice learning by implementing a recent policy of accreditation of practice teachers and requiring the approval of agencies as suitable to provide placements. These initiatives form part of the development of quality assurance systems for fieldwork learning.

In Hong Kong and in the People's Republic of China (PRC), there is no similar policy development or requirement that practice teachers must enrol in certain training programmes or undergo certain qualifying procedures before they can become practice teachers. In Hong Kong, it is the general practice for training institutes to provide practice teachers. These training institutes usually require that practice teachers have a Bachelor's degree in social work and have at least three years of post-qualifying social work practice experience prior to becoming a practice teacher. This is a minimum requirement to ensure that practice teachers have received formal and recognized social work training to the expected level and have sufficient practice experience themselves.

Social work educators in Hong Kong fully realize that experienced social workers do not automatically and necessarily become competent practice teachers. For practice teaching is not merely a process of transmitting experience from a practitioner to a novice. The integration of social work knowledge, skills and values and their application to life situations is an art to be acquired by students: this process cannot be achieved merely by taking the 'savings' from an experienced social worker's 'bank of knowledge' – in Freire's terms. Social workers, as practice teachers, are not just 'depositors' transferring knowledge and experiences from their own bank of knowledge to students (Freire, 1972). On the contrary, practice teachers have to understand the learning style and learning needs of students; explore a range of learning opportunities for students; develop a facilitative teaching–learning relationship with students; experiment with new elements of practice in safe situations and allow students to make rectifiable mistakes; encourage students to make choices in their own practice, and help students to develop their own practice theories and summarize experiences from practice through conscientious debate with students about what they are doing, what decisions they have made, and why they have chosen a certain course of action – all in all, a very demanding set of responsibilities.

In 1990, the Department of Applied Social Studies of Hong Kong Polytechnic started offering an extension course, Supervision and Professional Development, to train experienced social workers to supervise staff in social welfare agencies or to supervise social work students in fieldwork practice. In 1991, this extension course was converted to a module of a Postgraduate Diploma programme, and is now a module in a taught Master's programme within the department. In 1993, colleagues from the Department of Applied Social Studies of Hong Kong Polytechnic and Nottingham University (UK) offered an intensive practice teachers' training programme for social work educators, potential practice teachers and agency staff engaged in direct service work in Beijing, the People's Republic of China.

In the following sections, these two practice teachers' training pro-grammes in Hong Kong and in Beijing are compared by considering major factors, such as the characteristics of participants, the length and content of training, the educational philosophy adopted and the training methods and responses of participants.

Characteristics of participants

Hong Kong

In Hong Kong, the participants of the practice teachers' training course are all qualified social workers with a degree in social work and at least three years' social work experience. All of them are mature students; most of them have a full-time job and are enrolled in a part-time Postgraduate Diploma or Master's course. Studying for a Postgraduate Diploma or Master's course is not a prerequisite for experienced social workers to be promoted to higher positions in their agencies or to become practice teachers. Participants choose to enrol for a higher qualification for their own professional development – so their motivation is high. Participants are experienced in social work practice and have also experienced the role of being a student worker in fieldwork practice while studying for their Bachelor's degrees in social work. It was hoped that, using this range of experiences, they would easily be able to 'tune in' to the requirements of fieldwork placements and get a rough idea of what practice teaching is. However, the reality was not quite so simple!

Frequently, their own experience in direct practice and practice learning acted as a constraint on their ability to develop the skills of being a practice teacher. Some participants would unthinkingly transfer knowledge, values and skills used in their direct practice to practice teaching – that is, they would treat the student as a client, and assume that the worker–client re-lationship is the same as the supervisory or teaching relationship, that the objectives and tasks of working with clients are similar to those of working with students. Some other participants had another common frame of refer-ence which they applied to the teacher–learner relationship. They may have had an excellent or painful learning experience in their own fieldwork prac-tice when they were undergraduate social work students. Now, as they became practice teachers, they were determined either to try their best to model the practice of their respective practice teachers or to avoid doing to others what was done to them by their practice teachers.

The People's Republic of China

The social work students of Peking University in 1993/94 were the first cohort of students taking fieldwork practice in the history of social work education in the People's Republic of China. A practice teachers' training course was offered in April 1993 for those who would be providing placements, just six months before the commencement of students' fieldwork placements. The participants on the practice teachers' training course in Beijing included social work educators from universities, direct practitioners from the welfare agencies and postgraduate social work students. None of the participants had previously received any formal social work education, nor had they themselves had a fieldwork practice placement or received any fieldwork supervision before. Those participants who were social work educators or postgraduate students from the universities were mainly from the departments of sociology, education, philosophy, psychology or economics. They had no experience of direct contact with clients, nor did they even have the experience of working with others in helping relationships outside the school setting. Those participants who were practitioners from welfare agencies may not have had a university education, but they brought a wide range of experience to the course, having worked for a long time with people in need.

The social work educators and postgraduate students from the universities had previously developed an ability for academic study, analytical thinking and critical questioning and were able to learn new material quickly. But as they had little or no exposure to a social environment other than their schools, they had no in-depth understanding or experience of how to work with people from a variety of walks of life. Nor did they have any experience of direct contact with people in need.

The profile of the practitioners who came from welfare agencies was quite different. They had a lot of experience in working with people from varied backgrounds with a range of problems; they knew very well the nature of the social work environment. However, they had been absent from education for a long time, and it was quite difficult for them to adapt to the learner's role. Moreover, unlike those participants who came from universities, their existing learning and knowledge was not backed up by a strong theoretical understanding of social work and related studies, hence it was anticipated that it might be difficult for some of those in practice to absorb new materials. As they had not had the benefit of social work training before they entered 'people-helping work', some of the practitioners experienced another difficulty: they demonstrated an over-willingness to cling rigidly to imperatives derived from their practice experience. Without analysing, synthesizing or transferring their practice experiences to other contexts, some practitioners found that these experiences became a *hindrance* to developing their practice further, rather than providing a useful type of practice wisdom.

Analysing the participants of the practice teachers' training courses in Hong Kong and the PRC, we find that participants in the Hong Kong programme had similar backgrounds to each other, while participants of the course in Beijing had very varied experience and approached the course from different starting points and with different learning abilities. How could these factors be addressed in the design of the respective courses and in the teaching and learning strategies adopted?

Content of the practice teachers' training courses

Hong Kong

In Hong Kong, the practice teaching course consists of one half of a module entitled Supervision and Professional Development. This module is taught during the summer term and lasts for three months, from June to August.

During these three months, participants have to attend five $2\frac{1}{2}$-hour lectures and participate in four seminars and a practicum. This practicum requires that participants provide practice teaching for a Social Work Diploma student during a ten-week summer block fieldwork placement. As part of the practicum, the participants take part in two group consultation sessions and at least three individual consultations.

The sequence and topics of the lectures taught as part of the Supervision and Professional Development module are as follows:

- *Introductory Session* – the concept of professional development;
- *Functions of Supervision* – educational, administrative and supportive functions of supervision (Kadushin's model with local adaptation);
- *Process of Student Supervision* – analysing the student's learning needs; contracting with students; supervising and evaluating the students' performance;
- *Methods and Models of Supervision* – methods; individual, joint, peer, chain and group supervision models; apprenticeship, classical, therapeutic, caring, interventionist curriculum, adult-learning, and a model based on dialogue;
- *Theory–practice Integration* – defining theory and practice, and the relationship between these two elements; discussing the application of models, especially a bi-directional, co-evolving model of theory–practice integration.

Participants have a free choice of seminar topics, although they are required to study their chosen topic, make a presentation of their work in the seminar and facilitate discussion in the group. The participants may choose to present a theoretical discussion, for example:

What is the most important function of supervision? Or how can we facilitate students' use of theories in practice through a dialogue approach to supervision?

Alternatively, participants can examine the use of a particular skill or model, for instance:

Would the caring model of supervision encourage dependency of a young and inexperienced student? Or when would be the best time (how would we get the most desirable consequences) to confront a resistant and underperforming student in the supervision process?

Some participants were interested in examining a practical problem, such as:

How can we involve students actively in their learning?

Other participants wanted to research the issues, such as:

What exactly do we mean by theory–practice integration? How could it be realized in daily practice?

The participants had to write up a seminar paper at the end of the module.

The participants had to complete a 'practice teaching practicum' (a period of supervised learning as a practice teacher). During the practicum, participants had the opportunity of both supervising a social work student who is studying for a diploma and simultaneously being supervised (by a consultant) on their practice teaching. The consultants (the author and/or another co-opted teacher of this module) gave every participant at least three individual consultation sessions in order to facilitate and supervise the participants who were doing their practice teaching during the practicum. Some participants had difficulties in certain situations: for example, one participant was unable to compromise with a student on the selection of assignments in a fieldwork placement. Other participants needed more help in resolving some in-depth struggles: for instance, one participant had to deal with a student who was not meeting requirements and who seemed not to be committed to social work. In these and similar circumstances, the consultant had to spend more time and effort in supporting and facilitating participants to work through the practicum, while at the same time safeguarding the learning of the diploma student.

Group consultation was also provided. This can be carried out in many different ways, but the main objective was to provide opportunities for participants to learn from each other in a small group setting. We encouraged the participants to record part of their supervision session using either audiotape or videotape (with the consent of the diploma student), and to share the recorded supervisory interaction to illustrate a selected theme. For instance, one participant recorded part of a discussion which was mainly on 'how to practise client self-determination in social work practice when the client adopts a self-defeating attitude'. In the group consultation, after listening to the selected part of the taped supervision session, all participants were able to contribute and discuss the context of the supervision session. Key issues arising in this discussion tended to centre upon the practice teacher's and student's personal and professional values, the supervisor's skills and how to provide opportunities for participants to share experiences. The participants also suggested follow-up action to be taken by the practice teacher and ways of providing support while trying out certain courses of action.

All participants had to compile a practicum portfolio (a compilation of different pieces of work that provides evidence of competence); this included a selection of the student's work, such as a learning contract, a practice teacher's teaching plan, a practice teacher's self-evaluation and an evaluation of the student's performance.

The People's Republic of China

The practice teachers' training programme in the PRC lasts for two weeks and covers ten topics in eleven sessions. The sequence of the topics taught is as follows:

1 the nature and objectives of social work fieldwork practice;
2 the models of fieldwork practice and practice teaching;
3 the co-ordination of fieldwork practice;
4 the process of fieldwork practice teaching;
5 the functions of practice teaching;
6 the supervisory relationship between practice teacher and students;
7 mode and methods of practice teaching;
8 evaluation and assessment of fieldwork practice;
9 theory–practice integration;
10 skills of practice teaching (including: contracting; observing; listening; questioning; elaborating and assessing; empathic skills; reflection of feelings; summarizing; facilitative confrontation, and terminating skill).

We were unable to arrange a practicum for the participants; moreover, participants were not confident about immediately assuming the role of practice teacher.

The course consisted of a total of eleven three-hour sessions. Topics 1 to 9 were mainly taught through lectures, which included question and answer sessions, small group discussion and role-plays (in eight of the sessions). However, the skills training took three sessions, and we turned the classroom into a laboratory setting.

We selected ten basic skills which are essential and helpful for practice

teachers; the author (trainer for the practice teachers' training course) introduced each skill through a mini-lecture using relevant examples, then the
trainer would act as practice teacher, with a partner (in this case, the colleague from Hong Kong) acting as a student, to demonstrate the skill in a
role-play simulation. Hints and suggestions were given before the demonstration so that participants could make purposeful observations. After
observing the demonstration, there was a question and answer session to
facilitate relevant discussion. After this discussion, the trainer would invite
two participants to role-play a practice teacher and a student and try to practise the skills. These role-plays were videotaped and reviewed as a further
mechanism to promote debate.

There were several instances where the participants had difficulties
in identifying or using certain skills in role-plays. When this occurred,
the trainer would join the practice teacher, sit by their side and intervene
sparingly by selecting critical points and offering advice to the practice
teacher. For example, participants tended to ask closed questions or include
cues indicating expected answers – in some cases, the answer itself – in their
questions. The trainer sat by the participant who was playing the practice
teacher and asked the same questions, but in an open-ended way. This kind
of intervention was used naturally in participants' role-playing.

There were no planned seminars, but the participants actively brought up
issues and questions for discussion during the breaks or at lunch time. After
becoming acquainted, they started to exchange ideas among themselves.
Social work educators from different training institutes would start to share
their designs for fieldwork practice which formed a part of their social work
programme. They discussed the constraints and difficulties encountered in
providing social work education and welcomed comments and suggestions
from the trainer and other participants. The participants from Peking
University started to identify welfare agencies where they could place
students on placement, as Peking University intended to start social work
fieldwork placements at the earliest opportunity.

It can be observed that the practice teachers' training course in the PRC
included material about the co-ordination of fieldwork placements and the
significance of fieldwork practice in a social work educational curriculum –
none of these elements were mentioned in the Hong Kong course. In Hong
Kong, the importance and significance of high-quality fieldwork practice for
social work education have been well recognized, and social work educators
in the training institutes would usually co-ordinate and organize the fieldwork placements; practice teachers, generally speaking, do not get involved
in this co-ordination work. However, the co-ordination of fieldwork practice
is a basic issue for social work educators in the PRC. In the PRC, since the
social work profession has not been well known or developed, the co-ordinators of fieldwork practice might be expected to encounter many challenges

and difficulties. Moreover, according to the tradition of sociological education, 'fieldwork' means 'research or observation in the field' but not 'working in the field' with clients. With this background, we consider that preparing social work educators and agency workers to be able to understand *what social work fieldwork practice is and is for*, and *how to co-ordinate the effort of training institutes and welfare agencies to provide satisfactory learning environments for students* are essential and meaningful elements of a course for practice teachers in the PRC at present.

Moreover, the skills component was only present in the PRC, not in the Hong Kong practice teachers' training course. The reason is simple: the participants in the Hong Kong practice teachers' training course were all qualified and experienced social workers, so they did not lack social work skills; for them, a major concern was how to develop and adapt their inter-personal and interventive skills for use in a supervisory relationship within a supervisory setting. However, the participants of the PRC practice teachers' training course had no basic training in working with people. Consequently, the skills we selected were a combination of inter-personal skills and educational skills, adapted for use in a supervisory setting.

The educational philosophy behind the design of the courses

In designing the practice teachers' training courses, both in Hong Kong and in Beijing, we have incorporated three theoretical strands: the *adult learning theory* of Knowles; Rogers' concept of *whole person learning*, and Kolb's *experiential learning theory*.

Knowles' *adult learning theory* reminds us to attend to and make best use of an adult's self-concept and their own resources for learning. Knowles observes that adult learners have the following characteristics:

- Adults tend to see themselves as responsible, self-directing, independent personalities and tend to resist learning under conditions that are incongruent with their self-concept as autonomous individuals.
- Adults experience phases of growth as a result of engaging in developmental tasks. Each of these developmental tasks produces a 'readiness to learn' that, at the peak of learner involvement, presents 'a teachable moment'.
- Adults engage in learning, largely in response to pressures they feel from their current life problems: their time perspective is one where the immediate application of learning is important. They tend to enter any educational activity in a problem-centred frame of mind, so that

the learning meets a particular need at a given time. (Knowles, 1972, 1978, 1980)

As mentioned above, there is no requirement for a person to take a practice teachers' training course before they can become a practice teacher either in Hong Kong or in the PRC, so the participants in these training courses were all self-motivated, and they all actively chose to join the course. In the practice teachers' training courses, we included seminars, group consultation, group discussions and role-plays to facilitate participants' active involvement in learning and to promote the mutuality of learning from each other. In Beijing, when we started the practice teachers' training course, we incorporated this educational philosophy and explained the course design and rationale to course participants. There were only a few objections and hesitations. Previously, they were accustomed to and accepted the idea that teaching is 'lecturing', and that learning is 'listening to what the teacher said, jotting notes and memorizing the notes' (Ng et al., 1992). So the course started with lectures; group discussion and short role-plays were introduced gradually and in a natural manner. In this way, the course participants became familiar with new methods of teaching and learning.

Considering the *readiness to learn* or the *immediate application perspective* of adult learners, the practice teachers' training course in the PRC was the most judicious in its timing, as most of the participants were educators from various training institutes that intended to offer social work training to students in the near future. In particular, the participants from Peking University were offering a social work education programme and would have to arrange and co-ordinate fieldwork placements six months after the end of the practice teachers' course. During the course, the participants from social work agencies in the PRC began to be aware that the social work profession would be a new profession emerging in their work environment, and that it was important to offer fieldwork placements to facilitate this development. All participants had limited knowledge about social work education, and they seized every chance to learn about social work as a profession and about social work education. The participants knew that they would be practice teachers or co-ordinators of fieldwork placements in the near future, so the learning on the training course was of immediate use and meaningful.

Rogers' concept of *whole person learning* provides us with many insights. Learning involving the 'whole person' means to set free and utilize all aspects of the individual; so both the right brain (intuitive functions) and the left brain (cognitive functions) are brought together in harmony, whereas traditional learning emphasizes and uses mostly the capacity of the left brain – those parts of the brain that govern cognitive activity. Whole person learning has a special quality, because the learner is totally involved in both the feeling and cognitive aspects of a learning event (Rogers, 1983).

The design of practicum consultations included in the practice teachers' training course in Hong Kong made it impossible for participants to learn solely by rational thinking. It was evident, both in individual and group consultations, that many participants learned a lot through struggling with and sharing feelings – they found this type of learning invaluable. In the training course in the PRC, although we could not supervise the participants in a practicum, we designed the skills training workshop in such a way that participants' skills, personal values and feelings were shared, discussed, re-thought and re-organized as well as providing opportunities for the development of participants' rational thinking. In the author's experience of offering the practice teachers' training course, both in Hong Kong and in the PRC, it was discovered that adult learners who were engaged in a whole person style of learning found that their past experiences (including both their conceptual knowledge and feelings) are meaningful and become important resources for learning.

The more participants were willing to be involved in the learning process, the more they could actively and flexibly use different modes of learning. According to Kolb, there are four modes of learning: abstract conceptualization; active experimentation; concrete experience, and reflective observation (Kolb, 1984). *Concrete experience* and *abstract conceptualization* form the opposite poles of one dimension of learning called 'prehension'. This is concerned with the *grasping* of experience. The other two modes of learning form another dimension, called *transformation*, which denotes the ways by which grasped experience is processed. Knowledge is created when an experience is first grasped and then transformed by using one of these modes in the two dimensions of learning. For example, in learning basic communication skills, a student can listen to the teacher explaining the concepts and principles and then try these out in laboratory exercises: the student is then combining the use of abstract conceptualization and active experimentation (Tsang, 1990).

In our design for the practice teachers' training courses in Hong Kong and the PRC, we tended to require the students to begin the learning process on any topic with abstract conceptualization, as we started each section with lectures. After the introductory session, and when the group was comfortable with both the learning environment and the use of learning methods such as small group discussion, trainers' demonstrations, participants' involvement in role-playing and the Hong Kong participants' practicum, then other modes of learning were mobilized, either through a real-life situation or in a simulated environment. For example, when the participants heard about a certain skill or approach to practice teaching, they often thought that they understood the approach. However, only after trying the particular approach out themselves did they really appreciate the essence of the approach, and only then were they able to know their own strengths and weaknesses in using this method.

Responses of participants

Hong Kong

The participants in the practice teachers' training course in Hong Kong found that the requirements of this particular module were much greater than other modules, especially in terms of the amount of effort required. However, they responded well to this challenge, and most of them worked hard in the practicum. The participants expressed the view that the training was valuable – especially that the module provided an opportunity for further professional development in their career – and achieved the objectives for the particular module. After taking this course, participants realized the importance and value of fieldwork practice from an educational perspective, and they highly prized quality practice teaching and regarded it as an essential component in social work education. Although many participants felt anxious and pressurized during the practicum, they learned a lot from completing it. During the practicum, participants experienced the unique nature of a supervisory relationship. When they were in the role of practice teacher once again, they were able to re-evaluate both their own use of theories and the nature of their practice teaching. Also, they learned from the stimulating interactions with supervisees.

There was a unique side-effect for some participants in completing this training course – some course members had memories of painful experiences of being supervised on their own previous fieldwork practice; they faced and handled these vivid hurts and unhappinesses once again during the practicum. Those who were ready and had the courage to face these painful memories successfully overcame them.

The People's Republic of China

The participants of the practice teachers' training course in the PRC responded very positively to the course. They expressed the view that the course addressed the basic components of practice teaching and learning, and also that the content regarding social work education and the co-ordination of fieldwork placements was essential for them – taking into account the development of social work education in the PRC.

The participants felt that during the course they experienced a natural and gradual change of attitude towards using a range of teaching strategies, and also a greater understanding of concepts of teaching and learning. As mentioned before, initially, they objected to the idea of role-playing, discussion or 'learning from one another'. They valued greatly the inputs from the trainers, and they regarded the trainers' lectures as the most important, and in some cases, the *only* way of learning.

Starting from the third session, the trainer slowly introduced small group discussion, demonstration, question and answer sessions and role-plays in lectures; participants accepted these naturally and unconsciously. Moreover, the participants themselves celebrated their own success in the last three sessions – the skills laboratory. They had never learned and interacted like this before, in a classroom setting, but they gladly found that they could learn through role-playing and through a 'game-like' approach to teaching and learning. They also recognized that they could learn from active observation and discussion following the observation of others' performance – no matter if the performer were a trainer or a participant. They were amazed that they had the courage to be involved in role-playing and discussion in the skills laboratory. Moreover, they found that they enjoyed learning in this way.

Some participants revealed that they were frightened to learn a new professional role (being a practice teacher). However, at the end of the training course, they realized that their past training and experiences had provided them with valuable resources for their future learning and professional development in social work, although they had also discovered a brand-new and complex area for future learning.

Almost inevitably, the participants hoped that the trainers would stay longer, spend more time teaching, and that they would be able to share and discuss the course themes in greater depth and therefore have the opportunity to further their skill development. None the less, the participants fully understood the constraints upon the trainers and were grateful that in addition to the eleven three-hour sessions, the trainers provided some further sessions: there were three additional public lectures about the social work profession, social welfare and social policy, and in addition, the trainers spent evenings and lunch breaks with participants, providing for both individual and small group discussion.

Since there was no practicum arranged for participants, the trainers encouraged every participant to seek actively the opportunity to be a practice teacher as soon as possible, so that they could try out what they had learned and identify the skills, knowledge and values that they needed to develop further in the future.

Evaluation

Hong Kong

The author concurred with the Hong Kong participants' feedback that their workload during this course was too heavy, so that they felt too pressurized, and consequently, their learning was sometimes hindered. Therefore it would have been desirable either to prolong the length of the course but retain the same workload, or for participants to complete the practicum first, and then they could have used an extra month, without the pressure of a practicum, to organize their theoretical views and experiences to write up the seminar paper.

The author takes the view that in the practice teachers' training course in Hong Kong, less emphasis has been placed on the partnership with the service agencies which offer our students practice placements. This may be because colleagues from the Hong Kong training institutes have shouldered all the responsibilities and smoothed out any difficulties in the co-ordination of fieldwork placements. Hence, an analysis of learning environments and the co-ordination of fieldwork practice has been nearly invisible in this course, although it should not be forgotten that the establishment of co-ordination with agencies and the development of partnerships between agencies and training institutes are of vital importance in the process of developing both the social work profession and social work education.

The assumption that course participants are experienced social workers and consequently have developed basic competence in direct practice and inter-personal work stands in most cases. But the trainer still had to keep an open mind in observing every individual participant's strengths and weaknesses. In some cases, the trainer had to help participants to review very basic skills. The intensive and compact design of the course often seemed to leave little opportunity to meet these needs of participants.

The People's Republic of China

Although the author fully accepts that factors such as limited time, lack of sufficient staff and the difficulty of co-ordination all prevented the practice teachers' training course in the PRC incorporating a practicum, this is still a matter of regret. However, when considered overall, the design and structure of the course and the teaching and learning strategies adopted were a great success. The content which addressed the co-ordination of fieldwork practice and social work education both responded to the needs of the situation in the PRC and also introduced a conception of the interlocking nature of the relationship between training institutes and welfare agencies. This collaboration and co-operation is an essential step in development of both the social work profession and social work education. The participation of both agency staff and social work educators from training institutes on the course is one of the best ways to bring these two groups together. It offers them the same starting point for future communication and co-operation in development of the profession and education. The success of this recruitment strategy is indicated by follow-up research completed by the author one year after the practice teachers' training course in Beijing. For example, the co-ordination of practice teaching and fieldwork practice at Peking University had been developing steadily both during and after the training course. Colleagues at Peking University expressed the view that the course had provided them with the preliminary ideas about practice teaching and, most importantly, a framework to help them develop their own practice. When staff from the university co-ordinated with welfare agencies, they reached out to colleagues in agencies and tried to establish mutually agreed arrangements for fieldwork practice in agencies. Some agency staff generously helped by actively supervising students when they did their fieldwork practice. The division of labour between the practice teachers of the training institute and agency had been discussed, agreed and was tried out during the first fieldwork placement of Peking University (Ng-Wan, 1994b).

The response of the participants confirmed that the teaching and learning strategies of this course are appropriate for facilitating learning and preparing course members to be practice teachers. As in practice teaching, for most of the time, the practice teacher is not going to give lectures to students but will engage in discussion with students – resulting in the open exchange of ideas. In some instances, the practice teacher has to demonstrate skills such as role-play with the students; the course provided a good induction for practice teachers in using a variety of different teaching and learning strategies.

During the course of training, both the trainer and participants encountered issues of cultural difference. For example, in helping participants to develop skills in the 'reflection of feelings', there were no difficulties in introducing, explaining and giving examples of this skill. However, many participants could not try out this skill. The trainer discovered that the participants had seldom attended to or valued their personal feelings as part of their own social and emotional development. They tended to rationalize their feelings or just suppress them. Emotions have not been accorded priority in participants' emotional growth and in inter-personal relationships. The expression of recognition of feelings is rare and not encouraged. Hence, in Hong Kong or in Western society, the skills of 'reflection of feelings' are naturally accepted, but these skills and ideas need to be reconsidered when used in the context of Chinese society. In follow-up research on the co-ordination and supervision of social work fieldwork practice in the PRC, many interesting examples were identified that revealed the social and cultural differences between the environment of Hong Kong and the PRC, so an awareness of cultural and social characteristics in offering such courses is important for both the trainer and participants.

Conclusion

The follow-up research on the co-ordination and supervision of social work fieldwork practice in Beijing reveals that although there is still plenty of room for improvement, the experience of teaching and learning on the practice teachers' training course in Beijing was a fruitful one, both for participants and the trainer. It was especially useful to plan the initial stages of the course in collaboration with the potential participants (colleagues from Peking University). Also, the follow-up research provided a meaningful reflection of the outcome of the training course. In future, the trainer would consider involving Chinese colleagues in the whole process of planning of the course. This would add another rewarding dimension to the experience of training.

Postscript

Andrey M. Panov and Evdokia I. Kholostova

The original idea for this book developed from the Russian experience of social work education. It is fitting, therefore, that readers should know a little of that experience.

During the last four or five years, a new kind of profession has been developing in the Russian Federation – *social work*. At the same time, social work has become a new subject in the higher educational system – and a new academic speciality in the social sciences. From September 1991, more than twenty Russian institutes started basic training and re-training of specialists in social work. Currently, the number of institutes carrying out such training and re-training is about seventy.

Practice begins from the first year of students' study; usually, students have a practice placement. The main essence of this fieldwork practice is to heighten the student's knowledge about social problems and how the state attempts to solve them, to facilitate the acquisition of observation and communication skills and to learn how to provide help and support to clients. During the second year of the course, practice learning becomes more complex; the main aim of this period of practice is to provide training in the skills of social work. From the third year of the course, training in the specific specializations of social work begins. Nowadays, there are a considerable number of different specializations. During the final stage of training, a student has another period of practice which lasts for twelve weeks. So, in total, practice lasts for some twenty-two weeks during students' studies; it is therefore about 20 per cent of the whole curriculum. Is this too much or too little? It is small in comparison with many European training programmes, where, in many countries, often as much as 40–50 per cent of academic hours are devoted to practice. Hence, one of the issues for further consideration will be the possibility of enlarging the number of hours devoted to practice learning.

Looking critically at the present system of social work education in Russia, it might be said that the present system is a little rigid and inflexible. Some changes need to be made to facilitate the development of social work education – for instance, to reduce the number of specializations. It is also very important now to develop the necessary structures and methodology for the training and practice of social workers. This requires that the programmes of learning for each discipline of the main course and the various specializations are modified and amended to take account of recent developments. To achieve satisfactory programmes for learning about social work, it will be necessary to create sets of manuals, textbooks and reference books and to open experimental centres for social services, etc. (this book, *Social Work in a Changing World*, also published in Russian, will contribute to that process).

During the wide-ranging reconstruction of social welfare in the Russian Federation which has accompanied the transition to new economic structures, new social institutes and social phenomena have also been developing. Among them is social work, with its moral and intellectual potential for the promotion and creation of a social and civil society where the law is respected. Social work can become a guarantor of the constitutional rights of every individual who experiences complex problems and who needs state support and care.

Yet before social work can assume that role, there are many problems to be confronted and overcome in developing training for social workers in Russia. Each course for social workers must address some of the social problems that now face modern society in Russia.

In Russia, social work as a profession and as a science is in the early stages of development. For the future development and health of social work, it is necessary to subject recently-acquired knowledge to critical analysis, to create databases about professional social work with people and to promote the development of theory and practice about social work. That is why it is very important to use the experience of specialists' training accumulated in other spheres of knowledge (e.g. pedagogy, medicine) and to apply these disciplines to social work.

We wish to conclude by recognizing the importance of students' opinions: students often say that the fieldwork practice element of their course helps them to realize that they have made the right choice, and moreover, to understand that the profession of social work is a noble profession for enthusiastic people who ought to be professionally competent to fulfil the expectations of their work. In the words of one student:

> Poor and lonely people would be very unhappy if there was no social help. For such people, a social worker is like a light in the window.

Glossary

Rather than offer a definition of each and every word, we have decided to group similar terms together. The words cross-referenced and grouped under any one entry are not necessarily synonyms; they are linked as in a thesaurus. Even when different terms do appear to be synonymous by referring to the same activity or person (such as 'practice teaching', 'field instruction', 'student supervision'), very different meanings can be implied: the teaching of practice; instruction in fieldwork; a student supervised. One term which seems to be universal is 'student'!

academic setting see *class setting*
academic staff see *field liaison staff*
accreditation see *competencies*
agency see *practice setting*
alumni see *class setting*
assessment see *competencies*
block placement see *placement*
BSW see *acronyms*
CalSWEC see *acronyms*
CASSW see *acronyms*
CCETSW see *acronyms*
classroom see *class setting*
class setting see *class setting*
class(-based) teacher see *field liaison staff*
client see *practice setting*
college see *class setting*
college staff see *field liaison staff*
competencies see *competencies*
concurrent placement see *placement*
consultant see *consultant*

core competencies see	*competencies*
course see	*programme*
course teacher see	*field liaison staff*
CSWE see	*acronyms*
curriculum see	*placement*
DipSW see	*acronyms*
director of fieldwork see	*field liaison staff*
educational contract see	*placement*
educational establishment/ institution see	*class setting*
education programme see	*programme*
educator see	*field liaison staff*
employer see	*practice setting*
enterprise see	*practice setting*
establishment see	*class setting; practice setting*
evaluation see	*competencies*
faculty see	*field liaison staff*
field see	*practice setting*
field education see	*placement*
field educator see	*practice teacher/field instructor*
field instruction see	*placement*
field instructor see	*practice teacher/field instructor*
field liaison (staff) see	*field liaison staff*
field practice see	*placement*
field practicum manual see	*placement*
field programme see	*placement*
field setting see	*practice setting*
field supervision see	*placement*
field supervisor see	*practice teacher/field instructor*
field teacher see	*practice teacher/field instructor*
fieldwork see	*placement*
in-service training see	*programme*
institution see	*class setting; practice setting*
joint appointment see	*field liaison staff*
laboratory setting see	*class setting*
learning contract see	*placement*
learning goals or objectives see	*competencies*
lecturer see	*field liaison staff*
liaison staff see	*field liaison staff*
long-arm supervision see	*placement; practice teacher/ field instructor*
mentor see	*consultant*
MSW see	*acronyms*

organization see	*practice setting*
outcomes see	*competencies*
pedagogue see	*pedagogue*
performance criteria see	*competencies*
placement see	*placement*
placement agreement see	*placement*
placement of particular practice see	*placement*
placement team see	*field liaison staff*
polytechnic see	*class setting*
portfolio see	*competencies*
practice see	*practice*
practice assignment see	*competencies*
practice competence see	*competencies*
practice curriculum see	*placement*
practice setting see	*practice setting*
practice teacher see	*practice teacher/field instructor*
practice teaching/learning see	*placement*
practicum see	*placement*
practitioner see	*practice setting*
programme see	*programme*
programme provider see	*programme*
PTA see	*acronyms*
public welfare department see	*practice setting*
school (of social work) see	*class setting*
service organization see	*practice setting*
service setting see	*practice setting*
service user see	*practice setting*
social office see	*practice setting*
social (services) department see	*practice setting*
social welfare agency see	*practice setting*
specialist or semi-specialist	
practice teacher/field instructor see	*practice teacher/field instructor*
statutory agency see	*practice setting*
student supervisor see	*practice teacher/field instructor*
student unit organizer see	*practice teacher/field instructor*
supervision see	*placement*
training see	*programme*
training institute see	*class setting*
tutor see	*field liaison staff*
university see	*class setting*
university staff/teacher see	*field liaison staff*
voluntary (non-profit) agency see	*practice setting*
welfare agency see	*practice setting*
workload see	*practice setting*

Acronyms

The following acronyms are used in the book:

AASW

Australian Association of Social Work. This body accredits Australian schools of social work.

BSW

Bachelor of Social Work (basic qualifying degree in social work at baccalaureate level).

CalSWEC

California Social Work Education Center.

CASSW

Canadian Association of Schools of Social Work. This body accredits Canadian social work training programmes.

CCETSW

Central Council for Education and Training in Social Work. This body accredits UK social work training programmes.

CSWE

Council on Social Work Education. This body accredits social work training programmes in the USA.

DipSW

Diploma in Social Work (social work qualifying award in the UK).

MSW

Master of Social Work (postgraduate degree in social work).

PTA

Practice Teaching Award (post-qualifying award in practice teaching in the UK).

class setting

academic setting; alumni; classroom; college; educational establishment/institution; laboratory setting, polytechnic; school of social work; training institute; university

The class setting refers to the *educational establishment* or *institution* where students pursue their learning of social work. The learning in the class setting is associated with the *academic* content of the programme. This might take place in a *university, polytechnic, training institute* or *college*, and at postgraduate or undergraduate level. The word college is often used as a general term for the higher education setting. Graduates from any higher education course are sometimes referred to as *alumni*.

Colleges sometimes run classes which attempt to simulate the conditions found in practice in the agencies by creating a *laboratory setting*, often using skills training and video feedback.

competencies

accreditation; assessment; core competencies; evaluation; learning goals or objectives; outcomes; performance criteria; portfolio; practice assignment; practice competence

Social work students are *assessed* to see if they are competent to practise as social workers. The most important, generic competencies are often referred to as *core*. The practice teacher/field instructor usually makes a recommendation of 'pass', 'fail' or 'refer' for further work, or 'satisfactory'/'unsatisfactory'. In the UK, the notion of 'ready to practise' or 'not yet ready to practise' is developing.

Methods of assessment on placements vary. The most common has been a report written by the practice teacher/field instructor, which includes material and *practice assignments* by the student, such as case notes. There is an increasing move towards *competency-based assessment*, in which the *learning objectives* are carefully detailed, and the student is expected to provide evidence of achieving these objectives, using agreed *performance criteria*. In the UK, practice teachers also face an assessment if they wish to gain the Practice Teaching Award; they are assessed by means of a *portfolio*, which is a collection of evidence of ability collected over time. This system of *accreditation* is designed to guarantee the quality of practice learning available to the students.

The word *evaluation* has various meanings; sometimes it may refer to a formal measurement of a student's abilities at the end of placement, which is its most frequent usage in North America. Alternatively, it may refer to the quality of the placement (and the whole programme) in terms of helping students to achieve their *learning goals*. This is its most frequent usage in the UK.

consultant

mentor

Consultant or *mentor* usually refers to a person with considerable experience and expertise who is able to provide consultation and teaching. On training programmes for practice teachers/field instructors, a consultant or mentor helps the trainee to develop skills in practice teaching/field instruction.

field liaison staff

academic staff; class(-based) teacher; college staff; course teacher; director of field-work; educator; faculty; joint appointment; lecturer; placement team; tutor; university staff/teacher

The members of the *academic staff* at the educational establishment (university, college, etc.) who are responsible for communication with practice teachers/field instructors are called field liaison staff. This responsibility might fall to one or two people or be shared by a team of academic staff (*placement team*). The person with primary responsibility is sometimes designated the *director of fieldwork*. The term *tutor* is used in the UK to refer to a member of the *university staff* who is responsible for providing college support to the student while on placement.

There are other *class-based teachers*, members of the academic *faculty*, who are not involved in the student's learning outside the educational establishment. In the UK and Australasia, the general term for all college-based teachers, whether involved in liaison or not, is *lecturer*.

Some educational establishments have set up *joint appointments* with social work agencies, so that one person (or sometimes a pair) works partly as a member of faculty at the university and partly as a practitioner in the agency.

pedagogue

In the English-speaking world, there is no professional group known as pedagogues. In much of the European mainland, this is a distinctive profession, working with people in ways that are analogous to social work, but with a greater emphasis on the educative functions.

placement

block placement; concurrent placement; curriculum; educational contract; field education; field instruction; field practice; field practicum manual; field programme; field supervision; fieldwork; learning contract; long-arm supervision; placement agreement; placement of particular practice; practice curriculum; practice learning; practice teaching; practicum; student supervision

A placement is the period of learning that occurs when a student is located in a social work agency. What the practice teacher/field instructor does is referred to as *practice teaching, student supervision* or *field instruction*; what the student does is referred to as *practice learning*. Although these terms refer to the same activity, there are subtle differences between supervision, instruction and teaching.

Practicum is a North American term which brings together the notion of the placement and also what is to be learned on placement – the *practice curriculum*. The practice curriculum might be designed for general learning about social work or for a particular area of practice (such as child protection or mental health).

Most programmes provide a placement handbook or *field practicum manual* to guide the placement, with information about the *educational contract* or *placement agreement* which spells out expectations for the placement and the areas of practice to be learned (the *curriculum*), the regulations for assessing the level of a student's practice competence, and the placement arrangements, such as the required number of meetings between university staff, practice teachers/field instructors and students during a placement.

Arrangements for placements differ: for example, the overall length and whether they are *block* (five days a week) or *concurrent* (some part of the week on placement and some part in the class setting). Some students receive teaching in the form of *long-arm supervision* from a practitioner who is not their day-to-day supervisor.

Note: the term placement is also used by practitioners to refer to children placed in foster care, residential care, etc.

practice

This term is used in an alarming number of different ways in social work. At its most general, it refers to what social workers do (social work practice), and therefore what students need to learn to do. As a result, **practice setting** refers to the learning on placements in social work agencies. However, some social work programmes have practice classes which are based in the educational setting; these are designed to prepare the student for the practical work on the placement.

As a verb, 'to practise' can mean either to be engaged in social work practice, or to be rehearsing something – as in 'practice makes perfect'. Practice is also often put in opposition to theory, with a notion that theory takes place in the educational setting and practice in the work setting. This division is increasingly being challenged.

practice setting

agency; client; employer; enterprise; establishment; field; field setting; institution;

organization; practitioner; public welfare department; service organization; service setting; service user; social office; social (services) department; social welfare agency; statutory agency; voluntary (non-profit) agency; welfare agency; workload

The practice setting refers to the *agency, enterprise* or *organization* where students pursue their learning about social work practice (in other words, where the student is placed). The agency's principal responsibilities are to its *clients* and *service users,* not the student. The professional staff in the agency are often called *practitioners,* and some of these practitioners have students placed with them, as well as continuing to work with their *workload* of clients or service users.

Examples of types of practice setting are: residential care, group care, community work, children and family settings, hospitals, probation and correctional work. Generic terms for these kinds of agencies include *public welfare departments, social (services) departments* and *welfare agencies;* those with specific legal responsibilities, such as child protection, are called *statutory agencies. Voluntary agencies* are those which are non-governmental and do not make a profit. Agencies are sometimes characterized as urban or rural, and described along ethnic lines (for example, a Maori agency).

The practice setting is often summarized as the *field* – a location for social work students to learn about social work practice. The term field is most frequently used to distinguish from the class as a setting for learning.

practice teacher/field instructor

field educator; field supervisor; field teacher; long-arm supervisor; specialist or semi-specialist practice teacher; student supervisor; student unit organizer

These terms all refer to the person in a social work agency who has responsibility for teaching a student who is placed there. The term field instructor is usually found in North America; in the UK and New Zealand, the term has changed from *student supervisor* to practice teacher. Just to confuse matters, in the North American context, the term practice teacher is used to refer to persons in the educational setting who teach classes in social work practice! In this book, the term is used as it would be in the United Kingdom – except where stated otherwise.

Some students receive teaching from a person who is not involved in direct day-to-day supervision of their work, and this person is referred to as a *long-arm supervisor or teacher.* Some practitioners specialize in practice teaching/field instruction, so that – although they are employed in a social work agency – they spend a proportion of their time (*semi-specialist*) or all their time (*specialist*) teaching students. Sometimes, this might be organized around a *student unit* within the agency.

programme

course; education programme; in-service training; programme provider; training course

Together, the class-based learning (in the educational establishment) and agency-based learning (in the social work organization) make up the training programme; the balance of learning in the educational setting and the work setting varies, but can often be half and half. *Programme providers* is a collective term for all those who are responsible for the training programme.

In North America, the term *course* is used as a precise term to refer to specific elements in the programme; in the UK and Australasia, it is used to refer to the whole programme (although it often implicitly excludes the placement components, as in 'we haven't done that on the course yet', meaning the classroom).

There can be a tension between the training components of a programme (to produce competent agency workers) and the educative elements (to develop critical professionals). Some agencies provide *in-service training*, where their employees receive training while retaining a salary or stipend from the agency, and often the training is delivered by the agency itself.

Biographies of contributors

Svein Bøe works in the Department of Health Social Studies at the Telemark College in Skien, Norway. He graduated in 1976 from the University of Oslo with a degree in social pedagogy (minor subjects: sociology and history).

His experience has involved teaching and counselling at different educational levels. This includes five years' teaching and counselling at high school level, seven years' counselling work at a psychiatric agency, two years at the counselling department for high school education, and four years as a senior lecturer at college level.

From 1989 to 1992, he completed two studies concerning the working conditions of pupils in two different high schools. At present, he is working with two colleagues on a study of how the practice field affects students' learning processes in the area of social studies.

Marion Bogo, MSW, Adv. DipSW is Acting Dean and Associate Professor, and former Practicum Co-ordinator, at the Faculty of Social Work, University of Toronto. Professor Bogo's academic, educational, practice and consultative activities focus on social work education and social work practice in national and international contexts, including field practicum models, linkages to ethno-racial communities, and the development of professional competence and professional identity. She was co-principal investigator on two Canadian research projects on field education which led to the development of a teaching model and a training guide. Professor Bogo has been a consultant on field education programmes to schools of social work in the United States, Canada and Asia, particularly Japan and Sri Lanka.

Mark Doel is a lecturer in applied social studies at the University of Sheffield and Co-director of the Diploma in Practice Teaching. He is developing open and distance learning materials and programmes in the field of practice learning. During the 1980s, he had a joint appointment as a social worker with Sheffield Family and Community Services (a public welfare agency), where he was also a practice teacher. In 1991, he headed a research project in systems change for families with children with developmental disabilities at Portland State University, Oregon. As an independent training consultant, he is developing a number of post-qualifying programmes, including task-centred social work and group work skills. His published work in practice teaching includes a model for curriculum development in the field. Recent international work has included the making of a Russian training video for the education of social workers in countries of the former Soviet Union.

Bart Grossman, MSW, PhD is founding Executive Director of the California Social Work Education Center. He is Associate Adjunct Professor at the University of California at Berkeley School of Social Welfare and has been Field Director (currently on leave) for twelve years. Dr Grossman was a founder of the National Fieldwork Symposium and the North American Network of Field Directors and is a member of the Council on Social Work Education Commission on Fieldwork. He has published extensively on fieldwork in social work education, including *Field Education in Social Work: Contemporary Issues and Trends*, with Dean Schneck and Ronnie Glassman.

Karen Heycox, BSW, MA is a lecturer in the School of Social Work, University of New South Wales, where she has a major responsibility for practice learning on the Bachelor of Social Work course. She teaches a range of other subjects on the course, including a Women and Social Work elective. After many years as a practitioner in a variety of fields using a range of methods, she joined the university staff. She has worked mainly in health settings and has a special interest in older people, particularly women. She has been researching in the area of practice learning for a number of years and regards it as pivotal in the training of social workers.

Lesley Hughes, BA, BSoc. Stud., MSW, Cert HEd is a lecturer in the School of Social Work, University of New South Wales, where she has a major responsibility for practice learning in the Bachelor of Social Work course. She teaches a number of other subjects on the course, including a Women and Social Work elective. She came to the university after many years as a practitioner in a variety of fields using a range of methods. She has also worked in child and family welfare, is currently researching in the area of gender perspectives in Australian welfare history and has been researching in the area of practice learning for a number of years.

Evdokia I. Kholostova is currently Director of the National Institute for Social Work in Moscow. Previously, she worked at the Russian Social

Institute, teaching social work. She is particularly interested in the organization, development and theory of social work.

Iris Shuk-fong Ng-Wan is a lecturer in the Department of Applied Social Studies of Hong Kong Polytechnic University, Hong Kong.

She was born in Hong Kong, and she received her Bachelor of Social Science (Hons) with a Social Work major in the Chinese University of Hong Kong. She gained her Master of Science (Econ.) in Applied Social Studies at the University of Wales, College of Cardiff, United Kingdom.

She was a social worker of front-line practice for seven years, undertaking one year's part-time practice teaching at the Hong Kong Polytechnic (recently renamed the Hong Kong Polytechnic University), and is now a lecturer in the Hong Kong Polytechnic University.

She was a columnist for a youth magazine for several years and published three books on themes of personal growth, dating and courtship for youths in Hong Kong. She started to teach, research and write on practice teaching from 1991. She has been actively involved in co-ordinating social work students' fieldwork placements and teaching practice during the last five years. Being committed to the study and improvement of practice teaching, she had been enthusiastic in training of practice teachers in Hong Kong as well as in the People's Republic of China.

Andrey M. Panov is Deputy Minister at the Ministry of Social Protection for the Population of the Russian Federation. He is a Doctor of Pedagogy and has a particular interest in social work with children and families. He has been very involved in the international development of social work.

Robin Perry is currently a doctoral student at the School of Social Welfare at the University of California at Berkeley. In addition, he serves as a research assistant with the California Social Work Education Center. He obtained his MSW from the University of Windsor and received practice training at the Center for the Child and the Family at the University of Michigan. He has several years' experience in the public child welfare and family violence fields in Canada.

Shulamit Ramon is currently Professor of Interprofessional Health and Social Studies at Anglia University, and Visiting Professor at the Department of Social Work and Social Administration in the Moscow School of Social and Economic Sciences. She is also the co-ordinator of the TEMPUS programme to establish social work as a higher education discipline in the Ukraine. She has published extensively on mental health policies and practice in Britain and Europe, on community care and on social work education.

Ivo Reznicek was born in Czechoslovakia, where he graduated from Cornenius University in Bratislava and briefly worked as a psychologist, both there and in Brno. Following his emigration to the United States, he practised psychotherapy and then received his Doctorate in Social Policy and Research from the University of Pennsylvania in Philadelphia. Most of his work there was devoted to the study of mental health policy and programmes. Later, he taught research and social policy at the Catholic University in Washington, DC. For two years, he also taught social work practice and social policy and did research on homelessness and unemployment at Masaryk University in Brno. Experience from his sojourn forms the basis of his chapter. Following his return to the United States, he has been involved in cross-cultural work and development.

Gayla Rogers is an Associate Professor and Director of Field Education, Faculty of Social Work, the University of Calgary. She has pursued her interest in field education through research, presentations and publications. She has developed and taught courses and workshops for field instructors, has been a Master Teacher, and has provided consultation to social work programmes in Canada, the USA and the UK. She completed a PhD in 1995 at the University of Newcastle upon Tyne (UK), where she compared the training of field instructors in Canada and the UK.

Terry Sacco has been teaching at the University of the Witwatersrand, Johannesburg, since 1985. Areas of teaching include: preparing for practice; anti-oppressive social work practice; social work values and spirituality; social transformation; school social work, and the sociology of education. She is a founder member of Concerned Social Workers, an organization which politicized welfare in South Africa during the 1980s, and of the Detainee Counselling Service, an organization which provided services to ex-detainees and victims of political violence. She was also an activist within the anti-apartheid movement, specifically within the detainee movement, after she spent a time in solitary confinement under the Detention Laws of South Africa.

Steven Shardlow is the Associate Director of the MA/Diploma in Applied Social Studies course at the University of Sheffield, where he is also Co-director of the Diploma in Practice Teaching course. Since 1989, he has been the Chairperson of the Association of Teachers in Social Work Education. He is Joint Editor of the journal *Issues in Social Work Education*. His teaching interests, at Bachelors, Masters and Doctoral levels, include social work with children and families, especially child abuse; social work and 'race'; social work ethics and theories; practice learning in social work, and values and society. Current research interests are in the following areas: comparative social work practice; social work education, especially practice learning, and social work values and ethics. He has published widely in these fields, and his work has been translated into several languages.

R.R. Singh is Professor at the Department of Social Work, University of Delhi, India. He was the head of this department from 1987 to 1990. From 1960 to 1975, Dr Singh served on the faculty of two other schools of social work in India. He was the Convenor of the Panel on Social Work Education of the University Grants Commission from 1991 to 1993 and is currently the President of the Association of Schools of Social Work in India.

Harry Walker is a social worker with 25 years' experience who has been teaching a university social work course for five years. He was educated in rural New Zealand and raised by a mother and grandmother along with seven others in a 'rich' family which was both cash- and asset-poor! He gained a government bursary to attend university to attain a social work qualification and would never have attended university otherwise. He has worked with urban gangs, the unemployed, school drop-outs and alternative schools. His research interest area is the healing processes used by indigenous peoples and the social structures within which these processes are carried out, along with non-Western theories of social work practice and philosophy. Prior to his present employment, he worked as a Maori Welfare and Community Officer with the Department of Maori Affairs, a Tutor and Community Liaison Worker with the Wellington Polytechnic, a self-employed wood merchant, a Department of Social Welfare Social Work Trainer, and a Maori (Indigenous) Social Policy Advisor for the Department of Social Welfare.

Bibliography

Chapter 1

Syson, L. and Baginsky, M. (1981), *Learning to Practise: A study of practice placements in courses leading to the Certificate of Qualification in Social Work*, London: Central Council for Education and Training in Social Work.

Chapter 2

Arkava, M. and Brennen, E. (eds) (1976), *Competency Based Education for Social Work: Evaluation and curriculum issues*, New York, NY: Council on Social Work Education.

Barbour, R. (1984), 'Social Work Education: Tackling the theory–practice dilemma', *British Journal of Social Work*, 14 (6): 557–77.

Basso, R. (1987), 'Teacher and Student Problem-solving Activities in Educational Supervisory Sessions', *Journal of Social Work Education*, 23 (3): 67–73.

Belenky, M., Clinchy, B., Goldberg, N. and Tarule, J. (1986), *Women's Ways of Knowing: The development of self, voice, and mind*, New York, NY: Basic Books.

Bell, L. and Webb, S. (1992), 'The Invisible Art of Teaching for Practice: Social workers' perceptions of taking students on placement', *Social Work Education*, 11 (1): 28–46.

Berengarten, S. (1957), 'Identifying Learning Patterns of Individual Students: An exploratory study', *Social Service Review*, 31: 407–17.

Blyth, E. (1980), 'The Dilemma of Practice Teaching', *Community Care*, 9 October: 28–9.

Bogo, M. and Power, R. (1992), 'New Field Instructors' Perceptions of Institutional Supports for their Roles', *Journal of Social Work Education* 28 (2): 178–89.

Borland, M., Hudson, A., Hughes, B. and Worrall, A. (1988), 'An Approach to the Management of the Assessment of Practice Placements', *British Journal of Social Work*, 18 (3): 269–88.

Borrill, W., O'Sullivan, P. and Sleeman, S. (1991), *The Management and Reduction of Failing Placements: Report to the Department of Health*, Southampton: Department of Social Work Studies, University of Southampton.

Brandon, D. (1976), 'Out of the Lecture Room, into the Field', *Community Care*, 6 October.

Brennen, E. (1982), 'Evaluation of Field Teaching and Learning', in Sheafor, B. and Jenkins, L. (eds), *Quality Field Instruction in Social Work: Program development and maintenance*, New York, NY: Longman: 76–97.

Brookfield, S. (1986), *Understanding and Facilitating Adult Learning*, San Francisco, CA: Jossey-Bass.

Butler, B. and Elliott, D. (1985), *Teaching and Learning for Practice*, Aldershot: Gower.

Carew, R. (1979), 'The Place of Knowledge in Social Work Activity', *British Journal of Social Work*, 9 (3): 349–64.

Cassidy, H. (1969), 'Role and Function of the Coordinator or Director of Field Instruction', in Jones, B. (ed.), *Current Patterns in Field Instruction in Graduate Social Work Education*, New York, NY: Council on Social Work Education.

Casson, P. (1982), *Social Work Courses: Their structure and content*, Study 5, London: Central Council for Education and Training in Social Work.

CCETSW (1981), *Guidelines for Courses Leading to the Certificate of Qualification in Social Work* (revised edn) Paper 15.1, London: Central Council for Education and Training in Social Work.

CCETSW (1991a), *DipSW Rules and Requirements for the Diploma in Social Work* (2nd edn) Paper 30, London: Central Council for Education and Training in Social Work.

CCETSW (1991b), *Improving Standards in Practice Learning: Requirements and guidance for the approval of agencies and the accreditation and training of practice teachers* (2nd edn) Paper 26.3, London: Central Council for Education and Training in Social Work.

Clancy, C. (1985), 'The Use of the Andragogical Approach in the Educational Function of Supervision in Social Work', *The Clinical Supervisor*, 3 (1): 75–86.

Clapton, G. (1989), *Support Groups for Individual Practice Teachers*, London: National Organisation for Practice Teaching.

Cocozzelli, C. and Constable, R. (1985), 'An Empirical Analysis of the Relation Between Theory and Practice in Clinical Social Work', *Journal of Social Service Research*, 9 (1): 47–64.

Collins, S. and Ottley, G. (1986), 'Practice Teaching: Reflections, steps before reflection and some steps for the future', *Social Work Education*, 6 (1): 11–14.

Coulshed, V. (1986), 'What do Social Work Students Give to Training?', *Issues in Social Work Education*, 6 (2): 119–27.

Curnock, K. and Hardiker, P. (1979), *Towards Practice Theory: Skills and methods in social assessments*, London: Routledge and Kegan Paul.

Davies, H. and Kinoch, H. (1991), 'Improving Social Work Practice Teaching: Steps towards the goal', *Social Work Education*, 10 (2): 20–37.

Davies, M. (1981), 'What We Have to Learn About Social Work Education', *Community Care*, 15 January: 18–22.

Dwyer, M. and Urbanowski, M. (1981), 'Field Practice Criteria: A valuable teaching/learning tool in undergraduate social work education', *Journal of Education for Social Work*, 17 (1): 5–11.

Evans, D. (1987), 'The Centrality of Practice in Social Work Education', *Issues in Social Work Education*, 7 (2): 83–101.

Faria, G., Brownstein, C. and Smith, H. (1988), 'A Survey of Field Instructors' Perceptions of the Liaison Role', *Journal of Social Work Education*, 24 (2): 135–44.

Fellin, P. (1982), 'Responsibilities of the School: Administrative support of field instruction', in Sheafor, B. and Jenkins, L. (eds), *Quality Field Instruction in Social Work*, New York, NY: Longman: 101–15.

Fisher, T. (1990), 'Competence in Social Work Practice Teaching', *Social Work Education*, 9 (2): 9–24.

Fortune, A., Feathers, C., Rook, S., Scrimenti, R., Smollen, P., Stemerman, B. and Tucker, E. (1985), 'Student Satisfaction with the Field Placement', *Journal of Social Work Education*, 21 (3): 92–104.

Foulds, J., Sanders, A. and Williams, J. (1991), 'Co-ordinating Learning: The future of practice teaching', *Social Work Education*, 10 (2): 60–8.

Fox, R. and Guild, P. (1987), 'Learning Styles: Their relevance to clinical supervision', *The Clinical Supervisor*, 5 (3): 65–77.

Gardiner, D. (1984a), 'Learning for Transfer', *Issues in Social Work Education*, 4 (2): 95–105.

Gardiner, D. (1984b) 'Social Work Education and the Transfer of Learning – A comment', *Issues in Social Work Education*, 4 (1): 55–7.

Gardiner, D. (1987), 'Towards Internal Monitoring and Evaluation of Social Work Courses', *Issues in Social Work Education*, 7 (1): 53–5.

Gardiner, D. (1989), *The Anatomy of Supervision: Developing learning and professional competence for social work students*, Milton Keynes: Society for Research into Higher Education/Open University Press.

Gelfand, B., Rohrich, S., Nividon, P. and Starak, I. (1975), 'An Andragogical Application to the Training of Social Workers', *Journal of Social Work Education*, 11 (3): 55–61.

Goldmeier, J. (1983), 'Educational Assessment, Teaching Styles and Case Assignment in Clinical Field Work', *Arete*, 8: 1–12.

Gordon, M. (1982), 'Responsibilities of the School: Maintenance of the field program', in Sheafor, B. and Jenkins, L. (eds), *Quality Field Instruction in Social Work*, New York, NY: Longman: 116–35.

Gray, I. (1987), 'Some Key Problems in the Current Organisation of Practice Teaching', in CCETSW (ed.), *Accreditation of Agencies and Practice Teachers in Social Work Education: Workshop papers* (Supplement to Paper 26.1), London: Central Council for Education and Training in Social Work.

Gray, J. (1986), 'Learning for Transfer – The special case of practising social work in different countries', *Issues in Social Work Education*, 5 (2): 145–9.

Gregorc, A. (1982), *Gregorc Style Delineator: A self-assessment instrument for adults*, Columbia, CT: Gregorc Associates.

Grimwood, C. and Fletcher, J. (1987), 'The Growing Problem of Attempting to Find Placements for Students', *Social Work Today*, 18 (38): 12–13.

Hamilton, N. and Else, J. (1983), *Designing Field Education: Philosophy, structure, and process*, Springfield, IL: Charles C. Thomas.

Hardiker, P. (1981), 'Heart or Head – The function and role of knowledge in social work', *Issues in Social Work Education*, 1 (2): 85–111.

Harris, R. (1983), 'Social Work Education and the Transfer of Learning', *Issues in Social Work Education*, 3 (2): 103–17.

Hearn, J. (1982), 'The Problem(s) of Theory and Practice in Social Work and Social Work Education', *Issues in Social Work Education*, 2 (2): 95–118.

Hersh, A. (1984), 'Teaching the Theory and Practice of Student Supervision: A short-term model based on principles of adult education', *The Clinical Supervisor*, 2 (1): 29–44.

Howe, D. (1990–91), 'Three Ways to Train a Social Worker', *Social Work and Social Sciences Review*, 2 (1): 45–50.

Hutchison, E. (1977), 'Social Work Education: A view from the field', *Social Work Today*, 2 February: 10–12.

James, A., Morrissey, M. and Wilson, K. (1990), 'The Resource Implications of Practice Placements', *Issues in Social Work Education*, 10 (1&2): 92–111.

Johnson, S. (1989), *Implications of Better Practice Teacher Use: Project Report from West Midlands Teaching Consortium*, Rugby: Central Council for Education and Training in Social Work.

Kadushin, A. (1976), *Supervision in Social Work,* New York, NY: Columbia University Press.

Kadushin, A. (1992), *Supervision in Social Work* (3rd edn), New York, NY: Columbia University Press.

Knight, C. and Glazer-Semmel, E. (1990), *The Skills of Field Instruction: A study of BSW and MSW students' perceptions of effective supervision,* paper presented at the 36th Annual Program Meeting of the Council on Social Work Education, Reno, NV.

Knowles, M. (1970), *The Modern Practice of Adult Education: Andragogy versus pedagogy,* New York, NY: Association Press.

Knowles, M. (1972), 'Innovations in Teaching Styles and Approaches Based Upon Adult Learning', *Journal of Education for Social Work,* 8 (2): 32–9.

Kolb, D. (1976), *Learning Styles Inventory Technical Manual,* Boston, MA: McBer.

Kondrat, M. (1992a), *Education for Reflective Practice: Formal, substantive, and critical rationality in field education,* paper presented at the 38th Annual Program Meeting of the Council on Social Work Education, Kansas City, MO.

Kondrat, M. (1992b), 'Reclaiming the Practical: Formal and substantive rationality in social work practice', *Social Service Review,* 66 (2): 237–55.

Kruzich, J., Friesen, B. and Van Soest, D. (1986), 'Assessment of Student and Faculty Learning Styles: Research and application', *Journal of Social Work Education,* 22 (3): 22–30.

Lacerte, J., Ray, J. and Irwin, L. (1989), 'Recognizing the Educational Contributions of Field Instructors', *Journal of Teaching in Social Work,* 3 (1): 99–113.

Larsen, J. and Hepworth, D. (1982), 'Enhancing the Effectiveness of Practicum Instruction: An empirical study', *Journal of Education for Social Work,* 18 (2): 50–8.

Lemberger, J. and Marshack, E. (1991), 'Educational Assessment in the Field: An opportunity for teacher–learner mutuality', in Schneck, D., Grossman, B. and Glassman, U. (eds), *Field Education in Social Work,* Dubuque, IA: Kendall/Hunt: 187–97.

Mezirow, J. et al. (1990), *Fostering Critical Reflection in Adulthood: A guide to transformative and emancipatory learning,* San Francisco, CA: Jossey-Bass.

Mitchell, D. (1992), 'Practice what you Teach', *Community Care,* 5 November: 21–2.

Munson, C. (ed.) (1979), *Social Work Supervision: Classic statements and critical issues,* New York, NY: The Free Press.

Myers, I. (1976), *Introduction to Type,* Gainesville, FL: Center for Applications of Psychological Type.

Paley, J. (1984), 'The Devolution of Social Work Knowledge', *Social Work Education,* 3 (2): 19–24.

Paley, J. (1987), 'Social Work and the Sociology of Knowledge', *British Journal of Social Work,* 17 (3): 169–86.

Papell, C. (1978), 'A Study of Styles of Learning for Direct Social Work Practice', *Dissertation Abstracts International,* 39: 1842A–1843A.

Papell, C. and Skolnik, L. (1992), 'The Reflective Practitioner: A contemporary paradigm's relevance for social work education', *Journal of Social Work Education,* 28 (1): 18–26.

Parsloe, P. (1977), 'How Training may "Unfit" People', *Social Work Today,* 9: 15–18.

Payne, M. (1990), 'Relationships Between Theory and Practice in Social Work: Educational implications', *Issues in Social Work Education,* 10 (1&2): 3–23.

Perry, F. (1990), *Improving Practice Placement Provision: Report of feasibility study on the establishment of a clearing house for practice placements,* Leeds: Central Council for Education and Training in Social Work.

Pettes, D. (1967), *Supervision in Social Work,* London: Allen & Unwin.

Pettes, D. (1979), *Staff and Student Supervision: A task-centred approach*, London: Allen & Unwin.

Rachlis, R. (1988), 'The Social Work Practicum: Who should deliver it?', *Canadian Social Work Review*, 5 (1): 91–105.

Ramsden, P. (1985), 'Student Learning Research: Retrospect and prospect', *Higher Education Research and Development*, 4 (1): 51–69.

Raskin, M., Skolnik, L. and Wayne, J. (1991), 'An International Perspective of Field Education', *Journal of Social Work Education*, 27 (3): 258–70.

Raynor, P. (1992), 'Needs and Resources in Practice Learning: Findings from the Welsh placement survey', *Social Work Education*, 11 (1): 16–27.

Rodway, P. and Rogers, G. (1993), 'A Comparison of the Academic and Articulated Approaches to Field Education', *The Clinical Supervisor*, 11 (2): 37–54.

Rogers, G. and McDonald, L. (1989a), *Field Instruction Methods for Agency Field Supervisors*, paper presented at the Canadian Association of Schools of Social Work Annual Meeting and Conference, Quebec City, PQ.

Rogers, G. and McDonald, L. (1989b), 'Field Supervisors: Is a social work degree necessary?', *Canadian Social Work Review*, 6 (2): 203–21.

Rosenblatt, A. and Mayer, J. (1975), 'Objectionable Supervisory Styles: Students' views', *Social Work*, 2: 184–9.

Rosenblum, A. and Raphael, F. (1983), 'The Role and Function of the Faculty Field Liaison', *Journal of Social Work Education*, 19 (1): 68–78.

Rosenfeld, D. (1988), 'Field Instructor Turnover', *The Clinical Supervisor*, 6 (3/4): 187–218.

Rothman, J. (1977), 'Development of a Profession: Field instruction correlates', *Social Service Review*, 51 (2): 289–310.

Rubenstein, G. (1992), 'Supervision and Psychotherapy: Toward redefining the differences', *The Clinical Supervisor*, 10 (2): 97–116.

Saari, C. (1989), 'The Process of Learning in Clinical Social Work', *Smith College Studies in Social Work*, 60 (1): 35–49.

Sawdon, D. (1986), *Making Connections in Practice Teaching*, London: National Institute for Social Work.

Sawdon, D. (1991), 'Practice Teaching in the 1990s: An exercise in conflict-management', *Issues in Social Work Education*, 11 (1): 69–84.

Sawdon, D. and Sawdon, C. (1987), 'What Makes for a Good Practice Learning Experience?', *Social Work Education*, 6 (3): 3–5.

Schön, D. (1983), *The Reflective Practitioner: How professionals think in action*, New York, NY: Basic Books.

Schön, D. (1987), *Educating the Reflective Practitioner: Toward a new design for teaching and learning in the professions*, San Francisco, CA and London: Jossey-Bass.

Secker, J. (1992), 'More than Tea and Sympathy', *Community Care*, 2 July: 12–13.

Shapiro, C. (1989), 'Burnout in Social Work Field Instructors', in Raskin, M. (ed.), *Empirical Studies in Field Instruction*, New York, NY: Haworth Press: 237–47.

Shardlow, S. (1988), 'The Economics of Student Help', *Insight*, 3 (23): 24–5.

Shatz, E. (1989), Preface, in Raskin, M. (ed.), *Empirical Studies in Field Instruction*, New York, NY: Haworth Press: xxv–xxvii.

Sheldon, B. (1978), 'Theory and Practice in Social Work: A re-examination of a tenuous relationship', *British Journal of Social Work*, 8 (1): 1–22.

Sibeon, R. (1982), 'Theory–practice Symbolisations: A critical review of the Hardiker/Davies debate', *Issues in Social Work Education*, 2 (2): 119–47.

Sibeon, R. (1989–90), 'Comments on the Structure and Forms of Social Work Knowledge', *Social Work and Social Sciences Review*, 1 (1): 29–44.

Siporin, M. (1982), 'The Process of Field Instruction', in Sheafor, B. and Jenkins, L. (eds), *Quality Field Instruction in Social Work*, New York, NY: Longman: 175–97.

Skolnik, L. (1989), 'Field Instruction in the 1980s – Realities, issues, and problem-solving strategies', in Raskin, M. (ed.), *Empirical Studies in Field Instruction*, New York, NY: Haworth Press: 47–75.

Slater, P. (1992), ' "What's in it for practice agencies?": Joint provision of social work education and training', *Journal of Training and Development*, 2 (3): 41–5.

Smith, H., Faria, G. and Brownstein, C. (1986), 'Social Work Faculty in the Role of Liaison: A field study', *Journal of Social Work Education*, 22 (3): 68–78.

St John, D. (1975), 'Goal-directed Supervision of Social Work Students in Field Placement', *Journal of Education for Social Work*, 11 (3): 89–94.

Syson, L. and Baginsky, M. (1981), *Learning to Practise: A study of practice placements in courses leading to the Certificate of Qualification in Social Work*, Study 3, London: Central Council for Education and Training in Social Work.

Taylor, K. and Marienau, C. (eds) (1995), *Learning Environments of Women's Adult Development: Bridges toward change*, San Francisco, CA: Jossey-Bass.

Thompson, N., Osada, M. and Anderson, B. (1990), *Practice Teaching in Social Work*, Birmingham: PEPAR.

Timms, N. (1970), *Social Work – An outline for the intending student*, London: Routledge & Kegan Paul.

Tolson, E. and Kopp, J. (1988), 'The Practicum: Clients, problems, interventions and influences on student practice', *Journal of Social Work Education*, 24 (2): 123–34.

Towle, C. (1954), *The Learner in Education for the Professions as Seen in Education for Social Work*, Chicago, IL: University of Chicago Press.

Watt, S. and Thomlison, B. (1981), 'Trends and Issues in the Field Preparation of Social Work Manpower: Secondary analysis of data', *Canadian Journal of Social Work Education*, 7 (3): 1–18.

Webb, N. (1988), 'The Role of the Field Instructor in the Socialization of Students', *Social Casework*, 69 (1): 35–40.

Whittington, C. (1986), 'Literature Review: Transfer of learning in social work education', *British Journal of Social Work*, 16 (6): 571–7.

Whittington, C. and Holland, R. (1985), 'A Framework for Theory in Social Work', *Issues in Social Work Education*, 5 (1): 25–49.

Williamson, H., Jefferson, R., Johnson, S. and Shabbaz, A. (1989), *Assessment of Practice: A perennial concern?*, Cardiff: School of Social and Administrative Studies, University of Wales.

Young, P. (1967), *The Student and Supervision in Social Work Education*, London: Routledge & Kegan Paul.

Chapter 3

Ba, S.W. (1973), *The Concept of Negritude in the Poetry of Leopold Sedar Senghor*, Princeton, NJ: Princeton University Press.

Barretta-Herman, A. (1994), 'Revisioning the Community as Provider: Restructuring New Zealand's social services', *International Social Work*, 37 (1): 7–21.

Constable, R.T. (1983), 'Values, Religion, and Social Work Practice', *Social Thought*, 9: 29–41.

Faver, C.A. (1986), 'Religion, Research and Social Work', *Social Thought*, 18: 20–9.

Fox, M. (1988), *The Coming of the Cosmic Christ*, New York, NY: HarperCollins.

Goldstein, H. (1986), 'Toward the Integration of Theory and Practice: A humanistic approach', *Social Work*, 5: 352–7.

Gowdy, E.A. (1994), 'From Technical Rationality to Participating Consciousness', *Social Work*, 4: 362–70.

Mbiti, J. (1971), *African Religions and Philosophy*, London: Society for Promoting Christian Knowledge.

Moore, T. (1992), *Care of the Soul*, New York, NY: HarperCollins.

Poertner, J. (1994), 'Popular Education in Latin America: A technology for the North?', *International Social Work*, 37 (3): 265–75.

Saleeby, D. (1994), 'Culture, Theory, and Narrative: The intersection of meanings in practice', *Social Work*, 39 (4): 351–9.

Sengor, L.S. (1966), 'Negritude', *Optima*, 16: 1–8.

Setiloane, G.M. (1986), *African Theology: An Introduction*, Johannesburg: Skotaville.

Sherraden, M.S. and Martin, J.J. (1994), 'Social Work with Immigrants: International issues in service delivery', *International Social Work*, 37 (4): 369–84.

Shutte, A. (1993), *Philosophy for Africa*, Cape Town: UCT Press.

Toor, D. (1994), *Songs from the Mountains*, New York, NY: St Martin's Press.

Chapter 4

Abell, N. and McDonnell, J.R. (1990), 'Preparing for Practice: Motivations, expectations, and aspirations of the MSW class of 1990', *Journal of Social Work Education*, 26 (1): 57–64.

Alicea, V.G. (1978), *Community Participation, Planning and Influence: Toward a conceptual model of coalition planning*, Doctoral Dissertation, New York, NY: Columbia University.

Butler, A.C. (1990), 'A Re-evaluation of Social Work Students' Career Interests', *Journal of Social Work Education*, 26 (1): 45–56.

CalSWEC (1991), 'Results from the California Work Force Study', Berkeley, CA: California Social Work Education Center, unpublished.

Golden, D., Pins, A. and Jones, W. (1972), *Students in Schools of Social Work: A study of characteristics and factors affecting career choice and practice concentration*, New York, NY: Council on Social Work Education.

Grossman, B., Laughlin, S. and Specht, H. (1992), 'Building the Commitment of Social Work Education to Publicly Supported Social Services: The California model', in Briar, K.H., Hansen, V.H. and Harris, N. (eds), *New Partnerships: Proceedings from the National Public Welfare Training Symposium 1991*, North Miami, FL: Florida International University: 55–72.

Harris, N., Kirk, R.S. and Besharov, D. (1993), *State Child Welfare Agency Staff Survey Report*, Washington, DC: National Child Welfare Leadership Center.

Hendrickson, R.M. and Axelson, L.J. (1985), 'Middle-class Attitudes Toward the Poor: Are they changing?', *Social Service Review*, 59 (2): 295–304.

Imbrogno, S. (1994), 'The Emergence of the Profession of Social Work in the Russian Republic', in Constable, R. and Mehta, V. (eds), *Education for Social Work in Eastern Europe: Changing horizons*, Chicago, IL: Lyceum Books: 91–103.

Reeser, L.C. and Epstein, I. (1990), *Professionalization and Activism in Social Work: The sixties, the eighties, and the future*, New York, NY: Columbia University Press.

Rubin, A. and Johnson, P.J. (1984), 'Direct Practice Interests of Entering MSW Students', *Journal of Education for Social Work*, 20 (2): 5–16.

Rubin, A., Johnson, P.J. and DeWeaver, K.L. (1986), 'Direct Practice Interests of MSW Students: Changes from entry to graduation', *Journal of Social Work Education*, 22 (2): 98–108.

Santangelo, T. (1992), 'The 1991 Report on Entering MSW Student Demographics and

Characteristics for the State of California', Berkeley, CA: California Social Work Education Center, unpublished.

Thomlison, B. and Watt, S. (1980), 'Trends and Issues in the Field Preparation of Social Work Manpower: A summary report', *Journal of Social Work Education*, 6 (2&3): 137–58.

Watt, S. and Kimerley, D. (1981), 'Trends and Issues in the Field Preparation of Social Work Manpower: Part II, policies and recommendations', *Journal of Social Work Education*, 7 (1): 99–108.

Chapter 5

Doel, M. and Shardlow, S. (1993), *Social Work Practice – Exercises and activities for training and developing social workers*, Aldershot: Gower.

Hope. A. and Timmel, S. (1984), *Training for Transformation 1 – A handbook for community workers*, Gweru, Zimbabwe: Mambo Press.

Social Welfare Department (1986), *Puao-te-ata-tu – The New Dawn*, Wellington, NZ.

Tibble, Te Kakapaiwaho (1984), *Maori Economic Development Conference*, Paper 58, Wellington, NZ.

Victoria University, Social Work Department (1994a), *Practice Placement Handbook*, Wellington, NZ.

Victoria University, Social Work Department (1994b), *Social Work Practice Work Book*, 811/511A, Wellington, NZ.

Chapter 6

Brewer, C. and Lait, J. (1980), *Can Social Work Survive?*, London: Temple Smith.

Butler, B. and Elliott, D. (1985), *Teaching and Learning for Practice*, Community Care Practice Handbooks, Aldershot: Gower.

CCETSW (1995), *Review of CCETSW Paper 30*, London: Central Council for Education and Training in Social Work.

Doel, M. (1987), 'The Practice Curriculum', *Social Work Education*, 6 (3): 6–9.

Doel, M. (1988), 'A Practice Curriculum to Promote Accelerated Learning', in Phillipson, J., Richards, M. and Sawdon, D. (eds), *Towards a Practice-Led Curriculum*, London: National Institute for Social Work: 845–60.

Doel, M. and Shardlow, S. (1993), *Social Work Practice: Exercises and activities for training and developing social workers*, Aldershot: Gower.

Doel, M. and Shardlow, S. (1996), 'Simulated and Live Practice Teaching: The practice teacher's craft' (accepted for publication by *Social Work Education*).

Evans, D. (1987), 'Live Supervision in the Same Room: A practice teaching method', *Social Work Education*, 6 (3): 13–17.

Meinert, R.G. (1972), 'Simulation Technology: A potential tool for social work education', *Journal of Education for Social Work*, 8 (3): 50–9.

Payne, C. and Scott, T. (1982), *Developing Supervision of Teams in Field and Residential Social Work*, Paper No. 12, London: National Institute for Social Work.

Phillipson, J., Richards, M. and Sawdon, D. (eds) (1988), *Towards a Practice-Led Curriculum*, London: National Institute for Social Work.

Richards, M. (1988), 'Developing the Content of Practice Teaching', in Phillipson, J., Richards, M. and Sawdon, D. (eds), *Towards a Practice-Led Curriculum*, London: National Institute for Social Work.

Sawdon, C. (1985), 'Action Techniques' (printed handout).

Thompson, N. (1993), *Anti-Discriminatory Practice*, Houndmills, Basingstoke: Macmillan.

Chapter 7

Bogo, M. and Power, R. (1992), 'New Field Instructors' Perceptions of Institutional Supports for their Roles', *Journal of Social Work Education*, 28 (2): 178–89.

Brandon, J. and Davies, M. (1979), 'The Limits of Competence in Social Work: The assessment of marginal students in social work education', *British Journal of Social Work*, 9 (3): 295–347.

Cimino, D., Cimino, F., Neuhring, L. and Wisler-Waldock, B. (1985), 'Student Satisfaction with Field Work', *Contemporary Social Work Education*, 5 (1), 68–80.

Cobb, N. and Jordan, C. (1989), 'Students with Questionable Values or Threatening Behaviour: Precedent and policy from discipline to dismissal', *Journal of Social Work Education*, 2: 87–97.

Cole, B.S. and Lewis, R.G. (1993), 'Gatekeeping Through Termination of Unsuitable Social Work Students: Legal issues and guidelines', *Journal of Social Work Education*, 29 (2): 150–9.

Coulshed, V. (1980), 'Why is Placement Failure so Rare?', *Australian Social Work*, 33 (4): 17–21.

Dore, M.M., Newman Epstein, B. and Herrerias, C. (1992), 'Evaluating Students' Macro Practice Field Performance: Do universal learning objectives exist?', *Journal of Social Work Education*, 28 (3): 353–61.

Duncan, P., Fernandez, E., Hawkes, J. and Koonin, R. (1990), *Field Education in the 1990s: Policy and curriculum*, Final Report of the Australian Association of Social Work and Welfare Education (AASWWE) National Working Party on Field Education, Sydney: AASWWE.

Faria, G., Brownstein, C. and Smith, H. (1988), 'A Survey of Field Instructors' Perceptions of the Liaison Role', *Journal of Social Work Education*, 24 (2): 135–44.

Fernandez, E. (1994), 'Promoting Teaching Excellence in Field Education: Facilitating the transition from practitioner to educator', paper presented at the 27th Congress of the International Association for Schools of Social Work, Amsterdam, July.

Gardiner, D. (1989), *The Anatomy of Supervision: Developing learning and professional competence for social work students*, Milton Keynes: Society for Research into Higher Education/Open University Press.

Gitterman, A. and Gitterman, N. (1979), 'Social Work Student Evaluation: Format and method', *Journal of Education for Social Work*, 15 (3): 103–8.

Hughes, L., Heycox, K. and Eisenberg, M. (1994), 'Fear of Failing: Field teachers and the assessment of marginal students in field education', in *Advances in Social Welfare Education*, Melbourne: Monash University.

Kimber, S. (1982), 'Competence is Incompetence: Evaluation of a social work student's practice', *Contemporary Social Work Education*, 5 (2): 93–104.

Lindsay, F. and Fook, J. (1994), *Current Issues in Field Education*, Report on the National Survey on Field Education, presented at the Australian Association of Social Work and Welfare Educators (AASWWE) Conference, Perth, September.

McRoy, R., Freeman, E., Logan, S. and Blackman, B. (1986), 'Cross-cultural Field Supervision: Implications for social work education', *Journal of Social Work Education*, 22 (1): 50–6.

Moore, L. and Urwin, C. (1991), 'Gatekeeping: A model for screening baccalaureate students for field education', *Journal of Social Work Education*, 27 (1): 8–17.

Raphael, F. and Rosenblum, A. (1989), 'The Open Expression of Difference in the Field Practicum: Report of a pilot study', *Journal of Social Work Education*, 24 (2): 109–16.

Reeser, L.C. (1992), 'Students With Disabilities in Practicum: What is reasonable accommodation?', *Journal of Social Work Education*, 28 (1): 98–109.

Rosenblatt, A. and Mayer, J. (1975), 'Objectionable Supervisory Styles: Students' views', *Social Work*, 2: 184–9.

Rosenblum, A. and Raphael, F. (1987), 'Students at Risk in the Field Practicum and Implications for Field Teaching', *The Clinical Supervisor*, 5: 53–63.

Slocombe, G. (1991), 'A Framework for Understanding the Liaison Process', *Australian Social Work*, 44 (2): 29–35.

Vayda, E. and Bogo, M. (1991), 'A Teaching Model to Unite Classroom and Field', *Journal of Social Work Education*, 27 (3): 271–8.

Wilson, J. and Moore, D. (1989), 'Developing and Using Evaluation Guidelines for Final Practicum', *Australian Social Work*, 42 (1): 21–7.

Chapter 8

Bogo, M. (1981), 'An Educationally Focused Faculty/Field Liaison Program for First-time Field Instructors', *Journal of Education for Social Work*, 17: 59–65.

Bogo, M. and Power, R. (1992), 'New Field Instructors' Perceptions of Institutional Supports for their Roles', *Journal of Social Work Education*, 28 (2): 178–89.

Bogo, M. and Power, R. (1994), 'Educational Methodologies and Group Elements in Field Instructor Training', *The Clinical Supervisor*, 12 (2): 9–25.

Bogo, M. and Vayda, E. (1987), *The Practice of Field Instruction in Social Work: Theory and process*, Toronto, Ont: University of Toronto Press.

Bogo, M. and Vayda, E. (1993), *The Practice of Field Instruction in Social Work: A teaching guide*, Toronto, Ont: University of Toronto Custom Publishing.

Brundage, D. and MacKeracher, D. (1980), *Adult Learning Principles and their Application to Program Planning*, Toronto, Ont: Ministry of Education.

Fortune, A.E. and Abramson, J.S. (1993), 'Predictors of Satisfaction with Field Practicum Among Social Work Students', *The Clinical Supervisor*, 11 (1): 95–110.

Fortune, A.E., Feathers, C.E., Rook, S.R., Scrimenti, R.M., Smollen, P., Stemerman, B. and Tucker, E.L. (1985), 'Student Satisfaction with the Field Placement', *Journal of Social Work Education*, 21 (3): 92–104.

Hunt, D. (1987), *Beginning with Ourselves*, Cambridge, MA: Brookline Books.

Knowles, M. (1972), 'Innovations in Teaching Styles and Approaches Based Upon Adult Learning', *Journal of Education for Social Work*, 8 (2): 32–9.

Kolb, D., Rubin, I. and McIntyre, J. (1984), *Organizational Psychology* (4th edn), Englewood Cliffs, NJ: Prentice-Hall.

Kruzich, J., Friesen, B. and Van Soest, D. (1986), 'Assessment of Student and Faculty Learning Styles: Research and application', *Journal of Social Work Education*, 22 (3): 22–30.

Tolson, E.R. and Kopp, J. (1988), 'The Practicum: Clients, problems, interventions and influences on student practice', *Journal of Social Work Education*, 24 (2): 123–34.

Chapter 9

Bandura, A. (1969), *Principles of Behaviour Modification*, New York, NY: Holt, Rinehart and Winston.

Bandura, A. (1977), *Social Learning Theory*, Englewood Cliffs, NJ: Prentice-Hall.

Berger, P. and Luckmann, T. (1967), *The Social Construction of Reality in 'The Sociology of Knowledge'*, Garden City, NY: Anchor Books.

Bøe, S. (1993), 'På leting etter barnevernpedagogen identitet' (Searching for the identity of the child and welfare worker), Art, *Milepælen* 3: 14–20.

Bøe, S, Haarberg-Aas, K. and Sundt-Rasmussen, S. (1992), *Praksistedet som læringsarena* (The agency as learning seat) (unpublished study), Oslo: Norwegian State College of Public Administration and Social Work.

Buber, M. (1992), *Ich und Du* (I and You), Leipzig: Insel-Verlag.

Crib, I. (1992), *Modern Social Theory*, New York, NY: Harvester Wheatsheaf.

Freire, P. (1970), *Pedagogy of the Oppressed*, New York, NY: Herder and Herder.

Habermas, J. (1975), *Legitimation Crisis*, Boston, MA: Beacon Press.

Habermas, J. and Luhman, N. (1971), *Theorie der Gesellschaft* (Social theory), Frankfurt-on-Main: Suhrkamp.

Hellesnes, J. (1976), *Sosialisering og Teknokrati* (Socialization and technology), Oslo: Gyldendal Forlag.

Josefson, I. (1988), *Från Larling till Mastare: om kunnskap i vården* (From apprentice to master: about knowledge in social care), Stockholm: The Swedish Union of Health and Social Care.

Mead, G.H. (1934), *Mind, Self and Society*, Chicago, IL: University of Chicago Press.

Moxness, P. (1981), *Læring og ressursutvikling* (Learning and development of resources), Oslo: Institute of Social Science.

Schön, D. (1983), *The Reflective Practitioner*, New York, NY: Basic Books.

Schön, D. (1987), *Educating the Reflective Practitioner*, San Francisco, CA and London: Jossey-Bass.

Skinner, B.F. (1974), *About Behaviorism*, New York, NY: Alfred A. Knopf.

Skjervheim, H. (1974), *Deltakar og tilskodar* (Participant and viewer), Oslo: University of Oslo.

Vygotskij, L.S. (1971), *Tænkning og Sprog I* (Thought and language I), Copenhagen: Reizel.

Vygotskij, L.S. (1974), *Tænkning og Sprog II* (Thought and language II), Copenhagen: Reizel.

Vygotskij, L.S. (1978), *Mind in Society: The development of higher psychological processes*, Cambridge, MA: Harvard Press.

Wadel, C. (1990), *Den samfunnsvitenskapelige konstruksjon av virkeligheten* (The scientific construction of reality), Flekkefjord: SEEK.

Chapter 10

Charvátová, D. (1990), *Metody sociální práce* (Methods of social work), Prague: SPN (Statni pedagogicke nakladatelstvi).

Kanerova, M.C. (1992), 'Social Policy in Czechoslovakia', in Deacon, B. (ed.), *Social Policy Past, Present and Future*, London: Sage: 91–117.

Nerudová, L. (1980), *Vybrané problémy sociální politiky v ÈSSR* (Selected problems of social policy in the Czechoslovak Socialist Republic), Prague: SPN (Statni pedagogicke nakladatelstvi).

Novotná, V. and Schimmerlingová, V. (1992), *Sociální práce, její vyvoj a metodické postupy* (Social work, its development and methodical approaches), Prague: Charles University.

Pachl, I. et al. (1991), *Návrh koncepce politiky sociálního zabezpeèení* (Outline of the concept of social security), Prague: Ministry of Labour and Social Affairs of the Czech Republic (mimeographed paper).

Pippin, J.A. (1980), *Developing Casework Skills*, Beverly Hills, CA: Sage.

Reznicek, I. (1991), *Current Trends in Social Work Education in Czechoslovakia*, contribution presented at the Colloquium on Social Work Education in Budapest, Brno: Department of Sociology, Social Policy and Social Work, FF MU (Filosoficka Fakulta Masarykovy University) (mimeograph), October.

Reznicek, I. (1994), 'Social Work Practice and Social Work Education in the Czech Republic', in Constable, R. and Mehta, V. (eds), *Education for Social Work in Eastern Europe*, Chicago, IL: Lyceum Books: 35–41.

Schimmerlingová, V. (1992), 'Pôístupy institucí a sociálních pracovníkù kôesení sociálních situací obèanù' (Approaches of institutions and social workers toward solution of social situations among citizens), in *Sborník vybranych pøednásek z I. a II. konference sociálních pracovníkù v ceské republice* (Collection of selected presentations from the 1st and 2nd conferences of social workers in the Czech Republic), Prague: Ministry of Labour and Social Affairs of the Czech Republic.

Sheafor, B.W., Horejsi, C.R. and Horejsi, G.A. (1991), *Techniques and Guidelines for Social Work Practice* (2nd edn), Boston, MA: Allyn and Bacon.

Slavíková, J. (1992), 'Vysledky vyzkumu k nìkterym otázkám sociální péèe' (Results of research concerning some questions of social care), in *Sborník vybranych pøednásek z I. a II. konference sociálních pracovníkù v ceské republice* (Collection of selected presentations from the 1st and 2nd conferences of social workers in the Czech Republic), Prague: Ministry of Labour and Social Affairs of the Czech Republic.

Chapter 11

Erikson, E.S. (1963), *Childhood and Society*, New York, NY: Norton.

Kalra, R.M. and Singh, R.R. (1987), *Curriculum Construction for Youth Development*, New Delhi: Sterling Publishers.

Manshardt, C. (1967), *Pioneering on Social Frontiers in India*, Bombay: Lalvani Publishers.

Singh, R.R. (1994), 'Social Work Education through Distance Mode?', *The Social Work Educator, Newsletter of the Association of Schools of Social Work in India*, 1 (New Series) (2): 1–8.

Taber, A. (1994), 'Report on a Child Guidance Centre Project', 9 December (unpublished paper).

UGC (1990), *Report of the Curriculum Centre in Social Work Education*, New Delhi: University Grants Commission.

Verma, R. (1994), 'Intervention with Rural Families', in Desai, M. (ed.), *Family and Interventions: A Course Compendium*, Bombay: Tata Institute of Social Sciences: 265–80.

Chapter 12

Butler, B. (1983), 'Learning to Teach Social Work Practice', in CCETSW (ed.), *Research in Practice Teaching*, London: Central Council for Education and Training in Social Work.

Freire, P. (1972), *Pedagogy of the Oppressed*, Harmondsworth: Penguin.

Knowles, M.S. (1972), 'Innovations in Teaching Styles and Approaches Based Upon Adult Learning', *Journal of Education for Social Work*, 8 (2): 32–9.

Knowles, M.S. (1978), *The Adult Learner: A Neglected Species*, Houston, Texas: Gulf Publishing.

Knowles, M.S. (1980), *The Modern Practice of Adult Education*, Chicago, IL: Follett Publishing.

Kolb, D.A. (1984), *Experiential Learning*, Englewood Cliffs, NJ: Prentice-Hall.

Lu, M.H. (1991), 'The Development of Chinese Social Work Education', in APRSWEA and Peking University (eds), *Status Quo, Challenge and Prospect – Collected works of the Seminar of the Asian–Pacific Region Social Work Education Association*, Beijing: Peking University Press (published in Chinese), 38–41.

Midgley, J. (1981), *Professional Imperialism: Social Work in the Third World*, London: Heinemann.

Ng, I. et al. (1992), *Reflecting on Supervision: Supervising Students in Practice*, Hong Kong: Department of Applied Social Studies, Hong Kong Polytechnic.

Ng-Wan, Iris S. (1994a), *Training of Chinese Social Work Practice Teachers*, paper presented at the Conference on Development of Social Work Education in Chinese Societies, Asian & Pacific Association for Social Work Education, Beijing (published in Chinese).

Ng-Wan, Iris S. (1994b), *The Education of Social Work Fieldwork Supervisors and Coordinators in the People's Republic of China – Issues and future trends*, paper presented at the 27th Congress of the International Association of Schools of Social Work, Amsterdam, Netherlands.

Rogers, C.R. (1983), *Freedom to Learn for the 80s*, London: Charles, E. Merril, A. Bell and Howell.

Tsang, N.M. (1990), *Learning Styles and Associated Learning Barriers on a Social Work Course in Hong Kong*, PhD thesis, London: Middlesex University.

Wan, S.F. (1990), *Preparation for Social Work Practice – First undergraduate placements in a Hong Kong Family Casework Service Centre*, MSc dissertation, Cardiff: University of Wales.

Name index

Subject index

Personal Safety for Social Workers

Pauline Bibby

Commissioned by
The Suzy Lamplugh Trust
Foreword by
Diana Lamplugh OBE

This book is aimed at employers, managers and staff in social work agencies.

In part 1, *Personal Safety for Social Workers* deals with the respective roles and responsibilities of employers and employees are discussed, and offers guidance on developing a workplace personal safety policy. The design and management of the workplace are considered and guidelines provided for social workers working away from the normal work base. Part 2 contains detailed guidelines for use by individual social workers in a variety of work situations. Part 3 addresses training issues and provides a number of sample training programmes.

The message of this book is that proper attention to risk can reduce both the incidence of aggression and its development into violent acts.

1994   224 pages   1 85742 195 7   £16.95

Price subject to change without notification

arena

Assessing Needs AND Planning Care IN Social Work

Brian Taylor and Toni Devine

"...written clearly, is free of jargon and contains a wealth of information and thoughtful discussion. The theoretical content is skillfully related to examples of practice and I felt I was being gently lead through concepts which were sometimes complex and profound." **June Neill, Researcher, National Institute for Social Work**

"The authors have achieved a consolidation of current social work theory and practice concisely." **Community Care**

The focus of this book is on the development of the skills required at each stage of the social work process: assessment, care planning, implementation and evaluation. Throughout the book a balance is maintained between the focus on client involvement, and the role of the social worker in an agency. The latter part of the book addresses practical issues in developing new approaches to assessment and care planning: primary workers, individual support and managing change.

Brian J. Taylor, Assistant Principal Social Worker (Training), Northern Health and Social Services Board, Northern Ireland, and **Toni Devine**, formerly Lecturer in Social Care, North West Institute of Further and Higher Education, Londonderry.

1993   144 pages

Pbk   1 85742 144 2   £12.95   Hbk   1 85742 139 6   £28.00

Price subject to change without notification

arena

THE essential SOCIAL WORKER

An introduction to professional practice in the 1990s

THIRD EDITION

MARTIN DAVIES

This third edition has been radically revised and updated and contains an entirely new chapter providing a clear outline of the historical and policy-related framework within which social work operates in areas of particular practice - child care, disability, mental health, old age and criminal justice.

The Essential Social Worker defends the idea of a broadly based profession seeking to maintain disadvantaged people in the community. It bravely confronts the shallowness of many short-term fashions and argues that social work is a uniquely humane contributor to the achievement of welfare in the 1990s and beyond.

A careful reading will ensure that the student gains an understanding of the role of social work in a complex urban society and develops an awareness of the debates which surround it. Social work is often subject to public criticism, but, as the author shows, it has continued to grow in scale and in influence throughout the 20th century, and, although its structure will continue to evolve, social work will remain essential in any society which regards itself as democratic and humane.

Martin Davies is Executive Director of the School of Social Work, University of East Anglia.

1994   240 pages   Hbk   1 85742 100 0   £29.95
Pbk   1 85742 101 9   £12.95

Price subject to change without notification

Developing Skills for Community Care

A collaborative approach

Peter Beresford and Steve Trevillion

Fundamental reforms in community care and welfare generally, demand new skills, new ways of working and a new relationship with service users. Collaboration is a key idea at the heart of this cultural change. Until now, there has been little guidance to help practitioners turn the rhetoric into reality. For the first time, this book offers a practical basis for working in a collaborative way, which fully involves service users.

Drawing on a development project which included service users, carers, practitioners and managers, the book pioneers a collaborative approach to developing collaborative skills. It takes the reader through the processes involved and identifies essential skills. Key questions like: • What are collaborative skills? • How can they be evaluated? • What would a bottom-up approach to skill development look like? are answered through numerous examples and exercises.

Peter Beresford works with Open Services Project, is a member of Survivors Speak Out and teaches at Brunel University College. **Steve Trevillion** is a former neighbourhood social worker who now teaches at Brunel University College.

1995   173 pages   Hbk   1 85742 236 8   £32.50
Pbk   1 85742 237 6   £14.95

Price subject to change without notification

arena